Shrines
OF THE
Holy
Land

Shrines
OF THE
Holy
Land

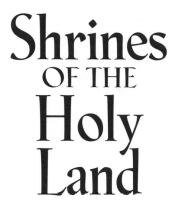

◆ *A Pilgrim's Travel Guide* ◆

Norman Wareham and Jill Gill

Foreword by Allan Weinert, C.Ss.R.
Editor in Chief of *Liguorian* Magazine

Liguori
LIGUORI, MISSOURI

Library of Congress Cataloging-in-Publication Data

Wareham, Norman.
    Shrines of the holy land : a pilgrim's travel guide / Norman Wareham and Jill Gill : foreword by Allan Weinert. — 1st ed.
       p. cm.
    Rev. ed. of: Every pilgrim's guide to the Holy Land. 1996.
    Includes bibliographical references and index.
    ISBN 0-7648-0180-5
    1. Christian shrines—Israel—Guidebooks. 2. Israel—Description and travel. 3. Christian shrines—West Bank—Guidebooks. 4. West Bank—Description and travel. I. Gill, Jill, 1936– . II. Wareham, Norman. Every pilgrim's guide to the Holy Land. III. Title.
DS107.5.W37 1998
263'.0425694—dc21   97–37775

Originally published in English under the title *Every Pilgrim's Guide to the Holy Land* by the Canterbury Press Norwich of St. Mary's Works, St. Mary's Plain, Norwich, Norfolk NR3 3BE U.K.

Printed in the United States of America
02 01 00 99 98 5 4 3 2 1
First Edition

CONTENTS

FOREWORD

PILGRIMAGES EVOKE images of people on a journey of faith, determined to discover a more profound truth about the events and circumstances in which God has made himself known. They serve as outward expressions of our inner response to the Lord's invitation to follow him. A pilgrimage to the Holy Land brings to life the people and places of the Bible. This mysterious land of barren slopes and desert continues to draw visitors from every corner of the world, exerting an appeal that is as powerful as our eternal search for the living God. A pilgrimage to the land of Jesus' birth, life, passion, death, and Resurrection can be a life-changing experience.

The pilgrim and the journey known as a pilgrimage are as old as our biblical forefathers. From earliest times these journeys were understood as unique expressions of the Israelite worship of God. The annual religious feasts of the early Hebrews were often celebrated in the context of elaborate pilgrimages to Jerusalem.

These journeys continued from the time of Moses down to the time of Joseph, Mary, and Jesus. In the Gospel of Luke, we see how even the Holy Family, obediently and religiously, participated in a yearly pilgrimage to Jerusalem to observe the feast of Passover. "And when Jesus was twelve years old, he went up with them according to the custom for this feast" (Luke 2:42). In much the same way, Christians in the first few centuries after Jesus' death and Resurrection journeyed from Europe and other parts of the globe to the sacred sites of the Holy Land. Eager to grow in their understanding of Jesus and identify with his early life, our Christian ancestors frequently set out from their homelands for the places made holy by Jesus when he walked among the villages and towns along the Sea of Galilee. Since that time, and throughout the spread of Christianity, Christians have traveled to experience firsthand the ordinary places made extraordinary by the presence of God.

What motivates a pilgrim to leave what is familiar and comfortable and set out for a remote place? Quite simply, moments of grace. People come back home changed. A pilgrimage to the Holy Land takes you not just around the world, but inside yourself. Traveling in the Holy Land is like crossing a bridge into the past. Pilgrims not only experience biblical history, they live it. People who live in Israel have a saying: "Pilgrims pass through the holy places, but the holy places pass through them." They are right.

The primary focus of the pilgrimage is on the person of Jesus. Even before arriving in the Holy Land, we know a great deal about him. We know that he was born of Mary. He lived in a struggling, dusty, obscure village called Nazareth. For thirty years he worked as a carpenter. He preached in Palestine. He died on a cross, then rose from the dead. People called him "Son of God" and "Savior."

As we meditate on the gospels, we find a more detailed portrait of Jesus. In them we see a man who lived simply and humbly. He loved people. He wept for his friends. He cared for those others despised. He sweat blood for himself. He was gentle, yet severe in his demands upon his disciples. He worked miracles, and he preached with amazing authority.

The knowledge and love you have for Jesus will deepen and become more vivid once you have been to the Holy Land and have seen it for yourself. Those who have been there will never again read or hear the Scriptures proclaimed in the same way again. At Ein Kerem you will visit the ruins of the house of Elizabeth and Zechariah, the birthplace of John the Baptist. Thousands of years have not diminished his voice, telling us to prepare the way of the Lord. And next Christmas, when you celebrate the birth of Christ, you will recall the fourteen-pointed silver star encased in marble located in the Church of the Nativity in Bethlehem. We have stored the gospel story of Christ's birth in our hearts for meditation and we know it so well: A census brought Joseph and Mary to the City of David. While they were there, the time came for her to be delivered. Mary gave birth to her firstborn son and wrapped him in swaddling clothes and laid him in a manger because there was no room for them where travelers lodged. The Word of God became flesh and made his dwelling among us. Jesus came to tell us, unimaginable as it may seem, that we are welcomed into the life of the Holy One. We no longer walk in darkness now that we have seen this great Light.

At the Church of the Beatitudes, you will hear again the words Jesus used to describe the kingdom of God. That kingdom is not fashioned out of large armies and huge treasuries but is a kingdom of love and respect. It is the kind of kingdom where Jesus could tell his believers, "Fortunate are those who have the spirit of the poor, for theirs is the kingdom of Heaven.... Fortunate are those with a pure heart, for they shall see God."

In Bethany you will visit the place where Jesus raised Lazarus from the dead. You will hear again Jesus' words to Mary and Martha, who were mourning the loss of their brother, "I am the resurrection; whoever believes in me, though he die, shall live" (John 11:25). Those words are meant to be a great consolation to those who have lost loved ones or who are preparing for their own death. If Jesus rose from the dead, then we too shall rise from the dead. This is our firm and unshakable conviction.

Next Lent, on Holy Thursday, you will recall the scene in the Upper Room where Jesus gathered his disciples together on the night before he died. Here Jesus taught us the meaning of life and death, love and service. He performed that ordinary gesture of washing the feet of his friends. In so doing he paid human beings the greatest compliment we could ever receive. He invited us to share with him in his work. That work is telling one another of the Father's love for us, and doing it in memory of Jesus.

And when you next pray the Stations of the Cross, you will remember the crowds and the narrow streets of Old Jerusalem pressing in around you. Not quite two thousand years ago Jesus walked this way from the place of judgment to the place of crucifixion and burial. The street winds through the Arab Quarter of the Old City. You will realize how hard it was for Jesus to negotiate those steps and passageways with the cross on his shoulder, how easy it was to fall, and why he welcomed the aid of Veronica, who wiped the blood and sweat from his face.

The Way of the Cross ends at the Church of the Holy Sepulchre, which contains stations ten through fourteen. The last station is located in the center of the rotunda, with an outer chamber and an inner burial chamber. The inner room contains the marble slab denoting the place where the body of Jesus was laid after it was taken down from the cross. This is also the place of the central mystery of our faith. An angel said to the women, "Do not be afraid, for I know that you are looking for Jesus who was crucified. He is not here, for he is risen as he said" (Matthew 28:5–6). The tomb is empty because Jesus is now among the living. Each of us can also say, "I, too, will rise. The tomb will be empty for me also." We celebrate what we long to believe in the deepest recesses of our being. The shattered, misshapen pieces of our lives will be lovingly gathered into the form of our best and truest selves.

The faith of pilgrims expands and deepens as a direct result of journeying with others to these holy places. But it is not enough to simply sign up for a trip and leave the rest to the planner. Even before they leave home, serious pilgrims prepare themselves for this exceptional faith journey to the very land where the Word became flesh among us. Pilgrims should pause to reflect on Christ's life, ministry, death, and Resurrection. Preparation for such a unique journey should not be taken lightly. Every facet of preparation makes us available to the certain graces that move powerfully in this land called *holy*. I encourage you to use *Shrines of the Holy Land* in preparation for your trip and during your stay in the Holy Land. Read carefully the descriptions and background of the places you will visit. This will help you walk in faith and bring you insight into the landscape of your own belief.

Fr. Allan Weinert, C.Ss.R.

PREFACE

FOR EVERY CHRISTIAN, a pilgrimage to the Holy Land should truly be the journey of a lifetime. To visit the country in which Jesus was born, proclaimed his gospel, was crucified, and overcame the power of death is not only a privilege but at the very least a gateway to a fuller understanding of his teaching. The greatest insight is perhaps in actually seeing some of the things that Jesus saw and relating many of his sayings to the background in which they were spoken. The experience often brings about a strengthening of faith and a desire to return to the land that has had such a profound influence upon humankind.

The purpose of this guidebook is threefold: to provide some background knowledge about each site together with details of how to reach it on foot or by car; to explain the site's main features in a "guide yourself" format; to supply some practical information about the available facilities. Included where appropriate are excerpts from one of the four gospels describing the events that occurred at, or very near, the shrines now commemorating the occasion. A full list of gospel references is given at the end of the book.

A pilgrimage to the Holy Land is often the fulfillment of a lifetime's ambition, and it is, therefore, important to ensure that the very best use is made of the precious time available. Our hope is that this book will provide exactly the right balance of background knowledge and practical information in an easily accessible format.

Authors' Notes

THE TEXT FOR each site opens with a brief description and usually ends with our personal comments.

The Scripture passages are from the *Christian Community Bible.* Each reading is followed by a few lines from a hymn, which are offered for prayerful reflection.

The sections describing the various shrines are arranged in a geographical sequence, but a comprehensive index at the end enables immediate reference to each individual site.

The general information supplied—in particular, opening/closing times and telephone numbers—has been carefully checked at the time of writing, but inevitably some of these may have changed since then.

Only sketch maps are included in this guide on the assumption that most pilgrims will have received detailed maps from their tour leader or travel agency.

Acknowledgments

WE WOULD LIKE to express our sincere appreciation to the following for their help in the preparation of this guide: McCabe Travel, London; Israel Government Tourist Office, London; Albina Tours, Jerusalem; Mohammed Joulani, Jerusalem. We should once again like to thank Terence Gill for drawing up the maps and plans.

Part 1

Background

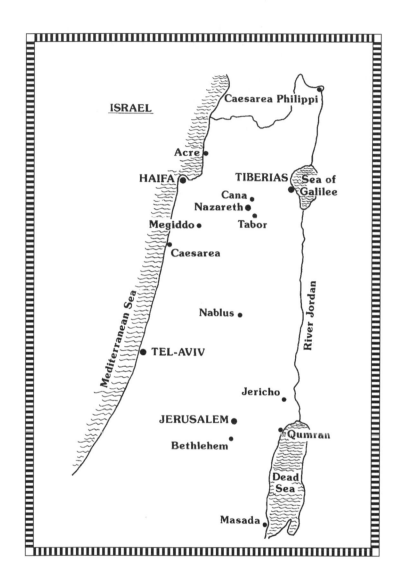

ISRAEL

Caesarea Philippi

Acre

HAIFA

TIBERIAS Sea of Galilee

Cana
Nazareth

Megiddo Tabor

Caesarea

Mediterranean Sea

Nablus

River Jordan

TEL-AVIV

Jericho

JERUSALEM

Bethlehem

Qumran

Dead Sea

Masada

3

Essentials

VISITORS TO ISRAEL must possess a passport, a return ticket, and sufficient funds for the trip. Visas are issued upon arrival in Israel and are valid for three months.

Checking with your medical insurance company before leaving is a good idea, as costs to cover medical emergencies can be very high in Israel.

Vaccinations and inoculations are no longer necessary, but if you have any doubt, it would be wise to seek medical advice.

Facts about Israel

The Land Itself

The country is surprisingly small—about the size of New Jersey. The distance from Jerusalem to the Sea of Galilee is less than one hundred miles.

The majority of the gospel sites are easily accessible and are mainly confined within three comparatively small areas: Jerusalem, Nazareth, and Galilee.

Clocks in Israel are normally seven hours ahead of those in New York, eight in Chicago, nine in Denver, and ten in Los Angeles.

English is widely spoken. In tourist areas most notices and road signs are in Hebrew, Arabic, and English.

General information and maps can be obtained from any travel agency or pilgrimage organization.

Climate

Temperatures vary enormously, and the mean annual rainfall is almost equal to that of San Francisco or Amarillo, but most of it falls between mid-November and mid-March. Sunset is within a narrow time-band throughout the year: 6:00–7:30 (times are different during the adjusted "Summertime"). There is very little twilight.

The most popular times with visitors are between April and mid-June or late September to mid-November, when the temperatures are not oppressive. Summer is generally hot, but winter can be surprisingly cold, particularly in Jerusalem, 2,500 feet above sea level, where night frosts and even snow are not uncommon.

The following table of average daily Fahrenheit temperatures has been supplied by the Israel Government Tourist Office. However, you should remember that evenings in Jerusalem can be quite chilly during spring and autumn. The Jordan Valley/Dead Sea area is consistently warm or very hot, while Tiberias is always much warmer than Jerusalem, with some degree of humidity.

	Jan	Feb	Mar	Apr	May	June	July	Aug	Sept	Oct	Nov	Dec
Jerusalem	53.0	57.4	60.8	69.4	77.4	81.3	85.3	85.5	81.9	77.9	66.6	56.1
Tiberias	64.9	67.1	72.3	80.1	89.1	94.8	97.9	98.8	95.0	89.2	78.3	68.2
Dead Sea	68.9	71.6	77.9	89.2	92.3	99.1	102.1	101.7	96.4	89.6	80.6	71.8

FINANCE

Banking hours are as follows:

Sunday, Tuesday, Thursday: 8:30–12:30, 4:00–6:00

Monday and Wednesday: 8:30–12:30

Friday and eve of Jewish Holy Days: 8:30–noon

The shekel (NIS) is divided into 100 agorots. Dollars are welcomed, but change will be given in shekels. Visa, American Express, and Diner's Club cards are accepted at most of the larger hotels and businesses. Traveler's checks are also accepted. Banks are often difficult to find in and around the Old City of Jerusalem, but plenty of moneychangers offer a good rate of exchange for cash or traveler's checks.

General Advice

Clothing

Mid-November to mid-March: Ordinary light winter garments and footwear; raincoats and umbrellas.

Late March and April: Light spring clothing, but a sweater will often be required in Jerusalem during the cool evenings.

May to mid-October: Very light casual clothing and comfortable footwear. Sun hat and sunglasses are essential, as the light is very dazzling.

Late October to mid-November: Dress as for March/April, but it can be warmer in the autumn than in the spring.

Medical

Medicines are best purchased before departure and should be clearly labeled.

All emergency treatment, doctor's visits, and prescriptions have to be paid for at the time, so allow sufficient funds. Insurance companies will wish to see receipts.

Stomach upsets are very common. During the hot months it is most important to drink plenty—and often—to avoid the very real danger of dehydration. A small thermos or water bottle might prove useful. Sunburn and blisters can also be a problem for the unwary visitor.

Tap water is normally safe, but if you have a delicate stomach you are strongly advised to purchase bottled water. All drinks in hotels are fairly expensive. Tea/coffee-making facilities are not normally provided in hotel rooms.

Electrical Equipment

Current is AC 220 volts, 50 cycles. The Israeli sockets are usually small three-pronged, but not of European design. A travel plug adaptor will be necessary. Airlines require electrical equipment to be carried in hand luggage.

A pocket flashlight will also be useful in some ancient sites where the lighting is poor. Take sufficient film and batteries for your photographic needs because these can be fairly expensive in Israel.

The Three Monotheistic Faiths

Jerusalem is a religious center for Jews, Muslims, and Christians. The three "Holy Days" can, therefore, cause some confusion! Friday for Muslims, Saturday for Jews, and Sunday for Christians, when their respective shops are closed. The Jews start their Sabbath (*Shabbat*) at sunset on Friday when all public transport operated by them ceases.

In mosques and churches visitors are required to dress modestly. Ladies should ensure that their shoulders and upper arms are covered—a light shawl would be useful for this purpose. Anyone in shorts will be refused admission.

SOUVENIRS

Consider bringing home leather goods, olive-wood carvings, mother-of-pearl items, diamond jewelry, copperware, embroidered clothes and linens, ceramics, dried fruits, nuts, herbs, and spices. Tax can be reclaimed on the more expensive items when leaving the country, but relevant receipts must be presented.

THE TOURIST "GREEN CARD"

This allows fourteen days unlimited admission to forty-three National Parks Authority sites, mostly of archaeological interest, of which eight are covered in this book. For those planning their own itinerary, the "green card" may be worth purchasing and is available from the National Parks Authority headquarters in Tel Aviv (4 Rav Alluf M. Makleff Street, Hakirya, 61070 Tel Aviv) POB 7028. Tel: (03) 695-2281, Fax: (03) 696-7643. The ticket offices at many of the sites also sell the cards.

JERUSALEM

Visitors should he particularly careful in the jostling crowds of the Old City to ensure that purses and wallets are not accessible to pickpockets and bag-snatchers.

Fruit is plentiful but should be thoroughly washed. Be wary of purchasing pressed orange juice—or any other unpackaged consumable—in the street.

TRANSPORT

The larger taxis, known as *sheruts*, seat seven passengers. Be prepared to share, but always agree on a price before departure. Taxi ranks are to be found at the Damascus and Jaffa Gates.

BUS STATIONS

Arab:

1. Opposite the city walls between Damascus and Herod's Gates: To Mount of Olives: No. 75; Bethlehem: No. 23; Bethany: No. 36; Jericho: No. 28.
2. Opposite Garden Tomb (Nablus Road): To El-Qubeibah: No. 45; Jacob's Well: No. 62.

Israeli:

Pick up near Jaffa Gate ("Egged" Buses):
To Ein Kerem: No. 17; Abu Gosh: No. 185; Yad Vashem: No. 20.

EMERGENCIES

American Embassy in Tel Aviv: telephone (03) 5197575.
American Consulate in Jerusalem: telephone (02) 6253288.
Emergency Services:

Police	100
Medical	101
Fire	102

USEFUL ADDRESSES FOR THE PILGRIM

The Christian Information Center is run by the Franciscans who administer the majority of the gospel sites. Enter the Old City by Jaffa Gate, follow the Citadel walls around to the right, and the entrance is almost opposite the bridge crossing the moat. A great deal of useful information is available here, including the times of religious services and also the language in which each is conducted. Bus timetables, current opening times of the sites, churches, mosques, and other places of interest, together with details of any special attractions, are also available. The hours are 8:30–1:00, but the center is closed on Sundays and holidays. POB 14308, 91140 Jerusalem. Tel: (02) 6272692. Fax: (02) 6286417.

The Tourist Information Office is just inside Jaffa Gate, on the left, in the Old City. POB 97911. Tel: (02) 6280382. The hours are Sunday–Thursday 8:30–6:00, Friday 8:30–2:00, closed on Saturday.

CHRISTIAN PERIODS AND DEVELOPMENT

HERE IS A brief explanation of the terminology used in the text:

Second Temple Period: 37 B.C. to A.D. 70. During this period King Herod the Great's magnificent building—so familiar to Jesus—was constructed. Strictly speaking, his temple was the third because the second, erected on a much smaller scale, came into being after the return of the Jews from exile in Babylon circa 587 B.C.

Judeo/Christian Period: A term used to describe the period between the Resurrection and the construction of the first Christian churches. During these three centuries the early Christians continued to worship in their synagogues and in house groups.

Constantinian Period: A definition applied to the very first churches to be built in the Holy Land on the specific instructions of Roman Emperor Constantine (c. 274–337) following his conversion to Christianity by his mother, St. Helena.

Byzantine Period: A rather loose term used to describe the churches built during the seven centuries that elapsed between the death of Constantine and the arrival of the Crusaders in the eleventh century. Most were totally destroyed by the Persians in A.D. 614, after which Christianity sank to a low ebb. However, the Church of the Nativity in Bethlehem survived, and the Church of the Holy Sepulchre in Jerusalem was twice rebuilt on a modest scale.

Crusader Period: 1096–1187. An incredibly industrious period of building and reconstruction during a span of less than one hundred years. Many of these churches were built upon the ruins of Byzantine foundations. Although the Crusaders were defeated in battle by Saladin in 1187, they continued to control the Port of Acre until 1291.

Middle Ages: After the Crusader Period the Muslims became the predominant influence throughout Palestine. However, as the Islamic faith acknowledges Jesus as a prophet, Muslims were not altogether intolerant of the followers of Christ. In consequence, some churches survived and were occupied during the Middle Ages by Christian monastic communities from all over Europe—in the main, the Augustinians, Benedictines, and Franciscans.

Modern Times: Toward the end of the nineteenth century there was a marked increase in Christian missionary activity, and a number of churches were built, some on Crusader and Byzantine foundations.

Since the inauguration of the state of Israel, many churches have been built or renovated. Thanks to the ease of modern travel, large numbers of pilgrims continue to flock to the Holy Land from all over the world.

Part 2

✜

Shrines
of the Holy Land

JERUSALEM

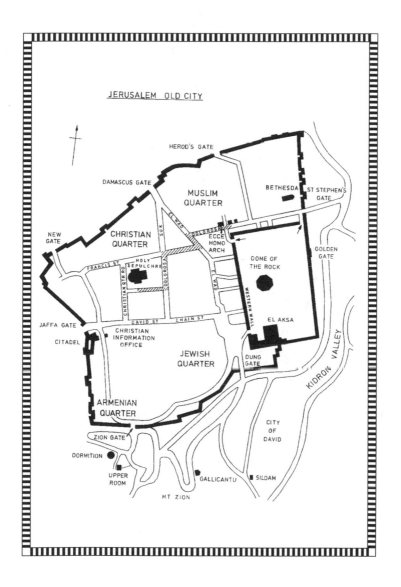

JERUSALEM OLD CITY

HEROD'S GATE

DAMASCUS GATE

MUSLIM QUARTER

BETHESDA ST STEPHEN'S GATE

NEW GATE

CHRISTIAN QUARTER

EL WAD

SUK

VIA DOLOROSA

ECCE HOMO ARCH

GOLDEN GATE

FRANCIS ST

HOLY SEPULCHRE

CHRISTIAN QTR RD

DOLOROSA

DOME OF THE ROCK

EL WAD

WESTERN WALL

JAFFA GATE

DAVID ST

CHAIN ST

EL AKSA

CITADEL

CHRISTIAN INFORMATION OFFICE

JEWISH QUARTER

DUNG GATE

KIDRON VALLEY

ARMENIAN QUARTER

ZION GATE

CITY OF DAVID

DORMITION

UPPER ROOM

GALLICANTU

SILOAM

MT ZION

Jerusalem is the "Holy City" for Jews, Christians, and Muslims. Here, a view of the city. *(Allan Weinert)*

One of the most ancient cities in the world, Jerusalem holds the unique distinction of being the "Holy City" for half the human race—for Jews, Christians, and Muslims. During the course of its long and turbulent history the city has been besieged on more than fifty occasions, has been conquered thirty-six times, and has suffered no less than ten total destructions.

These simple statements sum up the importance of this relatively small community that has played such an important role in the history of humankind.

Today it is difficult to realize that less than 150 years ago there were no houses outside the Old City walls. Even by the end of the British Mandate in 1948 Jerusalem had not developed extensively. However, since the Six-Day War in 1967 there has been a tremendous growth, which continues at a phenomenal pace. On the Judean hills, where previously shepherds tended their sheep, have sprung up the Israeli Parliament and other government buildings, an extensive university, the National Museum, and a number of tall hotels that now dominate the skyline. Furthermore, the city has recently been surrounded by large urban residential developments, some of which border the desert. An idea of the size of modern Jerusalem can be obtained from the high ground along the road to Bethlehem.

As can be seen from the map, the Old City today is divided into four distinct quarters—in addition to the Temple Area, which stands on its own and occupies most of the eastern boundary. Working clockwise from Jaffa Gate:

The Christian Quarter: In the northwest corner. This sector is roughly bounded by the road running east from Jaffa Gate and south from Damascus Gate. Within this area is the Church of the Holy Sepulchre and the residences of the Coptic, Greek Catholic, Greek Orthodox, and Roman Catholic patriarchs. Many other Christian communities are also represented, including the Abyssinians, Lutherans, Russian Orthodox, and Knights Hospitalers.

The Muslim Quarter: In the northeast corner. Roughly bounded by the road running south from Damascus Gate as far as the road continuing east from Jaffa Gate. Of particular Christian interest within this area is the Pool of Bethesda and the Crusader Church of St. Anne, the Roman Catholic Seminary of the Flagellation, the Convent of the Sisters of Zion, and also part of the Via Dolorosa.

The Jewish Quarter: Situated in the south, but west of the large plaza in front of the Western Wall of the Temple Area. Most of this sector was demolished after 1967 and rebuilt in sympathy with the original architecture. Bordering on this area is the Church of St. Mark, which the Assyrians claim is built over the site of the Upper Room.

The Armenian Quarter: This somewhat exclusive sector lies directly to the west of the modern Jewish Quarter and reaches as far as the western walls of the city. Within it is the Cathedral of St. James and the residence of the Armenian patriarch. To the north of this—before completing the circuit and reaching Jaffa Gate—is the Citadel, which occupies the site of Herod's Palace. Opposite the drawbridge is the entrance to Christ Church, the only Anglican church within the Old City.

The present walls were in the main built by Suleiman the Magnificent in the sixteenth century, and in them are eight gates: Jaffa Gate in the west; New Gate, Damascus Gate, and Herod's Gate in the north; St. Stephen's Gate and Golden Gate (sealed for several centuries) in the east; while in the southern walls are Dung Gate and Zion Gate.

To walk around the top of the walls is a rewarding experience and provides an excellent orientation. Access can be obtained from Damascus and Jaffa Gates, and about two-thirds of the total circumference is open to the public. Many of the buildings in the Old City, and in particular the covered *suqs* (markets), were constructed by the Crusaders and date from the twelfth century.

A Brief History

The earliest biblical record (Genesis 14:18) is from the time of Abraham, circa 2000 B.C., when reference was made to the habitation known as Salem, also the Hebrew word for peace. Many scholars consider that this was an abbreviated form of Jerusalem. There is also a strong tradition that Mount Moriah—upon which Abraham prepared to sacrifice his son Isaac in obedience to God—is the same mount on which were later built the Temples of Solomon, Herod, and the present Dome of the Rock.

PRINCIPAL DATES

1000 B.C.	King David captured the city from the Jebusites.
965	King Solomon, David's son, built the first Temple.
587	King Nebuchadnezzar captured the city, destroyed the Temple, and carried off the Jews to exile in Babylon.
538	The Jews returned, and a smaller Temple was rebuilt.
332	Alexander the Great captured the city.
167	The Hasmonean kings allowed the Jews independence.
63	The Romans captured the city.
37	Herod the Great was appointed king. The city was beautified and the Temple rebuilt on a magnificent scale.

The Birth of Jesus

A.D. 70	Roman Emperor Titus totally destroyed the city, including the Temple, following a Jewish revolt.
135	Hadrian, after crushing a second Jewish revolt, rebuilt the city as a typical Roman provincial town and renamed it Aelia Capitolina. The Jews were forbidden entry on penalty of death.
330	Roman Emperor Constantine was converted to Christianity by his mother, St. Helena. He built three principal churches: the Church of the Holy Sepulchre; "Eleona" on the Mount of Olives; and the Church of the Nativity in Bethlehem.
614	The Persians conquered the Holy Land and destroyed all its churches, with the exception of the Church of the Nativity in Bethlehem.
636	The Muslim Arabs gained control and held authority for nearly five hundred years.
1099	The Crusaders captured the city and built many churches.
1187	Saladin, the Muslim leader, defeated the Crusaders.

1517	The Turks captured the city and remained in control for the next four hundred years.
1917	General Allenby took possession of the city. Palestine came under mandatory British control with the authority of the League of Nations.
1948	The United Nations, at the end of British control, partitioned the country between Israel and Jordan. A year later the state of Israel was inaugurated.
1967	The Six-Day War between Arabs and Jews resulted in the Israeli occupation of the "West Bank" and the "Gaza Strip." The city is no longer arbitrarily divided, and the Jews are able to worship once again at the Western Wall.

MOUNT OF OLIVES

$$\frac{+\ ||\ +}{+\ ||\ +}$$

Place of the Ascension
Church of the Pater Noster
Dominus Flevit

The Mount of Olives is the high ground rising above the Kidron Valley to the east of the Old City. Sometimes known as Olivet, it is a gospel site in its own right, and there are many New Testament references to it. St. Luke records that it was from here that Jesus wept over the city as he foretold its destruction.

In addition to the three sites described in detail below, mention should be made of the slender tower on its summit, part of the Russian Orthodox Convent of the Ascension from where there are magnificent views. Unfortunately, the tower is rarely open to the public.

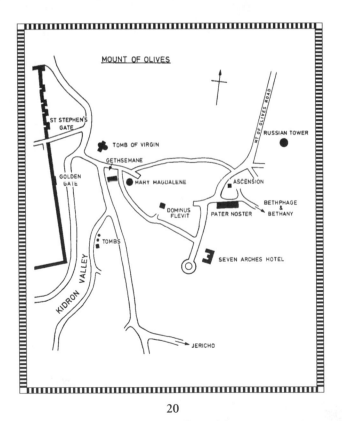

Place of the Ascension

A small octagonal shrine at the top of the Mount of Olives is built over the place where, according to tradition, Jesus ascended into heaven. St. Luke wrote in the Acts of the Apostles that the disciples came down from the Mount of Olives after the Ascension.

THE ASCENSION

Jesus led them almost as far as Bethany; then he lifted up his hands and blessed them. And as he blessed them, he withdrew (and was taken to heaven. They worshiped him). They returned to Jerusalem full of joy and were continually in the Temple praising God. (Luke 24:50–53)

All praise to thee who art gone up triumphantly to heaven;
All praise to God the Father's name and Holy Ghost be given.

ACCESS

ON FOOT

From St. Stephen's Gate (also known as Lion Gate) on the east side of the Old City, walk down the hill for two hundred yards and turn right into the main Jericho Road. Continue to the bottom of the Kidron Valley until reaching the stone wall surrounding the Church of All Nations in the Garden of Gethsemane. Take the narrow road to the left of the wall and go straight up the steep hill for about a quarter of a mile until reaching the road running north/south along the top of the Mount of Olives. Here turn to the right, pass the Mount of Olives Hotel, and shortly after, on the left, you will see the octagonal minaret of a mosque adjacent to the site. Allow a good half hour to reach the shrine.

BY CAR

The route above is also possible, but there is no point in starting from St. Stephen's Gate because it is at the end of a narrow cul-de-sac. Follow the city wall around from Damascus Gate until reaching the Garden of Gethsemane at the bottom of the Kidron Valley, then drive up the steep hill mentioned above.

DETAILS

Wide steps lead up to the site, which is owned by the Muslims, and if closed, it may be necessary to seek admission from the custodian of the mosque.

The earliest church here was built by Pomenia, a wealthy Roman lady, at the end of the fourth century, but this was destroyed by the Persians in A.D. 614. A little later Bishop Modestus erected a circular building that was open to the skies, and it is recorded that eight lamps shone brilliantly at night through the windows so that they could be seen from the city.

The existing structure is basically Crusader. In 1102 the Crusaders erected an impressive shrine comprising an outer colonnaded cloister, within which stood an octagon of slender columns and arches open to the sky. Upon the defeat of the Crusaders, the Muslims added a cupola to the central octagon and filled in the arches with stone blocks. The fine carved capitals are worth closer inspection. The encircling cloister was destroyed and the east wall re-aligned. The shrine today is a mere shadow of its previous splendor.

Within the structure is a rock upon which there is an indentation—dubiously reputed to be Christ's right footprint. It is worth remembering that Jesus is honored by the Muslims as a prophet—they are unable to accept the Crucifixion or the Resurrection, but they acknowledge the Ascension.

Annually, on the Feast of the Ascension, the Armenian, Coptic, Greek Orthodox, Roman Catholic, and Syrian Churches are each allowed to celebrate Mass within the compound. The metal rings high on the outer walls enable protective awnings to be erected above temporary altars.

AUTHORS' COMMENTS

It is not surprising that many pilgrims find this to be a somewhat bizarre site—more of a curiosity than a holy place.

Opening Times: ring the bell; there is a small admission fee

Souvenir Shop: a limited number of souvenirs beside the shrine

Toilets: none

Custodian: The Muslims

Church of the Pater Noster
(Our Father)

Here on the Mount of Olives, according to tradition, Jesus taught his disciples The Lord's Prayer. Within the grounds of the French Carmelite convent are the thirteen-foot-high walls of an uncompleted church. Below the altar are the few remaining ruins of the "Eleona" Basilica, built in the fourth century by Emperor Constantine.

THE LORD'S PRAYER

When you pray, do not use a lot of words, as the pagans do, for they hold that the more they say, the more chance they have of being heard. Do not be like them. Your Father knows what you need, even before you ask him.

This, then, is how you should pray:
Our Father in Heaven,
holy be your name,
your kingdom come,
your will be done
on earth as in heaven.
Give us today the kind of bread we need.
Forgive us our debts
as we forgive those
who are in debt to us.
Do not bring us to the test
but deliver us from the Evil One.

If you forgive others their wrongs, your Father in Heaven will also forgive yours. If you do not forgive others, then your Father will not forgive you either. (Matthew 6:7–15)

> *"Forgive our sins as we forgive"*
> *you taught us, Lord, to pray;*
> *But you alone can grant us grace*
> *to live the words we say.*

ACCESS

The church and convent lie at the junction of the roads that run north/south and east/west over the Mount of Olives (see access instructions for

Place of the Ascension on page 21). Pater Noster is one hundred yards farther along the road from that site. Allow a good half an hour to walk from St. Stephen's Gate.

TOUR

From the entrance gate, descend the three short flights of steps that lead down into the uncompleted church. Mounted on the wall, immediately to the left, is a white limestone plaque upon which the Lord's Prayer is inscribed in Aramaic and ancient Hebrew. Below the modern altar platform, steps lead down to the somewhat scanty remains of the "Eleona" Basilica (Greek: "Olive Tree"). This was one of the three original churches built in the Holy Land on the orders of Emperor

Within the Church of the Pater Noster, the Lord's Prayer is inscribed on the walls in more than sixty languages. Here, the Aramaic and Hebrew versions. *(George Martin)*

Constantine in A.D. 330. The others were the Church of the Holy Sepulchre and the Church of the Nativity in Bethlehem.

Below the altar platform, the apse of the crypt of the original basilica is clearly visible, and this was partially built within a cave. In addition to commemorating the place where Jesus taught the disciples his own prayer, tradition holds that near here he spoke to them of the destruction of Jerusalem and the nature of the coming kingdom. At the back of the ancient crypt are some first-century A.D. tombs.

The basilica was destroyed by the Persians in A.D. 614. In the twelfth century the Crusaders built another church on the site, but after their defeat the Muslims occupied the ruins.

In 1868 the Princess de la Tour d'Auvergne bought the land and erected the present convent with its cloister for the Carmelite sisters. In 1918 the French launched an appeal to build a new basilica dedicated to the Sacred Heart. Work commenced in 1920, but funds ran out; today the unfinished church remains open to the skies.

The Lord's Prayer is inscribed on the walls of the cloister, and more recently on the walls of the church, in more than sixty different languages. The English translation can be found by passing through the small doorway on the south side of the uncompleted church, turning left up the steps, and then following the cloister around to a vestibule on the right. It is interesting to see how one ceramic tile has been changed to conform with modern grammar: "which art in heaven" has now been amended to "who art in heaven." Adjacent to this vestibule is the tomb of the Princess de la Tour d'Auvergne.

AUTHORS' COMMENTS

An obvious place in which to say the Lord's Prayer but also—because the Church is on the Mount of Olives and open to the skies—a suitable site in which to call to mind our Lord's Ascension into heaven.

Opening Times: 8:30–11:45, 3:00–4:45; closed Sundays
Souvenir Shop: inside the entrance gate on the left
Toilets: none
Custodian: The French Carmelite Sisters
Telephone: (02) 6264904

Dominus Flevit (The Lord Wept)

A small, tear-drop shaped church halfway up the Mount of Olives, Dominus Flevit commemorates the occasion when Jesus wept over the city and foretold its destruction.

JESUS WEEPS OVER THE CITY

When Jesus had come in sight of the city, he wept over it and said, "If only today you knew the ways of peace! But now your eyes are held from seeing. Yet days will come upon you when your enemies will surround you with barricades and shut you in and press on you from every side. And they will dash you to the ground and your children with you, and leave not a stone within you, for you did not recognize the time and the visitation of your God." (Luke 19:41–44)

O pray for the peace of Jerusalem:
they shall prosper that love thee.

ACCESS

FROM GETHSEMANE

The approach is via a steep single-track road that rises to the right immediately behind the Church of All Nations. Allow about twelve minutes walking.

FROM THE TOP OF THE MOUNT OF OLIVES

Take the road that runs from north to south, and between the Convent of Pater Noster and the Seven Arches Hotel, steps lead down beside the Tombs of the Prophets—Haggai, Malachi, and Zechariah. From here allow about five minutes to descend the steps and steep path to the site.

TOUR

From the entrance gate the path leads through flowering shrubs to the little church that was built in 1955 to a design by the Italian architect Antonio Barluzzi. At the end of the path, bear left (to avoid passing in front of the altar window and obstructing the view from inside) and walk down to the terrace from where there are magnificent views of the Temple Area and the Old City across the Kidron Valley.

To the north side of the church are traces of earlier Byzantine and Crusader buildings. Before entering the doorway, notice on the ground to the left a fine fifth-century mosaic. The outstanding feature of this lovely little church is the "Chalice" window that frames, very movingly, the city beyond. The mosaic on the front of the altar is of a hen gathering her chicks under her wings, as mentioned in St. Luke's Gospel (13:34). The Latin inscription on the

The small church named Dominus Flevit commemorates Jesus' weeping in sorrow over the coming destruction of Jerusalem.
(George Martin)

wall is also from St. Luke, recording how Jesus wept over the city before entering Jerusalem on Palm Sunday. Notice on the floor at the back how the apse of an earlier church followed the Christian tradition of facing east rather than west. Some of the mosaics from this building are also incorporated in the modern floor.

On returning to the site entrance, notice on the left, before reaching the gate, the ancient tomb complex containing sarcophagi and ossuaries that date from circa the second century B.C. to the fourth century A.D.

AUTHORS' COMMENTS

The site is a very suitable place for meditation because it overlooks so much that is mentioned in the gospel narrative.

Opening Times: 8:00–noon, 2:30–5:00 daily
Souvenir Shop: none
Toilets: to the left of the terrace
Custodian: The Franciscans
Telephone: (02) 6274931

GETHSEMANE

+‖+
+‖+

Church of the Agony
Cave of the Olive Press
Tomb of the Virgin Mary
Church of St. Mary Magdalene
Kidron Valley

Gethsemane is situated in the Kidron Valley outside the eastern wall of the Temple Area. From St. Stephen's Gate, also known as Lion Gate, proceed down the hill for about two hundred yards and turn right into the main Jericho Road. Bear around to the left, and the Church of the Agony is ahead. Allow eight minutes walking.

+‖+
+‖+

Church of the Agony

Commonly called the Church of All Nations, the Church of the Agony has a striking west façade consisting of a colonnaded portico with a fine mosaic above. Inside the church is a bare rock upon which, according to tradition, Jesus prayed before his arrest on Maundy Thursday night. On the north side of the church is a walled garden containing eight ancient olive trees.

Down in the Kidron Valley, next to the Garden of Gethsemane, is the Church of the Agony, a beautiful structure commemorating Christ's agony in the garden before his arrest. *(Anthony F. Chiffolo)*

THE AGONY, BETRAYAL, AND ARREST OF JESUS

After this Jesus left to go as usual to Mount Olivet and the disciples followed him. When he came to the place, he told them, "Pray that you may not be put to the test."

Then he went a little further, about a stone's throw, and kneeling down he prayed, "Father, if it is your will, remove this cup from me; still not my will but yours be done." And an angel from heaven appeared to give him strength.

As he was in agony, he prayed even more earnestly and great drops of blood formed like sweat and fell to the ground. When he rose from prayer, he went to his disciples but found them worn out with grief, and asleep. And he said to them, "Why do you sleep? Get up and pray, so that you may not be put to the test."

Jesus was still speaking when a group of men appeared and the man named Judas, one of the Twelve, was leading them. He drew near to Jesus to kiss him, and Jesus said to him, "Did you need this kiss to betray the Son of Man?"

Those with Jesus seeing what would happen, said to him, "Master, shall we

Within the Church of the Agony, also known as the Church of All Nations, is the reputed rock, shown here in the foreground, upon which Jesus sweat blood before his arrest. *(Allan Weinert)*

use the sword?" And one of them struck the High Priest's servant and cut off his right ear. But Jesus stopped him, "No more of this." He touched the man's ear and healed him.

Then Jesus spoke to those coming against him, the chief priests, officers of the Temple and elders and he said to them, "Did you really set out against a robber? Do you need swords and clubs to arrest me? Day after day I was among you teaching in the Temple and you did not arrest me. But this is the hour of the power of darkness; this is your hour."

Then they seized him and took him away, bringing him to the High Priest's house. (Luke 22:39–54)

Thine own disciple to the Jews has sold thee,
With friendship's kiss and loyal word he came;
How oft of faithful love my lips have told thee,
While thou has seen my falsehood and my shame.

TOUR

The entrance gate is fifty yards along the narrow road to the left of the wall protecting the ancient olive trees. Once inside, turn right to circumvent the garden. The largest of the trees has a girth of over eighteen feet. It is impossible to date them specifically, although in 1982 the University of California carried out carbon-dating tests, the results of which indicate that some

of the wood may be 2,300 years old.

Proceed around the garden to the portico of the west façade and enter the church. Inside, the overall impression is one of quiet solemnity, and this is greatly enhanced by the subdued violet-blue light coming through the alabaster windows. The focal point of the church

The peaceful Garden of Gethsemane, where Jesus and his apostles undoubtedly rested and prayed. *(Allan Weinert)*

is the area of bedrock, preserved in front of the main altar, upon which it is claimed that Jesus prayed to his Father before his arrest. St. Luke mentions that it was a "stone's throw" from where the disciples were sheltering and had fallen asleep. This is consistent with the proximity of the Cave of the Olive Press. The mosaic above the altar depicts the scene.

The iron wreath partially enclosing the rock represents the crown of thorns. Centrally, on three sides, a pair of thorn birds are featured in front of a Communion cup, symbolizing souls who wish to share the chalice of Christ's Passion. In each corner a silver dove is depicted caught in the thorns. The iron wreath was a gift from Australia.

Through a glass panel in the floor of the south aisle, you can see some original fourth-century Byzantine mosaics that were part of the first church. The modern floor is an exact copy. The apses of the north and south aisles have been designed so as to incorporate some lower stone courses from this same early church, which was reduced to ruins by the Persians in A.D. 614.

The Crusaders built another church on the site, but at an angle across the original foundations. You can see some remains of this twelfth-century structure on the south side of the modern basilica.

The present building, constructed on the line of the Byzantine foundations, was completed in 1924. Antonio Barluzzi, an Italian architect, succeeded in creating an atmosphere that reflects the anguish in the garden on that first Maundy Thursday night. The basilica is often referred to as the Church of All Nations because many countries contributed toward its cost. Their respective coats of arms are depicted in the twelve domes of the ceiling. Facing east, and working from the apses: on the left the cupolas represent Argentina, Brazil, Chile, and Mexico; in the middle, Italy, France, Spain, and England; on the right, Belgium, Canada, Germany, and the United States. The mosaics in the apses were donated by Ireland, Hungary, and Poland.

After leaving the church, cross the main road and turn to admire the fine west façade. Surmounting the Corinthian columns are statues representing the four great evangelists: Matthew, Mark, Luke, and John. Above them is an inscription in Latin from Hebrews 5:7: "Christ, in the days of his mortal life, offered his sacrifice with tears and cries. He prayed to him who could save him from death, and he was heard because of his humble submission." The mosaic depicts Christ as the mediator between God and humankind on whose behalf he gives his very heart, which an angel is shown receiving into his hands. To Christ's left there is a throng of lowly folk who, through their tears, look to him with confidence. To his right, the powerful and wise acknowledge the shortcomings of all their might and learning. On the summit two bronze stags flank the cross.

AUTHORS' COMMENTS

Undoubtedly one of the most important gospel sites in the Holy Land. Its devotional atmosphere makes a profound impression upon many pilgrims.

Opening Times: 8:00–noon, 2:30–6:00 daily (winter closes at 5:00)
Souvenir Shop: none (beware of persistent street traders outside)
Toilets: none
Custodian: The Franciscans
Telephone: (02) 6283264

+ + / + + /
Cave of the Olive Press

Here, according to tradition, Jesus and his disciples often sheltered.

ACCESS

The cave, and the entrance to the Tomb of the Virgin Mary, are to be found about one hundred yards north from the façade of the Church of the Agony. Immediately behind the small domed monument to a fifteenth-century Arab writer, descend the flight of steps leading down into a sunken courtyard. This was constructed in the twelfth century over an enormous water cistern. Ahead is the arched Crusader doorway to Mary's Tomb, but before entering it, take the narrow walled passageway to the right that leads to the Cave of the Olive Press.

DETAILS

The Hebrew words *gat shemen,* from which the area derives its name, means "olive press." Archaeological evidence found in the cave indicates that in our Lord's time an olive press was situated in the recess where the altar now stands. Notice beneath it the bronze figures depicting two of the sleeping disciples. At seasons other than harvest, the cave would have been used as a shelter and as such was known to Jesus and his followers. There is also evidence of Christian devotion here since the fourth century. You can see fragments of a mosaic floor and a pre-Christian water cistern at the back of the cave.

AUTHORS' COMMENTS

This site is often omitted from pilgrimage itineraries—which is a pity because here is a place that is basically unchanged and must have been familiar to Jesus.

Opening Times: 8:30–noon, 2:30–5:00 daily
Souvenir Shop: none
Toilets: none
Custodian: The Franciscans
Telephone: (02) 6283264

Tomb of the Virgin Mary

This is sometimes referred to as the Church of the Assumption. The Crusader doorway gives access to a long flight of steps leading down into the crypt, which is all that now remains of a fourth-century church containing the reputed tomb of the Mother of our Lord.

ACCESS

See the instructions for Cave of the Olive Press.

TOUR

The plain arched Crusader entrance to the shrine is on the north side of the sunken courtyard. From the entrance door, forty-four steps lead down through the gloom to a dungeonlike crypt, which is all that now remains of the original fourth-century Byzantine church. The crypt, therefore, is the oldest most complete religious building in Jerusalem, and this in itself justifies a visit.

The Tomb of the Virgin Mary is the reputed final resting place of the Blessed Virgin. As seen here, the interior features beautiful gold and silver lamps hanging from the ceiling. *(George Martin)*

The Franciscans were relieved of the custodianship of the shrine in 1857, and it is now used by the Eastern Orthodox churches: the Armenians, Copts, Greeks, and Syrians. The Muslims are also allowed to worship here because they reverence Mary as the Mother of the Prophet Jesus. There is a *mihrab* (prayer niche) to the right of the tomb. The atmosphere is typical of Eastern Orthodox churches, and illumination is confined to bare electric light bulbs.

At the bottom of the steps on the right is an altar behind which is an aedicule built over the reputed tomb of the Mother of our Lord. It is not unlike that in the Church of the Holy Sepulchre except, in this instance, much of the original hewn rock still remains. The architect separated it from the adjoining rocky mass, destroying other graves in the area. It is worth remembering that in the Turkish city of Ephesus there is another tomb claimed to be that of Mary. St. John, into whose care Jesus entrusted his mother, lived in that city toward the end of his life.

Hanging from the ceiling are a myriad of gold and silver lamps, while around the walls are many icons and other religious paintings. The use of candles has blackened the roof over the centuries, and on the Feast of the Assumption the light from hundreds of tapers carried by worshipers enhances the whole appearance.

On ascending the marble steps toward the daylight, notice, about halfway up on the right, a chapel dedicated to St. Joseph, Mary's husband. On the left is another dedicated to her parents, St. Joachim and St. Anne.

AUTHORS' COMMENTS

A typical Eastern Orthodox setting. Well worth a visit because of the antiquity of the site. Take a flashlight to illuminate the icons and paintings.

Opening Times: 6:00–11:45, 2:30–5:00 daily; a small donation is expected
Souvenir Shop: none
Toilets: none
Custodians: The Greek Orthodox Church

Church of St. Mary Magdalene

This impressive Russian Orthodox Church on the rising ground behind the Church of the Agony is distinguished by its seven gold onion-shaped domes.

ACCESS

Take the road to the right immediately behind the Church of the Agony. The entrance to the convent is on the left.

DETAILS

Czar Alexander III had this distinctive church built in 1888 in a typical seventeenth-century Russian style in memory of his mother. Visitors are allowed to view the interior from the back of the nave only, but you can see a number of nineteenth-century paintings and icons. Outside, there is a splendid view from the terrace across the Kidron Valley to the eastern wall of the Temple Area. Within the garden is buried Princess Alice of Greece, Mother of HRH Prince Philip, Duke of Edinburgh.

AUTHORS' COMMENTS

The exterior of the Church is the main attraction, and the surrounding compound is very peaceful. It is worth trying to gain admission to hear the nuns singing vespers.

Opening Times: 10:00–11:30 Tuesdays and Thursdays only; ring the bell

Souvenir Shop: none

Toilets: none

Custodian: The White Nuns of the Russian Orthodox Church

Telephone: (02) 6284371

The Russian Orthodox Church of St. Mary Magdalene, distinguished by its onion-shaped domes, is just up the hill from the Church of the Agony. *(George Martin)*

Kidron Valley

Also known as the Valley of Jehoshaphat, the literal meaning of which is "God judges." In the book of Joel (3:2) is found the prophesy that here all the

The Kidron Valley, as seen from the walls of Jerusalem. At the bottom of the valley is the Church of the Agony, and behind it is the distinctive Church of St. Mary Magdalene.
(Anthony F. Chiffolo)

nations of the world shall be judged, and since the period of the First Temple the slopes of the Kidron Valley have been a favored site for burials.

There has been a considerable in-fill of the valley over the centuries; nevertheless, the Kidron Brook still flows through it during the winter months. Much of the water is piped underground, but in places there is an open concrete channel, visible in the orchard immediately to the west of the Church of the Agony. During the summer months it is totally dry.

A little farther down the valley you will see the conical roof of what is generally known as the Tomb of Absalom. This, together with other tombs hewn out of the same rockface, dates from the first century B.C. They are among the few surviving artifacts upon which Jesus would undoubtedly have cast his eyes and as such are of particular significance to the Christian.

There is also the moving thought that on Maundy Thursday night Jesus, having been arrested in the Garden of Gethsemane, must have passed this way to his trial and been all too conscious of the fact that on the morrow he himself would lie in a tomb.

TEMPLE AREA

Western Wall
Mosque of El–Aqsa
Dome of the Rock

This extensive area encompassing the summit of Mount Moriah is sacred to followers of the three great monotheistic faiths: Jews, Christians, and Muslims—half the human race.

Western Wall

ACCESS

See map on page 15. The Temple Area with its Western Wall is situated in the southeast corner of the Old City and comprises a fifth of its area.

ON FOOT

From Jaffa Gate or Zion Gate, walk due east and look for the signs. From Damascus Gate, keep to the left and walk

Encompassing the summit of Mount Moriah, the Temple Area is sacred to Judaism, Christianity, and Islam. *(Allan Weinert)*

straight ahead for about a half mile until reaching an underpass that leads to the large piazza in front of the Western Wall. To the right of the wall, a narrow path leads up to a gate giving access to the Temple Area.

BY CAR

Park outside Dung Gate in the south wall of the Old City. Once inside the gate, walk straight ahead to the security check, and beyond it take the narrow path immediately on the right, which leads up to a gate giving access to the Temple Area.

HISTORY

There is an ancient tradition that here Abraham prepared to sacrifice his son Isaac in obedience to God.

In 1000 B.C. King David "built an altar unto the Lord," having purchased the ground from Araunah, the last of the Jebusite kings, who had used it as a threshing floor.

King Solomon, David's son, built the First Temple on the site in 950 B.C. It became a permanent resting place for the Ark of the Covenant. His temple was destroyed in 587 B.C. by the Babylonians when the Jews were taken into exile. Fifty years later they were allowed to return and rebuild to the same plan. Apart from a further interruption of worship during the Maccabean Revolt in 167 B.C., the area continued to be the religious center for the Jews.

Construction of the existing Temple platform, an area of about thirty-five acres, was begun by Herod the Great in 20 B.C. and today bears witness to the incredible achievement of his engineers. Upon this platform Herod built the magnificent Second Temple, which was still being completed in our Lord's time.

Here Jesus was presented as a baby, and here, at the age of twelve, his parents found him lingering among the teachers. Later, it is recorded that he was tempted by the devil to throw himself down from "The Pinnacle."

Jesus often worshiped and taught within the Temple precincts when visiting Jerusalem for one of the major festivals. Shortly before his arrest, he overturned the tables of the moneychangers, protesting that his Father's house should be a place of prayer and not a den of thieves.

In A.D. 70 when Jerusalem was sacked by Roman Emperor Titus, the Temple was totally destroyed and has never been rebuilt. In 135 Emperor Hadrian reconstructed the city as Aelia Capitolina, giving it the layout typical of a Roman town. He virtually ignored the Temple platform, and it lay almost derelict for the next five hundred years, although some scholars suggest that a statue or a temple to Venus was erected on the site.

The Muslims believe that in the middle of the seventh century their prophet Mohammed ascended into heaven on his winged stallion Al-Burak from the Temple Mount. For the last thirteen hundred years, therefore, the area has been sacred to Islam.

Today, strict Orthodox Jews are forbidden from entering the area. Because it was the resting place of the Ark of the Covenant, the ground is still regarded as too sacred to walk upon. Instead, they worship at the Western Wall, which increasingly has become the focal point of Jewish religious life.

JESUS EXPELS THE TRADERS
AND HEALS THE BLIND AND LAME

So Jesus went into the Temple and drove out all who were buying and selling in the temple area. He overturned the tables of the money changers, and the stools of those who sold pigeons. And he said to them, "It is written: My house shall be called a house of prayer. But you have turned it into a den of thieves."

The blind and the lame also came to him in the Temple and Jesus healed them.

The chief priests and the teachers of the Law saw the wonderful things Jesus had just done, and the children shouting in the temple area, "Hosanna to the Son of David!" They became indignant and said to Jesus, "Do you hear what they say?" Jesus answered them, "Yes. Have you never read this text: From the mouths of children and infants you have got perfect praise?"

So leaving them he went out of the city and came to Bethany where he spent the night. (Matthew 21:12–17)

> *All glory, laud, and honor*
> *to thee, Redeemer, King,*
> *To whom the lips of children*
> *Made sweet hosannas ring.*

TOUR

From the approach path there is a good view, on the left, of the Western Wall. The first seven courses of huge stone blocks above the present pavement level are Herodian. In our Lord's time a deep valley ran beside the wall, and eight additional lower courses were also visible. Through the centuries this valley, the Tyropean, has been progressively filled in with masonry and rubble. Originally, a wide bridge spanned the valley beyond the Western Wall so that people could reach the Temple from the Upper City. On the right of the approach path, jutting out from the wall, you can clearly see the stub of an arch that supported the upper platform of a stairway running west and then south down to the paved thor-

Since the Six-Day War in 1967, when Israel occupied the West Bank, the Jews are once again able to worship at the Western Wall. *(Anthony F. Chiffolo)*

oughfare below. This is known as Robinson's Arch, named after its discoverer the American archaeologist, Dr. Edward Robinson.

Inside the entrance gate and on the right is the Islamic Museum, while straight ahead is the Mosque of El-Aqsa. You can purchase an admission ticket to the museum and the mosques from the booth in the middle of the open courtyard on the right. The Muslims strictly control the area; consequently, pilgrims should be warned that group readings, prayers, and hymns are forbidden. Visitors are also prohibited from sitting on the grass, and any unseemly behavior means instant expulsion because the guards are anxious to maintain the sanctity of the site.

It seems likely that somewhere in this southern section of the Temple platform Jesus would have overturned the tables of the moneychangers. Beyond the Mosque of El-Aqsa, at the far southeast corner, is a sheer drop of about 130 feet from the top of the walls to the bedrock below. This has traditionally become known as "The Pinnacle," from which Jesus was tempted by the devil to throw himself down and be upheld by the angels. However, access to this point is often forbidden. You can get a good view of "The Pinnacle" from the Kidron Valley.

$$+\!\!\parallel\!\!+$$
$$+\!\!\parallel\!\!+$$

Mosque of El-Aqsa

Before entering the building, visitors must remove their shoes in the Muslim tradition, and for security reasons cameras and hand-baggage are not allowed. Nevertheless, a visit is worthwhile because the interior is most impressive and the sense of space is truly awesome. There is room for more than four thousand Muslims to prostrate themselves on the carpets during their worship, which takes place five times a day.

The name means "the farthest" (from Mecca). Although considerable reconstruction and restoration have been carried out since 1938, the lines of the present building date from the eleventh century, and its structure was based on an earlier mosque built in A.D. 715 by Caliph Al-Wail. During the Crusader Period the building was converted for Christian use and became known as the Templum Solomonis, headquarters of the Knights Templars. After their defeat in 1187 it was once again used as a mosque. In 1927 serious earthquake damage occurred, and more than a third of the structure had to be totally rebuilt. Tragically, on August 21, 1969, a visitor deliberately started a fire, causing considerable damage to the ancient marble paneling and mosaics at the far end of the building, but the most serious loss was the total destruction of the splendid twelfth-century pulpit beautifully inlaid with mother-of-pearl and ivory.

The roof is supported by seventy-five columns and pillars, which divide the building into a wide nave and six aisles. The circular marble columns are modern and were quarried in Italy, but the massive square pillars on the right date from the eleventh century. The nave and all to the left of the building have been reconstructed since 1938. The forty-two clerestory windows containing contemporary colored glass throw a subdued light on the beautifully decorated ceiling, a gift from King Farouk and the Egyptian government. The Oriental carpets are Turkish, while the green-and-white prayer rugs were a gift from Saudi Arabia. The oldest part of the building is the far end, where the wall and the *mihrab* (indicating the direction of Mecca) date from the eighth century. The windows flanking this area contain copies of twelfth–fourteenth-century stained glass. Notice the modern Western-style clock on the left with additional faces indicating sunrise and sunset, and also the variable prayer times throughout the day.

On Fridays the Temple Area is closed all day to tourists when this great mosque, together with the courtyard outside, is filled with thousands of Muslim worshipers.

On leaving the main entrance, walk straight ahead toward the Dome of the Rock and observe, in passing, the ritual cleansing fountain, which is in daily use.

Dome of the Rock

Sometimes called the Mosque of Omar, it is not, however, a congregational mosque, but rather a place for private prayer, contemplation, and pilgrimage. This truly magnificent shrine, the earliest surviving Muslim building in existence, was built in A.D. 692 by Abd-al-Malik, and its basic structure has successfully withstood the ravages of time. It was erected over the exposed rock at the summit of Mount Moriah, where, according to tradition, Abraham prepared to sacrifice his son Isaac, and also in a sacred area where once stood Solomon's Temple, and later the Temple built by Herod the Great that was so familiar to our Lord. During the Crusader Period the building was used as a church, the Templum Domini, when for a short time the Christian cross replaced the half crescent.

The perfect geometric proportions and the brilliant blue exterior are particularly striking. Originally, the dome was covered in gold and the walls

The Dome of the Rock is a magnificent Muslim shrine, designed for private prayer, contemplation, and pilgrimage.
(Anthony F. Chiffolo)

with mosaics. In the sixteenth century the mosaics were replaced with blue Turkish tiles, and at the end of the nineteenth century, a decorative band bearing quotations from the Koran was added at the top of the outer walls. Considerable restoration has taken place in recent years: the gold covering on the dome has been replaced three times, and the wall tiles have been faithfully renewed.

Entrance for visitors is normally through a door in the west face. Again, shoes must be removed, and there are the usual security arrangements.

The interior at first appears to be rather dark, but the eyes soon adjust to the soft light filtering through the fifty-six stained-glass windows. From the doorway, walk toward the center where you can see the exposed rock of the top of Mount Moriah; it is protected by a twelfth-century cedarwood screen. The dome above, decorated with magnificent gold-and-red stucco, was rebuilt in 1022 but has been partially restored on five separate occasions. The drum supporting it is covered in superb mosaics, which follow the original designs. During the Crusader Period a Christian altar was placed upon the rock. The entire area had to be protected by marble because pieces were being chipped away to be used as relics all over Europe.

In the right-hand corner of the rock is a tall wooden shrine with gilded grilles and cupola. It is said to contain a hair from the prophet Mohammed's beard.

Continue around the rock until reaching sixteen steps leading down to an ancient cave below. This is a place of great sanctity, and many fables and legends are attached to it in Jewish and Islamic traditions. During the Crusader Period the cave was used as a confessional.

Before leaving the main building, notice the splendid mosaics in gold and green at the top of the arcade of outer pillars and arches. Most of the decoration here is original and dates from A.D. 692. Above it, in gold lettering on a green background, is the founder's inscription running around the building on both sides of the arcade for a total length of about 825 feet. It is the oldest Arabic script in existence. The Caliph al-Ma'mun, in carrying out restoration in 830, erased the name of the founder, Abd-al-Malik, and inserted his own—but he neglected to alter the date!

Once outside the Dome of the Rock, walk to a point on the east of the building to view the little Dome of the Chain. Some scholars suggest that it was used as a builder's model for the main mosque and was never dismantled. The seventeen marble pillars from earlier Byzantine churches are arranged in such a way that they can all be seen simultaneously from any angle. This delightful aedicule is devoid of walls except for a *mihrab* facing Mecca. It derives its name from an ancient legend that here on the site of David's Place of Judgment a suspended chain was used as a lie detector.

Continue in an easterly direction to descend a wide flight of steps from where there is an attractive view of the Mount of Olives. At the bottom, take the path to the left, and on the right of it can be seen the rear of Golden Gate. According to Jewish tradition, it is sealed until the Day of Judgment, when the righteous will be accepted into the Holy City.

Visitors are discouraged from closely inspecting the structure, which is an impressive one dating possibly from the middle of the fourth century. The gate has not been opened since the Crusader Period, and then only on Palm Sunday and on the Feast of the Exultation of the Cross.

Before leaving the Temple Area, walk along the north side of the compound to notice, on the right, the remaining foundations of Herod's massive Fortress of Antonia built directly upon the bedrock. Here was stationed the Roman garrison whose duty was to maintain public order in the Temple precincts.

Opening Times: 8:00–11:30, 12:30–2:00; 7:30–10:00 only during Ramadan; closed Fridays and Muslim public holidays

Souvenir Shop: none

Toilets: ask one of the guards for directions

Custodian: The Supreme Muslim Council

Telephone: (02) 6283313

POOL OF BETHESDA

Church of St. Anne

Excavations have uncovered a small area of the pool some thirty-three feet below today's ground level. St. John records that here Jesus healed the man who had been paralyzed for thirty-eight years.

The Crusader Church of St. Anne is built over the reputed site of the home of St. Joachim and St. Anne, the parents of the Virgin Mary.

ACCESS

Refer to the map on page 3. Approximately sixty yards inside St. Stephen's Gate (also known as Lion Gate), on the right of the street, is the entrance to the compound of the Greek Catholic seminary occupied by the French White Fathers. There is an inscription to this effect above the doorway. Within the area are located both the Pool of Bethesda and the Church of St. Anne.

DETAILS

From the entrance door, walk straight ahead across the pleasant courtyard past the west façade of St. Anne's Church toward the railings that mark the perimeter of the excavations. At first sight the ruins are somewhat bewildering; it is, therefore, worth studying the archaeological plan close at hand.

The diggings, carried out since 1956, have revealed the remains of a very large fifth-century Byzantine church—the Church of the Paralytic—part of which was built over a small area of the Pool of Bethesda. The Persians destroyed the church in A.D. 614, and its masonry fell into the pool. Today, a series of stairways eventually leads down to a level where it is possible to see small pockets of rather stagnant water among the ruins.

In our Lord's time the pool was an

The ruins of the Pool of Bethesda, built as a reservoir. The waters were believed to have therapeutic qualities. *(Allan Weinert)* elongated trapezoid shape approximately 330 by 165 feet and about 20 feet deep. It was carved out of the rock as two separate basins. These were surrounded by five colonnades, one on each side and another across the dividing wall. St. John refers to them in his gospel. The pool was originally built as a reservoir to collect the winter rains that drained into it for use in the Temple during the summer months. The water was believed to have therapeutic qualities, and it is interesting to note that the east end of the Byzantine church was built over a pagan temple to Aesculapius, the Greek god of healing.

In the twelfth century when the Crusaders built the Church of St. Anne, they also erected a small chapel on the remains of the northern nave of the Byzantine basilica. This can be distinguished very clearly above ground level and affords an excellent example of one church being built upon another.

THE HEALING OF THE PARALYTIC

Now, by the Sheep Gate in Jerusalem, there is a pool (called Bethzatha in Hebrew) surrounded by five galleries. In these galleries lay a multitude of sick people—blind, lame and paralyzed.

(All were waiting for the water to move, for at times an angel of the Lord would descend into the pool and stir up the water; and the first person to enter after this movement of the water would be healed of whatever disease he had.)

There was a man who had been sick for thirty-eight years. Jesus saw him, and since he knew how long this man had been lying there, he said to him, "Do you want to be healed?" And the sick man answered, "Sir, I have no one to put me into the pool when the water is disturbed; so while I am still on my way, another steps down before me."

Jesus then said to him, "Stand up, take your mat and walk." And at once the man was healed, and he took up his mat and walked. (John 5:2–9)

All your commands I know are true,
your many gifts will make me new,
into my life your power breaks through
Living Lord.

Church of St. Anne

DETAILS

This is one of the finest examples in the Holy Land of a large Crusader church. From the outside the robust structure gives a fortresslike appearance. Inside, its lines are powerful and rather austere, looking very much as they must have done eight hundred years ago.

From the south aisle, twenty-three steps lead down to the crypt, which dates from the fifth century. According to tradition, the original Byzantine church was built over a cave that had been part of the home of Joachim and Anne, the parents of the Virgin Mary. The crypt contains two small altars.

A Crusader church, the Church of St. Anne was built in 1140 over the reputed home of Joachim and Anne, the parents of the Virgin Mary. *(George Martin)*

The earliest recorded associations with Mary date from the third century, when there was an oratory on the site. Queen Eudoxia, the Byzantine empress, built the first church over the oratory in A.D. 438. The Persians destroyed it at the beginning of the seventh century, but it was rebuilt soon afterward. The Crusaders erected the present church in 1140, and after they had been driven out half a century later, the Muslims used the buildings as an Islamic theological school, although Christians were still allowed into the crypt. Above the west door outside you can see an inscription in Arabic from this period.

In 1856 the Turks presented the site to the French in appreciation for their help during the Crimean War. Extensive restorations took place before the church was entrusted to the care of its present occupants, the White Fathers.

It is interesting to note that the site was previously offered to Queen Victoria—but this gesture was declined in favor of the Island of Cyprus!

AUTHORS' COMMENTS

The area is a very peaceful haven from the noise of the street outside. St. Anne's Church is striking in its simplicity and possesses a fascinating acoustic. Even a small group singing can sound like a large congregation in a great cathedral.

Opening Times: summer 8:00–noon, 2:00–6:00; winter 8:00–noon, 2:00–5:00; closed on Sundays

Souvenir Shop: postcards and a guidebook are available

Toilets: inside the entrance to the compound

Custodian: The French White Fathers (a Greek Catholic Community)

Telephone: (02) 6283285

VIA DOLOROSA
(The Way of Sorrows)

The Stations of the Cross

"The Way of the Cross," the route Jesus took to Calvary, was not defined in its present form until the fifteenth century. There are fourteen stations of the cross: nine along the Via Dolorosa, and the remainder within the Church of the Holy Sepulchre. Their locations are, in the main, only commemorative: nine are based on the gospel narratives, while the other five are traditional. It is not really practical for large groups to stop for devotions except in the early morning before the shops are opened.

JESUS BEFORE PILATE. THE WAY OF THE CROSS

Early in the morning, the chief priests, the elders and the teachers of the Law (that is, the whole Council or Sanhedrin) had their plan ready. They put Jesus in chains, led him away and handed him over to Pilate.

Pilate asked him, "Are you the King of the Jews?" Jesus answered, "You say so." As the chief priests accused Jesus of many things, Pilate asked him again, "Have you no answer at all? See how many charges they bring against you." But Jesus gave no further answers, so that Pilate wondered.

At every Passover festival, Pilate used to free any prisoner the people asked for. Now there was a man called Barabbas, jailed with the rioters who had committed murder in the uprising. When the crowd went up to ask Pilate the usual favor, he said to them, "Do you want me to set free the King of the Jews?" For he realized that the chief priests had handed Jesus over to him out of envy. But the chief priests stirred up the crowd to ask instead for the release of Barabbas. Pilate replied, "And what shall I do with the man you call King of the Jews?" The crowd shouted back, "Crucify him!" Pilate asked, "What evil has he done?" But they shouted the louder, "Crucify him!"

As Pilate wanted to please the people, he freed Barabbas and after the flogging of Jesus had him handed over to be crucified.

The soldiers took him inside the courtyard known as the praetorium *and called the rest of their companions. They clothed him in a purple* cloak and twisting a crown of thorns, they forced it onto his head. Then they began saluting him, "Long life to the King of the Jews!" With a stick they gave him blows on the head and spat on him; then they knelt down pretending to worship him.

When they had finished mocking him, they pulled off the purple cloak and put his own clothes on him.

The soldiers led him out of the city to crucify him. On the way they met Simon of Cyrene, father of Alexander and Rufus, who was coming in from the country, and forced him to carry the cross of Jesus. (Mark 15:1–21)

> O dearest Lord, thy sacred head
> with thorns was pierced for me:
> O pour thy blessing on my head
> that I may think for thee.

ACCESS

Reference to the map on page 3 will show that there are many approaches, but it is best to enter the Old City from the east through St. Stephen's Gate, also known as Lion Gate because of the four lions in bas-relief on its façade. Suleiman the Magnificent had this gateway and the present walls built in the sixteenth century. From the gate, walk straight ahead for three hundred yards.

Stations of the Cross

All the stations are described in detail below; however, some pilgrims leave out eight and nine and proceed straight to number ten within the Church of the Holy Sepulchre.

STATION I: JESUS IS CONDEMNED TO DEATH

Located three hundred yards from St. Stephen's Gate within the court-yard of Al'Omariyeh College, an Arab school, which now stands over part of the site of the Fortress of Antonia, where, according to tradition, Jesus stood trial before Pilate. The station, however, is not specifically marked. To reach the school, ascend a flight of steps on the left of the road. The premises are not normally open, but the gatekeeper occasionally gives permission to enter. However, the Franciscans organize a procession commencing here at 3:00 on Friday afternoons when a heavy wooden cross is carried along the Via Dolorosa. Members of the public are welcome to join them.

In our Lord's time the Antonia Fortress was an enormous military garrison, built by Herod to defend the northern boundary of the city and to maintain order in the Temple Area. Many scholars support the view that Pilate would have stayed in the fortress whenever he visited Jerusalem from his headquarters at Caesarea beside the Mediterranean. In consequence, the traditional Via Dolorosa starts at this point, although some suggest that the procurator may have stayed in Herod's Palace, which was on the west of the city beside the present Jaffa Gate.

STATION II: JESUS TAKES UP THE CROSS

Like the first station, the second is not specifically defined. However, pilgrims meditate upon its significance in the street a little farther along from

the steps leading up to Al'Omariyeh College. Ahead, the arch with the windows above it is known as "Ecce Homo" (Behold the Man). It is built on the site of the gateway where by tradition Pilate addressed the crowd.

If time allows, there are three important Christian shrines in the immediate vicinity that the pilgrim should visit. It is widely believed that these are also on part of the site of the Fortress of Antonia. To reach them, walk back along the road for a few yards and enter a doorway on the left just before a smaller arch that spans the street toward Al'Omariyeh College. The door leads into a courtyard belonging to the Franciscans. Immediately ahead is the entrance to a Roman Catholic theological college, while on the right is…

Built on the reputed site of the gateway from which Pilate addressed the crowd, the "Ecce Homo" arch commemorates Jesus' taking up his cross.
(George Martin)

CHAPEL OF THE FLAGELLATION

This was rebuilt in 1929 to a design by the Italian architect Antonio Barluzzi. The main features are the ceiling above the altar representing a crown of thorns, and the three stained-glass windows. These depict Jesus scourged at the pillar, Pilate washing his hands, and the triumph of Barabbas.

CHAPEL OF THE CONDEMNATION

This chapel is on the left of the courtyard. Here behind the altar is a moving portrayal in relief of Jesus leaving the Fortress of Antonia to receive his cross. Notice the enormous flagstones at the back of the chapel. These are a continuation of the Lithostrotos, the major part of which can be seen within the adjoining Convent of the Sisters of Zion. Opposite the chapel entrance is a model of Jerusalem in the first century showing how the sites of Calvary and the tomb were outside the city walls.

LITHOSTROTOS

Lithostrotos is the Greek name for pavement; it is *gabbatha* in Aramaic, the spoken language of some of the Jews in our Lord's time. The entrance is forty yards farther along the street from the courtyard of the Chapels of the Flagellation and Condemnation. At this point, turn right into a narrow alley; the door is immediately on the left.

The Via Dolorosa commemorates the route Jesus traveled to Calvary. This mosaic is found within the Convent of the Sisters of Zion. *(Anthony F. Chiffolo)*

Ring the bell for admission. A small entrance fee is payable at the desk, and a leaflet explaining the archaeological discoveries will be provided. In the reception area are three information bays, and below each lectern are some useful explanatory diagrams.

Follow the arrows around the site; the various features are clearly marked. There are many steps to negotiate, so the less mobile are advised to turn right at the bottom of the first flight, proceed ahead under an arch, then turn right again toward the Roman pavement.

The more agile can continue down another flight of steps, almost immediately below the first flight, leading to the Struthion Pool, which still holds a large volume of water. This reservoir dates from the Herodian Period, and its original purpose was to provide water for the Fortress of Antonia and its environs. Hadrian had the vaulted roof constructed here in A.D. 135, and it supports a section of the Roman pavement above.

Continue following the arrows around the complex until reaching a level area near the bottom of the first flight of stairs leading down from the entrance foyer. Walk straight ahead and pass over a grille through which you can see, directly below, the waters of the Struthion Pool. A little farther along you'll reach the Roman pavement.

In this area silence is particularly requested because the low ceiling is very resonant. An altar has been erected in the center for the celebration of Mass.

Notice how the flagstones have gullies cut into them to carry away the rainwater; other sections are striated to prevent horses from slipping, while some of the holes were most probably used to support streetlamps.

Proceed to the far end, passing the altar on the left, and notice on the wall a modern mosaic depicting Jesus on the pavement with his cross.

Now turn back, passing the altar on the other side, and just beyond on the left is one of the most interesting features of the whole area. Here, etched into a flagstone, you can clearly distinguish the outline of a dice game played by the Roman soldiers. This was known as the "King's Game," and occasionally, the soldier who won it was given the robe of the prisoner to be crucified. The game, therefore, has particular significance in relation to the gospel story.

Archaeologists have now confirmed that the pavement, as it is seen today, was laid in A.D. 135 by Hadrian when Jerusalem became a Roman city known as Aelia Capitolina. Although this was a century after the Crucifixion, it seems improbable that in the reconstruction Herod's enormous flagstones would have been totally discarded merely to be substituted by others of similar proportions. It is more likely that many of them would simply have been recut and relaid when the area became a Roman forum. If this assumption is correct, then there are grounds for believing that Jesus may have walked on some of these stones.

The exit from the pavement is on the right. Ascend a metal stairway leading to a vestibule from which a revolving steel door gives access to the street. Turn right, walk under the "Ecce Homo" arch, and then ascend a flight of steps on the right. These lead into a vestibule from where you can see the interior of the chapel belonging to the Sisters of Zion. The archway behind the altar is Roman. When it was built in A.D. 135, it formed part of Hadrian's Triumphal Arch, the central span of which straddled the street outside.

Return to the Via Dolorosa, walk down the hill for about a hundred yards, and turn sharply left at the end. Continue for another fifteen yards to the next station, on the left.

STATION III: JESUS FALLS FOR THE FIRST TIME

A very small chapel, running parallel to the street, commemorates this station. Above the entrance is a stone-relief of Jesus falling with his cross. Beside the doorway are two ancient pillars. The building was restored in

1948 with donations from Polish soldiers who served in Palestine during the Second World War. Continue along the road for twenty-five yards to the next station on the left.

STATION IV: JESUS MEETS HIS MOTHER

A stone-relief above a doorway depicts the scene. Here pilgrims are reminded of Mary's grief. The doors lead into a small Armenian Catholic chapel, but it is rarely open to the public. Walk along the road for another twenty-five yards and then turn right. On the corner is the next station.

STATION V: SIMON OF CYRENE IS COMPELLED TO CARRY THE CROSS

The gospels record how this casual visitor from North Africa became involved in the Passion story. The lintel of a doorway is clearly marked with an inscription, on the left of which is the Roman numeral V. Behind the door is a Franciscan oratory, but again it is not often open to the public. Now start ascending the steps up the hill, and a hundred yards on the left you'll find the next station.

STATION VI: ST. VERONICA WIPES THE SWEAT FROM JESUS' FACE

This station is reputed to be on the site of the home of St. Veronica who, according to tradition, used her veil to wipe the face of Jesus. The imprint of his features remained on the cloth. The veil is said to have been responsible for a number of miracles and since A.D. 707 has been preserved in St. Peter's in Rome.

To identify the station, look for a wooden door with studded metal bands upon it. The center panel bears the Roman numeral VI. The chapel behind is not open to the public, but ten yards farther on, up a flight of steps, you can view the Greek Church of the Holy Face and St. Veronica through a metal door. This delightful chapel, built in 1882 on the site of a sixth-century monastery, was tastefully restored in 1953 by the Italian architect Antonio Barluzzi. It belongs to the Little Sisters of Jesus, a Greek Catholic order.

Continue up the hill for seventy-five yards. From a position at the end of a very dark archway, look directly ahead to identify the next station.

STATION VII: JESUS FALLS FOR THE SECOND TIME

On the wall, above a window over a doorway, is the Roman numeral VII. Often hidden by market stalls, the door is usually locked. Behind the façade are two chapels, one above the other, and in the lower is a second-century pillar, in its original position, which was part of the wide colonnaded main street of the Roman city Aelia Capitolina. The thoroughfare, known as the Cardo, ran from Damascus Gate in the north to Zion Gate in the south.

It is important to realize that the position of this station marks the west boundary of Jerusalem in our Lord's time. According to some scholars, the "Gate of Judgment" would have been here. From this point on, therefore, Jesus carried his cross outside the city walls on his way to the mound known as "Golgotha" (Place of the Skull), upon which crucifixions took place in full view from the walls.

Pilgrims leaving out Stations VIII and IX should take the following route to the Church of the Holy Sepulchre: Turn left at the top of the hill by Station VII and proceed along the busy main street for 150 yards. Here turn right, then shortly left and right again into a wide thoroughfare. Continue straight ahead for eighty yards, and go through a small archway above which are the words "Holy Sepulchre."

Otherwise, walk straight across the main thoroughfare into the narrower street, and after only thirty yards look out on the left for the next station.

STATION VIII: JESUS CONSOLES THE WOMEN OF JERUSALEM

Of all the stations, this is the most difficult to identify, and it is not even marked with the Roman numeral *VIII*. Look for a small stone set at eye level distinguished by a cross carved upon it and flanked by the Greek letters IC XC NIKA ("Jesus is victorious"). Also cut into the stone is a hole in which a small candle is sometimes placed.

Instructions for reaching the ninth station are somewhat complicated because it is first necessary to retrace one's steps to the main thoroughfare. Here, turn right and walk along the very busy street for one hundred yards; on the right is a flight of twenty-eight wide steps. Ascend them, turning left at the top, and continue along a passageway for thirty yards, then turn right at the end.

Proceed for twenty yards, passing under an archway; turn left at the end and continue for another thirty yards until reaching the entrance to the Coptic Patriarchal Cathedral. To the left are three steps leading into the Ethiopian monastery. This is the next station.

STATION IX: JESUS FALLS FOR THE THIRD TIME

The station is not specifically marked, but pilgrims meditate upon its significance in the vicinity of the ancient Roman column set into the wall.

The remaining five stations of the cross are within the Church of the Holy Sepulchre. If the door to the Ethiopian monastery is open, it is possible to take a shortcut from this point. The first paragraph below gives instructions for the shorter route. If the door is closed, please read on to the second paragraph.

1. Step into the Ethiopian compound (details of the monastery will be found under "Church of the Holy Sepulchre" on page 58). Walk straight ahead and enter the second small door on the right with a low lintel. This leads into the upper chapel belonging to the Abyssinian monks. Walk to the back and descend some steps into the lower chapel. From here a door gives access to the courtyard in front of the main entrance to the Church of the Holy Sepulchre.
2. If the door is not open, it will be necessary to return to the main street. Here (at the bottom of the twenty-eight wide steps) turn right and proceed for another forty yards to the end. Now turn right, then shortly left and right again into a wide thoroughfare. Continue straight ahead for eighty yards toward a small archway, above which are the words "Holy Sepulchre," leading into the courtyard in front of the church.

Stations X to XIV are listed here to avoid interruption of the devotional sequence. Except for a brief explanation of the tomb, no attempt is made in this text to describe the surroundings. A more detailed account can be found under "Church of the Holy Sepulchre" on page 58.

From the courtyard in front of the Church of the Holy Sepulchre, enter the main door, and once inside, turn immediately right to ascend the nineteen very steep steps leading to the chapels constructed above the rock of Calvary. The four stations here are not specifically marked.

STATIONS X AND XI: JESUS IS STRIPPED OF HIS GARMENTS AND JESUS IS NAILED TO THE CROSS

The chapel at the top of the stairs belongs to the Roman Catholic Church. Devotions commemorating the tenth and eleventh stations take place here. The two sanctuaries on Calvary are divided by large pillars. Walk between them into the other chapel owned by the Greek Orthodox Church. This is Station XII.

STATION XII: JESUS DIES ON THE CROSS

The ornate altar here is built directly over the traditional site of the Crucifixion. On either side, through glass panels, you can see the natural bedrock of Calvary. To the right is the next station.

STATION XIII: JESUS IS TAKEN DOWN FROM THE CROSS

The small altar placed centrally between the two larger ones also belongs to the Roman Catholic Church. Upon it, protected by glass, is a statue of the Blessed Virgin Mary known as *Stabat Mater (Our Lady of Sorrows)*.

Leave Calvary by the other steps at the rear of the Greek Orthodox chapel, turn left at the bottom, and proceed past the Stone of the Anointing, above which hang eight lamps. According to tradition it was here that our Lord's body was prepared for burial. Continue straight ahead to the final station beneath the Rotunda.

STATION XIV: JESUS IS LAID IN THE TOMB

This area of the church is known as the Anastasis ("Resurrection"). In the center is a large aedicule built over the site of the tomb. It should be remembered that at the beginning of the eleventh century, the original tomb was totally destroyed on the orders of the fanatical Egyptian Caliph Hakim. Turkish authorities erected the present aedicule marking the sacred place of our Lord's burial less than two hundred years ago when relations between the East and West were at a very low ebb. The steel girders that had to be used to shore up the building following an earthquake in 1927 do not help the general impression.

The outer chamber is known as the Chapel of the Angel, and on a plinth in the center is reputed to be a piece of the original rolling stone. An inner chamber lined with marble and constructed in 1810 marks the site of the tomb itself. Inside there is just sufficient room for three people to kneel in devotion. Pilgrims should be warned, however, that the Greek Orthodox priest on duty will expect a monetary offering. Many find this a distasteful and distracting act within such a very holy place.

Flagellation and Condemnation

Opening Times: 8:00–noon, 2:00–6:00 daily; winter 8:00–noon, 1:00–5:00
Custodian: The Franciscans
Telephone: (02) 6282936

Lithostrotos

Opening Times: 8:30–12:30, 2:00–5:00; winter closes 4:30; closed on Sundays; there is an entrance fee

Toilets: beyond the reception area

Custodian: The French Sisters of Zion

Telephone: (02) 6277292

Holy Sepulchre

Opening Times: 4:00–8:00 P.M. daily; winter closes 7:00

Custodian: multidenominational

Telephone: (02) 6273314 (Franciscans)

CHURCH OF THE HOLY SEPULCHRE

This great basilica encompasses all that remains of the traditional rock of Calvary and the site of our Lord's tomb. Both are at the very heart of the Christian faith—the scene of humankind's redemption and the place where Jesus overcame the power of death. Of all the holy sites, it is undoubtedly the most difficult to come to terms with, and to appreciate the church, the pilgrim should first have some understanding of its complexity. The archaeological and historical evidence to support the validity of the site is very substantial.

Built over Jesus' traditional burial place, Church of the Holy Sepulchre is one of Christendom's holiest sites.

1. The basilica is not laid out in the traditional Western form, and at first sight the interior hardly resembles a church at all. The main entrance leads into a dark transept on the south side from which, immediately on the right, steps lead up to two ornate chapels built over the rock of Calvary.
2. Ironically, because of its importance, this central shrine of Christendom has, through the centuries, suffered from humankind's attempts alternately at desecration, preservation, and overzealous adornment. The Crusaders erected the present building, the fourth on the site, in the twelfth century. The original basilica, built by Roman Emperor Constantine in A.D. 335, was almost twice the length.
3. The Armenian, Coptic, Greek Orthodox, and Roman Catholic Churches share the building. Although today there is a greater degree of ecumenical tolerance between these branches of Christianity, it is hardly surprising that they jealously guard their ancient rights to hold their own forms of worship within its walls.

The very diverse services—and the particular "territories" owned by the custodians—are strictly governed by regulations known as the "status quo." Other Eastern Orthodox churches within the Holy City are also allowed specific privileges to conduct worship here.

Furthermore, a vast number of Christian pilgrims from all over the world come to pray in this holy place. To them must be added an even greater number of tourists who also wish to see inside the building. Consequently, be prepared for crowds at peak periods.

The most suitable time to visit is very early in the day, and especially from about six o'clock on Sunday morning onward, when this great basilica—more appropriately known by the Eastern Orthodox churches as the Church of the Resurrection—can be seen at its best and is alive with so many forms of liturgical worship.

ACCESS
See map on page 63.

FROM JAFFA GATE
Walk straight ahead into the Old City for one hundred yards until reaching the top of David Street, a main Arab trading thoroughfare. Descend the shallow steps for sixty yards, then take the first left under an archway. Continue along this street, Christian Quarter Road, for about one hundred yards, and look for the huge stone blocks that now form part of the pavement. These have been moved from their original position but date from the time of Herod the Great. Soon after this turn right into a covered street and walk to the end. Here, by the entrance to a mosque, turn left and descend some steps that lead into the courtyard in front of the Church of the Holy Sepulchre.

FROM DAMASCUS GATE
Pass through the gateway and walk straight ahead for sixty yards, keeping to the right. Now take the narrow arched street continuing on the right. Walk along this main thoroughfare to the end (a total distance of 350 yards). At a point where the *suq* (market) narrows and is traversed by another, turn right into a street open to the skies. Follow the S-bend around, and at the junction turn right toward the minaret of a mosque at the end of a wide street. Proceed straight ahead for eighty yards, and go through a small archway above which are the words "Holy Sepulchre." This leads into the courtyard in front of the church.

HISTORY AND VALIDITY OF THE SITE

For those familiar with the gospel story and the words of Mrs. C. F. Alexander's famous hymn recalling the green hill outside the city walls, it is bewildering to discover that the Church of the Holy Sepulchre is today almost in the center of the Old City. Scripture clearly records that Christ suffered "outside the gate" and in a place called Golgotha ("Place of the Skull"), adjoining which was a garden. It is hardly surprising, therefore, that some Christians find the Garden Tomb, situated a few hundred yards outside Damascus Gate, more in keeping with their expectations. Nevertheless, the hypothesis is very strong in support of the claim that the ground on which the church stands was in fact outside the city walls at the time of the Crucifixion.

THE EARLY ARCHAEOLOGICAL EVIDENCE

1. It is important to appreciate that in our Lord's lifetime the north wall of Jerusalem ran roughly from Herod's Palace (where the Citadel now stands) to the Fortress of Antonia. Indeed, one of the purposes of this great stronghold was to defend the city from the north. Golgotha was then outside this wall. However, the historian Flavius Josephus records that in the middle of the first century, some time after the Crucifixion, Jerusalem began to spread northward, and a suburb developed. This new area required protection, so two other walls were subsequently built.

   It was not until A.D. 135 when Roman Emperor Hadrian completely redesigned the city that the north wall was constructed in its final position. You can still see the lower courses of this Roman structure below Damascus Gate. Thus, the Church of the Holy Sepulchre is now well within the confines of the Old City—and has been for over 1,800 years.

2. In the 1960s the famous British archaeologist the late Dr. Kathleen Kenyon discovered in a deep excavation south of the church a stone quarry dating from the seventh century B.C. This contained only waste material, and she found no evidence of any building prior to the second century A.D. Consequently, she drew the conclusion that the site remained outside the occupied area, and, therefore, presumably outside the walls.

3. Inside the Church of the Holy Sepulchre and within a few yards of the site of our Lord's tomb are, hewn out of the bedrock, two complete first-century Jewish tombs. This proves that the area was outside the walls in our Lord's time because burials never took

place within the city confines as the ground was thus rendered unclean.

It is probable that there were other tombs in the area and that the rocky mound of Calvary was chosen for crucifixions simply because it could be seen from the walls and acted as a reminder of the consequences of breaking the law.

EARLY HISTORICAL EVIDENCE

During the four decades after the Resurrection, the followers of Jesus would undoubtedly have known the precise location of Calvary and the tomb. Many of them had been firsthand witnesses to the aftermath of this momentous event—not least among them were Mary Magdalene, Mary the mother of James, Peter, and the other disciple who hurried to the sepulchre on the first Easter morning. Indeed, the tomb itself most probably remained in Christian hands because it belonged to a follower of Jesus, Joseph of Aramathea.

It is important to bear in mind that at this stage these early Christians anticipated that Jesus would return in their own lifetimes. They did not then appreciate the significance of his promise that he would "be with them always"—in the unseen presence of the Holy Spirit. It was not necessary, therefore, to physically mark the tomb for future generations to identify, but it is surely reasonable to assume that his early followers venerated the site. They in turn must have passed on very accurate and reliable information as to its exact location. This was the beginning of the "oral tradition," and it was extremely strong.

In A.D. 70 Roman Emperor Titus sacked the city. Herod's magnificent Temple, the center of Jewish worship and culture, was totally destroyed, together with all other buildings of significance. Indeed, Jesus himself predicted that "not one stone would be left upon another." However, it seems most likely that Calvary and the tomb would have escaped the attention of Titus's troops, being already waste ground, an "unclean" burial place with no buildings erected upon it.

There then followed a very sad period in Jerusalem's history when the city lay in ruins, rather like some of those in Europe after the Second World War. However, domestic life gradually began to return to some degree of normality as the inhabitants had not been banished, although many of the Jewish leaders were slain. Thus the seeds of the early Church were able to survive.

Between Pentecost and the destruction of Jerusalem, Christianity spread rapidly throughout the whole of the Eastern Mediterranean due to the activities of St. Paul. Antioch became the missionary center of the Gentile church, but Jerusalem remained at its heart, and James, a brother of our Lord, became the first bishop.

In A.D. 135, sixty-five years after the sacking of the city by Titus, Hadrian finally banished the Jews and totally rebuilt Jerusalem in the form of a typical Roman colonial town renamed Aelia Capitolina. He constructed a large podium over the entire area of Calvary and the tomb, upon which were erected in honor of the Roman gods a statue of Jupiter and a temple to Venus. St. Jerome suggests that Hadrian did this to obscure the sites and prevent the Christians from venerating them. Whether this is true or not, the fact remains that his action marked their position for future generations to uncover.

Although Hadrian had banished the Jews, the Gentile church of Greco-Roman origin nevertheless continued. There is an extant record of all the Greco-Roman bishops, and Eusebius, who was bishop of Caesarea from A.D. 313, mentions that the Gentile church in Jerusalem flourished.

FOURTH-CENTURY DEVELOPMENTS

Early in the fourth century Roman Emperor Constantine was converted to Christianity by his mother, St. Helena. Macarius, the bishop of Jerusalem at that time, assured him that Calvary and the tomb were to be found beneath the temple to Venus and the statue of Jupiter. Constantine expressed a desire to "make that most blessed spot, the place of the Resurrection, visible to all and given over to veneration."

Consequently, in A.D. 325 work started on demolishing the temple and removing the podium. The whole area when cleared revealed the small mound of Calvary, while a little to the west rose the rockface containing the sepulchre. In a letter that Constantine wrote to Bishop Macarius he said, "No words can express how good the Savior has been to us....that the monument of his Holy Passion, hidden for so many years, has now at last been restored to the faithful and set free by the defeat of our common enemy, it is indeed a miracle. My great wish is, after freeing the site of impious idols, to adorn it with splendid buildings."

To construct his magnificent basilica encompassing these two holy sites, the ground had to be leveled, and to fit into the architectural plan the rock surrounding the tomb was cut away vertically. Calvary also received similar treatment (see diagrams). Eusebius wrote, "Is it not astonishing to see the rock standing isolated, in the midst of a level space, with a cave inside it."

A large rotunda was constructed to encircle the tomb with an open courtyard to the east of it. In the southeast corner of this cloister stood the tall

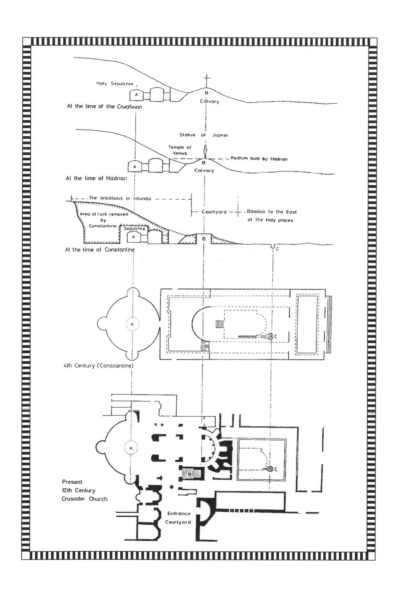

Holy Sepulchre

Calvary

At the time of the Crucifixion

Statue of Jupiter

Temple of Venus

Podium built by Hadrian

Calvary

At the time of Hadrian

The anastasis or rotunda

Area of rock removed by Constantine

Sepulchre

Courtyard

Basilica to the East of the Holy places

At the time of Constantine

4th Century (Constantine)

Present
12th Century
Crusader Church

Entrance
Courtyard

block of Calvary, surrounded by a metal grille and with a cross erected on the top. A depiction of this can be seen today in a contemporary fourth-century mosaic in the Church of Santa Pudenziana in Rome. Immediately to the east of the colonnaded cloister was built a large basilica known as the Martyrium, dedicated to the martyrdom of the Savior. Access was from the Cardo, the main Roman street of Jerusalem.

The remains of this entrance are still visible today in the Hospice of the Russian Excavations, in the cellars of the nearby Coptic convent, and also in the basement of Zelatino's Café at the foot of the steps that lead up to the Ethiopian monastery from the *suq*. The extent of the church is clearly visible in the famous sixth-century Madaba mosaic map. Reference to the diagram will explain the probable layout.

The basilica was consecrated on September 14, 335, in the presence of three hundred bishops. Thus for over sixteen and a half centuries the church has been a focus of Christian pilgrimage.

THE CRUCIFIXION

When they had led him to the place called Golgotha, which means the Skull, they offered him wine mixed with myrrh, but he would not take it. Then they nailed him to the cross and divided his clothes among themselves, casting lots to decide what each should take.

It was about nine o'clock in the morning when they crucified him. The statement of his offense was displayed above his head and it read, "The King of the Jews." They also crucified two robbers with him, one on his right and one on his left.

People passing by laughed at him, shook their head and jeered, "Aha! So you are able to tear down the Temple and build it up again in three days. Now save yourself and come down from the cross!"

In the same way the chief priests and the teachers of the Law mocked him saying to one another, "The man who saved others cannot save himself. Let's see the Messiah, the king of Israel, come down from his cross and then we will believe in him." Even the men who were crucified with Jesus insulted him.

When noon came, darkness fell over the whole land and lasted until three o'clock; and at three o'clock Jesus cried out in a loud voice, "Eloi, Eloi, lamma sabachthani?" which means "My God, my God, why have you deserted me?" As soon as they heard these words, some of the bystanders said, "Listen! He is calling for Elijah." And one of them went quickly to fill a sponge with bitter wine and, putting it on a reed, gave him to drink saying, "Now let's see whether Elijah comes to take him down."

But Jesus uttered a loud cry and gave up his spirit. And immediately the curtain which enclosed the Temple sanctuary was torn in two from top to bottom.

The captain who was standing in front of him saw how Jesus died and heard the cry he gave; and he said, "Truly, this man was the Son of God." (Mark 15:22–39)

> *O dearest Lord, thy sacred heart*
> *with spear was pierced for me;*
> *O pour thy spirit on my heart*
> *that I may speak for thee.*

A Brief History of the Four Churches Built on the Site

Constantine's Basilica

This remained in continuous use for nearly three hundred years until A.D. 614, when the Persian invaders destroyed it. However, only a few years passed before they in turn were defeated by Roman Emperor Heraclius. He gave instructions that the Christian places of worship should be rebuilt.

Modestus

The Bishop of Jerusalem at that time, Modestus set about reconstructing the church, although on completion his basilica lacked much of its former grandeur. In 637 the Muslims overran the city, but their leader, Caliph Omar, spared the building and allowed the Christians to continue to worship there. It should be borne in mind that Jesus is recognized as a prophet in the Islamic faith.

Worship continued for nearly four hundred years until A.D. 1009 when the fanatical Egyptian Caliph Hakim began persecuting the Christians. He gave orders that all the churches in the land should be destroyed—especially the Church of the Holy Sepulchre. There is an interesting account by an observer of how at first the rock of the tomb seemed almost impenetrable to the workmen's tools. However, they persevered, and eventually the damage was catastrophic. The tomb itself was hacked to pieces so that virtually nothing remained. The basilica then lay in ruins for almost four decades.

Monomachus

This Roman emperor, in exchange it is said for five thousand Muslim prisoners, was given permission to rebuild on the site in 1048. His basilica was on a scale even less lavish than that of Modestus, but worship resumed, and the building continued to be used for fifty years.

The Crusaders

The Crusaders finally captured the city on July 15, 1099, and immediately set about the total restoration of the church. The architecture was that of the Western tradition, and the finest craftsmen were employed from all over Europe. For the first time the rock of Calvary and the site of the tomb were enclosed under one roof, and a chapel was built over Calvary. A simple aedicule was constructed over the site of the tomb, and the rotunda surrounding it was embellished with magnificent carvings. A small crypt was dedicated to St. Helena as there was a tradition that, in an ancient cistern below it, she had discovered the true cross and the instruments of the Passion.

On July 15, 1149, a great service was held in thanksgiving for the complete restoration. The church must have been one of the finest in the world.

Upon the defeat of the Crusaders, the Augustinian monks became responsible for the building, and their monastery was constructed above the Chapel of St. Helena. This was destroyed during the Middle Ages, but the remains of the roof arches are still visible encircling the monastery of the Ethiopians, who now occupy the site.

In 1808 a fire seriously damaged the rotunda. At this time, when relations between the East and the West were at a particularly low ebb on account of the Napoleonic Wars, the Turks ruled Palestine. Consequently, it was left to the Christians in the East to carry out the restoration. They made a deplorable job of it. The tombs of the Crusader kings of Jerusalem were removed, the rich stone decorations destroyed, the ambulatory around the rotunda closed, many windows filled in, and the stone walls covered with plaster. The building took on a very dark and dismal appearance. Sadly, too, in 1810 the simple Crusader aedicule over the site of the tomb was replaced by the present somewhat ugly alabaster shrine.

To aggravate the situation further, in 1927 there was a serious earthquake, and British engineers had to temporarily shore up the whole building for fear of total collapse. Most of the unsightly girders have now been removed, but some can still be seen around the aedicule.

Since 1950 there has been a more favorable ecumenical climate, and a team of three architects representing the Armenian, Greek Orthodox, and Roman Catholic Churches has been appointed for the express purpose of trying to restore the building to some degree of its original splendor. The task, not surprisingly, is taking a very long time because the proposals have to be agreed upon by Christians from totally different cultural backgrounds. Nevertheless, considerable progress is being made, and each year there is some significant improvement.

THE RESURRECTION

Now, on the first day after the sabbath, Mary of Magdala came to the tomb early in the morning, while it was still dark and she saw that the stone blocking the tomb had been moved away. She ran to Peter and the other disciple whom Jesus loved. And she said to them, "They have taken the Lord out of the tomb and we don't know where they have laid him."

Peter then set out with the other disciple to go to the tomb. They ran together but the other disciple outran Peter and reached the tomb first. He bent down and saw the linen cloths lying flat, but he did not enter.

Then Simon Peter came following him and entered the tomb; he, too, saw the linen cloths lying flat. The napkin, which had been around his head was not lying flat like the other linen cloths but lay rolled up in its place. Then the other disciple who had reached the tomb first also went in; he saw and believed. Scripture clearly said that he must rise from the dead, but they had not yet understood that.

The disciples then went home again.

Mary stood weeping outside the tomb, and as she wept she bent down to look inside; she saw two angels in white sitting where the body of Jesus had been, one at the head, and the other at the feet. They said, "Woman, why are you weeping?" She answered, "Because they have taken my Lord and I don't know where they have put him."

As she said this, she turned around and saw Jesus standing there, but she did not recognize him. Jesus said to her, "Woman, why are you weeping? Who are you looking for?" She thought it was the gardener and answered him, "Lord, if you have taken him away, tell me where you have put him, and I will go and remove him."

Jesus said to her, "Mary." She turned and said to him, "Rabboni"— which means, Master. Jesus said to her, "Do not cling to me; you see I have not yet ascended to the Father. But go to my brothers and say to them: I am ascending to my Father, who is your Father, to my God, who is your God."

So Mary of Magdala went and announced to the disciples, "I have seen the Lord, and this is what he said to me." (John 20:1–18)

> Jesus lives our hearts know well
> Nought from us his love shall sever;
> Life, nor death, nor powers of hell
> Tear us from his keeping ever. Alleluia!

TOUR

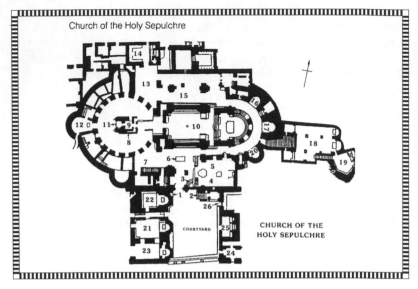

Church of the Holy Sepulchre

CHURCH OF THE
HOLY SEPULCHRE

Refer to the numbered plan on page above.

The façade of the church is in typical Crusader style. Notice the twelfth-century decoration around the window and door arches. The original carved lintels were removed to the Rockefeller Museum for safekeeping following the 1927 earthquake. The right-hand doorway has been blocked since the sixteenth century. In the pavement in front of this, under some wooden slats, is the tomb of the English knight Philip d'Aubigny, tutor to Henry III. In 1810 when all the other Crusader tombs were desecrated, it escaped destruction because it was hidden by the doorkeeper's bench.

Since the defeat of the Crusaders in 1187, the responsibility for locking and unlocking the door of this most important shrine in Christendom has remained with the Muslims. For the past four hundred years the same two families have shared the duty and zealously guarded their privilege. One has the custody of the key, while the other performs the actual opening. The Christians still have to pay them a fee for doing this!

The massive bell tower on the left (1) has been standing since the twelfth century, although the top story had to be dismantled in 1549 following an earthquake. The steps on the right (2) originally led up into a porchway giving access to the chapels above Calvary. Since the Middle Ages the entrance has been blocked, and today the area beneath the cupola is known as the

Chapel of the Franks. Below this is a small Greek oratory dedicated to St. Mary of Egypt.

Enter the church, and allow time to adjust from the bright light outside. Almost behind the front doors, turn immediately right to ascend nineteen very steep steps (3), which lead up to the two chapels above Calvary. The first belongs to the Roman Catholics and commemorates the nailing to the cross (4).

A view of the Greek Orthodox Chapel of Calvary, which shares the top of Calvary with the Roman Catholic chapel (not seen in this view) to the right. *(George Martin)*

In the ceiling in front of the altar, darker than its surroundings, is portrayed a figure of Christ—the only remaining Crusader mosaic in the entire building. The chapel was restored in 1937; however, the Florentine altar dates from 1588. The tenth and eleventh stations of the cross are venerated here. Through the grille on the right you can see the Chapel of the Franks, the original approach to the shrine.

On the left, beyond the central pillar, is the extremely ornate Greek Orthodox Chapel of Calvary (5). The altar is situated directly over the place where, it is believed, the cross stood. The glass panels on either side reveal the natural rock below. Also visible is a rent in the rock, which geologists agree was occasioned by an earthquake. It could well have been the one that occurred upon the crucifixion. The twelfth station of the cross is venerated here.

Between the two chapels is another Roman Catholic altar dedicated to *Stabat Mater (Our Lady of Sorrows)*. This is the thirteenth station of the cross and commemorates the place where Mary received the body of her son. The statue above it, enclosed in a glass case, was a gift from Queen Maria I of Portugal in 1778.

Descend the steep steps at the back of the Chapel of Calvary, and at the bottom turn left. Ahead, directly opposite the main entrance, flanked by candlesticks and beneath a row of eight hanging lamps you can see the Stone of the Anointing (6). It belongs jointly to the Armenians, Greeks, and Roman Catholics and commemorates the place where, according to tradition, the body of our Lord was prepared for burial. The polished red stone dates

The Stone of the Anointing commemorates the preparation of our Lord's body for burial. *(George Martin)*

from the time of the Turkish restoration in 1810. This is the fourteenth station of the cross.

Continue in the same direction toward four pillars surmounted by a marble canopy, which marks the place from where the three Marys are said to have viewed the Crucifixion (7). This area belongs exclusively to the Armenians. Their sacristy is on the left, while the stairs lead up to a small oratory.

From the position where the three Marys stood, the pilgrim today has the first glimpse of the shrine built over the site of the tomb (8). This is perhaps appropriate because on seeing it, many also experience a sense of bewilderment, incredulity, and disbelief. The present aedicule, less than two hundred years old and still encased in steel girders after the 1927 earthquake, is hardly edifying to Christians from the West.

The lofty circular stone structure encompassing this whole area is known as the rotunda, or Anastasis ("Resurrection"), and was built upon foundations laid over sixteen hundred years ago (see the diagram on page 68). Originally, the pillars were covered in marble, and the cupola glittered with gold mosaics. The interior of the Muslim Dome of the Rock in the Temple Area affords an idea of how splendid it might have looked. The interior of the dome was recently redone, with Greek Orthodox, Roman Catholics, and Armenians cooperating, and unveiled in an ecumenical ceremony in 1997.

The reputed tomb of Jesus Christ. Note how the surrounding rock has all been cut away from the tomb itself. *(George Martin)*

Now proceed to the front of the shrine. Above the doorway are numerous hanging lamps, and enormous candlesticks belonging to the Armenians, Greeks, and Roman Catholics flank the entrance. The inside is divided into two chambers. The first is the Chapel of the Angel (9), where in the center is a pilaster that contains, according to tradition, a piece of the original sepulchre. Some claim that it is part of the rolling stone. A low doorway leads into the second chamber resembling a tomb. It is lined in marble and hung with more lamps and holy pictures. There is just room for three people to kneel in prayer. A marble slab dating from the sixteenth century represents the place where, it is believed, the body of Jesus lay.

Pilgrims should be warned that during peak periods the Greek priest on duty in the chamber expects a monetary offering. Many find this a particularly distasteful and distracting act within such a very holy place.

Opposite the entrance to the tomb is the Greek Orthodox cathedral known as the Katholikon (10). Originally, this was the choir of the Crusader church. A great deal of restoration has taken place in recent years, and the lofty vaulted ceiling is reminiscent of those in many European cathedrals. Notice the large screen, the iconostasis, a feature of the Eastern Orthodox churches, which partially hides the altar from view. From the ceiling hangs an impressive modern chandelier, while on the polished marble floor stands the *omphalos* (navel). To the Greeks this symbolizes the center of the world.

Now walk to a position directly behind the tomb where the Coptic Church has erected a small chapel (11). Under the altar is displayed a portion of rock claimed to be part of the original sepulchre.

Directly opposite this little chapel, walk between two of the pillars supporting the rotunda into an extremely dilapidated room, the Chapel of the Syrian-Jacobites (12). On Sundays and feast days it is furnished and the tiered altar dressed for the celebration of Mass. Notice the curved wall at the back, which was part of one of the three apsed-chapels of the original Constantinian church.

Immediately on the left is the low entrance to a complete first-century Jewish tomb. This is extremely important because it proves that the site was outside the city walls at the time of the Crucifixion (see "Early Archaeological Evidence" number 3 on page 60).

Return to the rotunda, and turning left passing the Chapel of the Copts and the tomb, walk between the pillars of the rotunda on the left into an area that is exclusively owned by the Roman Catholics (13). Opposite the fine modern organ is an altar dedicated to St. Mary Magdalene commemorating the place where Jesus appeared to her on the first Easter morning. To the left of the altar is the Franciscans' private sacristy.

At the far end of this area, double doors lead into the Chapel of the Apparition (14). There is an ancient tradition that Jesus appeared to his mother after his Resurrection, although the event is not recorded in the gospels. The Franciscans have tastefully restored the chapel, and here the Blessed Sacrament is reserved. Inside, the scenes of the Passion are movingly depicted in wrought iron along the wall. It is a most suitable place for meditation.

On leaving the chapel, pass the altar dedicated to St. Mary Magdalene and turn left. Walk along a rather dark aisle known as the Arches of the Virgin containing pillars and other remains from earlier basilicas (15). Toward the end, divert to the left to see a small Greek chapel called the Prison of Christ. The reason for the name is unclear.

Return to the aisle, and ahead, at the end, are three other chapels constructed around an ambulatory. The first belongs to the Greeks and is dedicated to St. Longinus (16), the Roman soldier whose spear pierced our Lord's side, while next to it is another, belonging to the Armenians, commemorating the division of the raiment, or clothes, of our Lord (17).

Now begin descending, on the left, the twenty-nine steps to the Armenian Chapel of St. Helena (18), and notice on the walls hundreds of crosses inscribed by pilgrims. While it was formerly thought that Constantine's basilica had a crypt, scholars now reject this view and date the Chapel of St. Helena to Crusader times. Notice the dome in the ceiling, which outside is seen to be at ground level in the courtyard of the Ethiopian monastery. Since 1950 a major restoration of the chapel has taken place, and the walls and floor have been decorated with scenes from Armenian history.

Important archaeological excavations were begun in the 1970s when a most interesting cavernous area was discovered below a storeroom directly behind the main altar. If there is a priest on duty, it is worth seeking his permission to view the excavations, which you reach by way of a wrought-iron door on the left of the sanctuary. This gives access to part of the seventh-century B.C. quarry mentioned earlier (number 2, page 60); remnants of the foundations of the podium that Hadrian had constructed in A.D. 135, upon which he had his pagan temple erected; and also some of the foundations of the original basilica that Constantine had built in A.D. 330. In the center of the excavated cavern is an altar dedicated to St. Vartan and the Armenian martyrs, but of particular interest on a stone block to the right is a drawing of a fishing boat—a symbol of Christian pilgrimage—claimed to be over 1,600 years old.

Return to the main Armenian chapel and descend the twenty-two stairs on the right of the altar to the Franciscan Chapel of the Finding of the Cross, which has been built within part of the ancient quarry (19). Here, according to tradition, St. Helena discovered the true cross and the instruments of the Passion. The chapel is a quiet place away from the crowds and affords another opportunity for meditation.

Now return to the main body of the church, ascending all the steps, and turn left at the top. Almost immediately is the third of the chapels built around the ambulatory (20). This belongs to the Greeks and commemorates the mocking of our Lord by the crowd. Continue on, and in about ten yards notice on the left a glass screen that slightly protrudes into the aisle. Through it can be seen the natural rock of Calvary. Now, almost immediately, turn left into a small area that is directly under the Greek Orthodox Chapel of Calvary, where the rock can be seen again and is floodlit behind protective glass. The fissure in the middle is a continuation of the one in the chapel above.

This small place is designated in some guidebooks as the "Chapel of Adam." The Eastern Orthodox churches perpetuate a somewhat dubious, but nevertheless symbolic, legend that in a cave below the rock of Calvary, Adam was buried and the blood of Jesus fell upon the first guilty head. Consequently, in many Greek depictions of the Crucifixion a skull appears at the foot of the cross. St. Paul puts it more positively in his First Letter to the Corinthians (15:22): "All die for being Adam's, and in Christ all will receive life." A fitting thought with which to conclude a somewhat overwhelming tour of the Church of the Holy Sepulchre.

Opening Times: 4:00 A.M.–8:00 P.M. daily (winter closes 7:00 P.M.)

Souvenir Shop: none

Custodians: The Armenian, Greek, and Roman Catholic Churches

Telephone: Franciscans (02) 6273314

There are a number of other chapels, monasteries, and convents directly linked to the church, which the pilgrim may possibly gain permission to enter. If time permits you may obtain a plan of the whole area from the Christian Information Center opposite the moated entrance to the Citadel near Jaffa Gate (not to be confused with the Tourist Information Office just inside the gate). Five of these places are briefly mentioned below:

1. Three Greek Orthodox chapels on the west of the courtyard. It seems likely that the baptistery of the original fourth-century Constantinian basilica would have stood in this area. Archaeological excavation has not been possible, but the middle chapel is dedicated to St. John (21), and there is a very ancient baptistery within it.

The chapel directly under the Crusader belfry is in memory of the "Forty Martyrs," soldiers of the Twelfth Legion who were frozen to death in Armenia in A.D. 320 rather than renounce their Christian faith (22). The third chapel at the other end is dedicated to St. James (23). The Greek Orthodox community uses this as their parish church.

2. On the east of the courtyard, the door farthest from the basilica leads into the Greek Orthodox Convent of St. Abraham (24).

3. The central arched doorway, on this side of the courtyard, with the modern green and gold doors, gives access to the ornately decorated Armenian Chapel of St. John (25).

4. The door nearest to the basilica leads into a chapel owned by the Copts but used by the Ethiopian monks (26). Inside, on the left, a stairway ascends to the upper chapel. A passageway to the left of the altar gives access to the courtyard of the Ethiopian monastery. This is directly above the Armenian Chapel of St. Helena, the cupola of which is clearly visible at ground level in the center of the courtyard.

   The monastery is a fascinating complex, and the pilgrim might be forgiven for thinking that he or she was in Africa because the dark-skinned monks and nuns live in very simple whitewashed dwellings. From a position beside the far wall of the courtyard, there is a good view of the large apse of the Greek Orthodox Katholikon. Notice also on the left the remains of roof arches from the earlier medieval Augustinian monastery.

5. On leaving the courtyard in front of the Church of the Holy Sepulchre, turn left through the small archway and continue to the end of the street. The Hospice of the Russian Excavations is on the left. Ring the bell; an admission fee is charged. Here excavations carried out in 1883 have revealed part of Hadrian's podium and also one of the three entrances to Constantine's basilica.

GARDEN TOMB

This complete tomb, which almost certainly existed at the time of Christ, is approached through a lovingly tended garden. It is a most helpful visual aid to the events of the first Easter.

ACCESS

The site lies to the right of Nablus Road, 250 yards due north of Damascus Gate. It is sometimes known as "Gordon's Calvary" because in 1883 General Charles Gordon of Khartoum became convinced that here he had found the true site of Calvary and the tomb. The nearby rock face resembled Golgotha ("Place

No historical or archaeological evidence links the Garden Tomb to Jesus, but it undoubtedly gives pilgrims a sense of what Jesus' burial site might have been like. *(Anthony F. Chiffolo)*

of the Skull"), and the site lay outside the city walls, thus conforming to the description in the four gospels.

The tomb is one of a number of ancient sepulchres in the area, but sadly for many pilgrims there is no historical or archaeological evidence to support the validity of the site. However, it undoubtedly appeals to the imagination and is generally considered to be aesthetically more pleasing than the Church of the Holy Sepulchre.

AUTHORS' COMMENTS

A peaceful haven from the busy streets outside, it is well worth a visit. Many pilgrims find the atmosphere here more conducive to meditation than that of the Church of the Holy Sepulchre.

Opening Times: 8:30–noon, 2:00–5:30, closed on Sundays except for a service at 9:00

Souvenir Shop: at the main entrance; very well stocked with cards and books
Toilets: follow the signs from the shop
Custodians: The Garden Tomb Association
Telephone: (02) 6272745

CITADEL
(Tower of David)

The fortress today is mainly medieval, and the lines of the present walls date from the Crusaders in the twelfth century. Constructed partly on the remains of King Herod's Palace, the lower courses of Herodian dressed stone in the massive northeast tower date from the time of Christ. The buildings contain an imaginative museum tracing the history of Jerusalem over a period of three thousand years. An excellent open-air *son et lumière* (sound-and-light show) is also presented in English on some summer evenings.

Adjacent to Jaffa Gate, the Citadel now serves as a museum.
(Allan Weinert)

The Citadel is often referred to as "The Tower of David," but no connection with that king has ever been established. It was the Byzantines who incorrectly identified the area as the site of his palace—and the name has been handed on through the centuries.

ACCESS

The Citadel is situated in the west of the Old City adjacent to Jaffa Gate (see map on page 63). The main entrance is located on the east side of the compound and is approached via a flight of steps. There is an admission charge.

HISTORY

The earliest settlements on the site date from the seventh century B.C. During the reign of Hasmonean King John Hyrcanus (134–104 B.C.), a defensive city wall was built, part of which archaeologists have now uncovered running from north to south through the center of the compound. King

76

Herod erected his royal palace here on a grand scale. It extended much farther south, almost as far as the present city walls, and included a large garden. He built three towers and dedicated them to his brother, Phasael, his wife, Mariamne, and his friend Hippicus, but the positions of two of these have yet to be discovered. Some scholars are of the opinion that Pontius Pilate would have stayed in Herod's royal palace when he came up to Jerusalem at the time of the major festivals, in preference to residing in the Fortress of Antonia (see page 60). If this is true, then somewhere within the vicinity Jesus would have stood trial before Pilate and been scourged. In A.D. 66 the palace was burned down during a Jewish revolt. These uprisings led to Titus's sacking the city in A.D. 70. The Tenth Legion then used the area for the next two hundred years as a barracks.

In the twelfth century Crusader King Baldwin II used the site as his palace and constructed new buildings to the west beyond the old defensive city wall. The Marmelukes further adapted and fortified the Citadel at the beginning of the fourteenth century, as did Suleiman the Magnificent two hundred years later. He also rebuilt most of the present walls surrounding the Old City. In 1917 General Allenby proclaimed the British liberation of Jerusalem from Turkish rule from the steps in front of the entrance gateway.

Following the Six-Day War in 1967 the Citadel was converted into an attractive museum.

DETAILS

All the features are clearly marked, but be sure to climb to the top of the northeast tower (with its Herodian lower courses), from which there are fine views across the Old City to the Mount of Olives. It is now known as David's Tower, and there is an exhibition room on the first floor. The main museum comprises three separate areas, each covering a specific period of Jerusalem's history. Allow at least two hours to view the exhibits.

Opening Times: Sunday to Thursday 9:00–5:00 (winter 10:00–4:00); Friday, Saturday, and holiday eves 9:00–2:00

Souvenir Shop: more than one outlet

Toilets: available and well marked

Custodian: The Municipality of Jerusalem

Telephone: (02) 6274111

Son et Lumière: during the summer months performances in English are at 9:30 P.M. on Mondays and Wednesdays and 10:30 P.M. on Saturdays; warm clothing is recommended

CATHEDRAL OF ST. JAMES

This Armenian cathedral is undoubtedly one of the more important Christian places in Jerusalem. Its most significant relic is thought to be the head of St. James the Great, who was executed in A.D. 44. The cathedral is also reputed to be the burial place of St. James the Less and is the seat of the Armenian patriarch.

ACCESS

Admission times are very restricted; see details on page 80. Enter the Old City by Jaffa Gate and follow the road around the high walls of the Citadel, passing the bridge leading into the main entrance. Continue for about 150 yards; ahead is a narrow arch-covered passageway. Proceed through with caution because there is no pavement and hardly room for both cars and pedestrians. At the end, on the left, is the arched entrance to the cathedral.

BACKGROUND

The Armenians were the first people to adopt Christianity as their official state religion in A.D. 287. The present community in Jerusalem has deep roots in the city, and it is interesting to note that from the Crusader Period until the end of Turkish rule in 1918 the patriarch was considered to be the most senior Christian dignitary in the Holy Land.

The modern Region of Armenia lies south of the Caucasus Mountains and between the Black Sea and the Caspian Sea. Toward the end of the last century there was considerable unrest in the area, which resulted in mass genocide carried out by Turkish troops in 1909 and 1915, when it is said that nearly two million people lost their lives.

Today there are about two and a half million Armenians worldwide, but many have migrated throughout the Middle East and to the United States. At the beginning of the century some families, not surprisingly, joined their compatriots in Jerusalem. In more recent times there has been a movement away from Israel, and it is said that the population of the Armenian Quarter has decreased from many thousands to a few hundred. Nevertheless, the Armenian Church continues to have considerable influence among the Christian communities. It has sole jurisdiction over part of the Church of the Nativity in Bethlehem and also over the Chapel of St. Helena in the crypt of the Church of the Holy Sepulchre.

TOUR

The entrance to the cathedral from the street is through a tall archway that immediately leads into a vestibule. The doorkeeper's office is on the left. Walk diagonally across to the right, where an archway leads into a small courtyard. Here some of the inscriptions on the wall date from the twelfth century and include examples of the so-called Jerusalem Cross, which originated in Armenia in the ninth–tenth centuries. It was later adopted by the Crusaders and the Franciscans. Notice the finely decorated wrought-iron screen leading into the ceremonial entrance to the cathedral.

Ascend the steps on the right, and straight ahead are clappers, one in wood and the other in metal. These are still struck with a hammer to summon the faithful to worship—an alternative to bells, whose ringing was forbidden at some periods in the past. Notice above the cathedral's main entrance a painting depicting Christ seated in glory surrounded by the Virgin and other holy men and women. In front of the doorway hangs a heavy leather curtain, which effectively acts as a sound barrier.

The interior has many moods: on a sunny day, and particularly during worship when many of the hanging lamps are lighted, there is a sense of color and life; while on a cloudy day and when there is no worship, it can in contrast seem extremely dark. The cathedral is dedicated to St. James (the son of Zebedee and brother of St. John the Apostle) whom it is said was executed on this site by Herod Agrippa I, grandson of Herod the Great, circa A.D. 44 (see Acts of the Apostles 12:1–2). It is also dedicated to St. James the Less. Some scholars believe that this apostle, who became the first bishop of Jerusalem, was our Lord's brother.

The walls are partially covered in blue eighteenth-century Turkish tiles, and many ornate lamps are suspended from the ceiling. The main altar and the chapel to the right of it are dedicated to the Virgin Mary, while the chapel on the left is dedicated to St. John the Baptist. Notice the patriarchal throne of St. James the Less adjacent to the large northeast pillar. It was made in 1656 and is used only on ceremonial occasions. Beside it, on the east side of the pillar, is a low iron grille enclosing the reputed burial place of the saint.

On the north wall of the nave, the first small chapel on the left is dedicated to St. Macarius, bishop of Jerusalem at the time of Constantine, while next to it is the vestibule of the second slightly larger chapel dedicated to St. James the Great. This is the most important shrine in the cathedral and is reputedly built over the site where the saint was beheaded. It is said to contain his skull. According to ancient tradition, the body was taken to Santiago de Compostela in Spain. Notice the extremely fine eighteenth-century decoration on the doors inlaid with tortoise shell and mother-of-pearl.

Other chapels in the cathedral are not normally open to the public, but it is worth noting that the doorway beyond the shrine of St. James gives access to a complex of chapels, including that of the apostles and altars dedicated to St. Minas and St. Sargis. Also through the same archway is the entrance to the Church of St. Stephen, now used as a sacristy. Here, too, is the baptistery of the cathedral. Altars within this area are dedicated to St. Stephen himself; St. Cyril, bishop of Jerusalem in the fourth century; and St. Gregory the Illuminator. This is the oldest part of the building, some of which may date from the fifth century.

The present structure of the cathedral dates mainly from the twelfth century, and its original entrance was through the door in the south wall. The exterior of this doorway is in typical Crusader style, and originally it was approached from the south via an arched portico. This was filled in during the mid-seventeenth century to form the narrow Chapel of Etchmiadzin, named after a holy city in Armenia. The main feature here is the Altar of Sinai containing stones from Mount Sinai, Mount Tabor, and the Jordan River, which provide a focus for veneration for those who are not fortunate to make a pilgrimage to these places.

Opening Times: Monday to Friday 6:00–7:00, 3:00–3:30, Saturday and Sunday 6:00–9:30 A.M.

Telephone: (02) 6282331

CHURCH OF ST. MARK

This Syrian Orthodox Church is claimed to be on the site of the house of Mary, the mother of John Mark, author of the second gospel. If this claim is true, then it was here that St. Peter first came when an angel released him from prison (Acts of the Apostles 12:12–17). The Syrians, sometimes known as the Assyrians, also have a tradition that this was the site of the Upper Room, the scene of the feet washing and the Last Supper.

ACCESS

This small church situated within its monastery compound is difficult to find because it is in a somewhat isolated position east of the Armenian Quarter, northwest of the rebuilt Jewish Quarter, and south of David Street, which runs from Jaffa Gate toward the Temple Area. The best approach is to enter the Old City by Jaffa Gate and follow the road around the high walls of the Citadel, passing the bridge leading into the main entrance. Continue for about 150 yards, and just before entering a half-arch–covered passageway ahead, turn immediately left into St. James Road. Follow this road around to the left and then to the right, and proceed until reaching a junction. Here turn left and eventually pass through two covered passageways. At the end of the second, turn right. In twenty-five yards, on the right, is the door leading into the compound. Ring the bell.

TOUR

Inside, on the left of the low vaulted courtyard, steps lead up to the residence of the Syrian archbishop, while ahead are green double doors leading into the church. This is a very small Christian community, and sometimes the archbishop himself conducts visitors around the church.

The building dates from the Crusader Period, but much restoration has been carried out since the beginning of the eighteenth century. The nave walls are hung with a number of ancient religious paintings, while the sanctuary is richly decorated, although sometimes partly hidden by a curtain.

Just inside the door, set into a pillar, is a stone that was discovered during restoration work in 1940 and is said to date from the sixth century. On it is an inscription written in ancient Syriac—a language very similar to the Aramaic used by our Lord. The translation is as follows:

This is the house of Mary, mother of John, called Mark. Proclaimed a church by the holy apostles under the name of Virgin Mary, mother of God, after the ascension of our Lord Jesus Christ into heaven. Renewed after the destruction of Jerusalem by Titus in the year A.D. 73.

Against the south wall of the nave is a font with an ornate canopy. Here there is an ancient portrait on parchment of the Virgin Mary, which the Syrians claim was painted by St. Luke himself. They also believe that the Virgin was baptized by the holy apostles within the original house of John Mark.

Two other significant events that, according to Syrian tradition, took place on this site are the election of Matthias as an apostle to replace Judas Iscariot, and the coming of the Holy Spirit on the assembled company at Pentecost.

The small and devout Syrian (Jacobite) congregation regularly uses the church. Some pilgrims find St. Mark's a fitting place from which to commence their Maundy Thursday devotional walk because it is within the city walls and geographically is still on Mount Zion. If it is not feasible to gain admission to the church in the evening, devotions can be conducted in the quiet street outside. Canon Ronald Brownrigg in his book *Come, see the Place* goes so far as to suggest that, by prior arrangement, groups might be able to seek entry and also to persuade one of the Syrian priests to read the words of the institution of Communion—"This is my body…This is my blood"—in a language that would have been recognizable by the apostles.

Opening Times: 8:00–5:00 (closed on Sundays); winter closes 4:00

Telephone: (02) 6283304

OPHEL ARCHAEOLOGICAL EXCAVATIONS

Officially called the Archaeological Garden, the area directly below the south wall of the Temple platform is of particular Christian interest. The extensive excavations include the remains of a wide flight of steps that Jesus would undoubtedly have used when he went up to the Temple to pray and teach.

ACCESS

The ticket office is immediately inside Dung Gate (see the map on page 15).

The Ophel Archaeological Excavations, in the area directly below the south wall of the Temple platform, include the remains of a wide flight of stairs that Jesus would have used to go up to the Temple. *(George Martin)*

DETAILS

Thorough excavation took place here between 1968 and 1984. Previously, the east end had been a grassy slope where sheep were often seen grazing. Six periods of occupation have been revealed: First Temple, Hasmonean, Second Temple, Byzantine, Omayyad (early Muslim), and Medieval.

From the entrance gate, only half the excavated area is visible. The southeast section containing the ancient steps is beyond the Ottoman wall that divides the site.

Below the southwest corner of the Temple platform, further excavation of the ruins has been carried out, and it is now possible to look down onto the Herodian paved street level of the deep Tyropean Valley, which used to run along the west side of the platform. This valley, filled with rubble over the centuries, continued under the modern wide pavement immediately in front of the Western Wall. Here, above ground level, seven courses of huge stone blocks form the sacred part of the wall, but below them are a further eight courses—giving an idea of the depth of the valley at this point in the first century.

Also visible from the excavations, near the south end of the Western Wall, is the stub of an arch that originally supported the upper platform of a stairway running west and then south down to the paved thoroughfare below. This is known as "Robinson's Arch," so named after the American archaeologist who discovered it in 1835. The foundations of the west pier of the supporting arch have also been revealed directly opposite the protruding stub.

As a matter of interest a second archway, known as "Wilson's Arch," still exists to the north of the present sacred area of the Western Wall. It is within the buildings to the left of the pavement reserved for male worshipers. Underneath the span is a prayer hall.

The steps from the Second Temple Period, at the far end of the site, gave access to the Temple Mount by way of a double gate in the wall, which is now almost hidden by later buildings. These also cover half the width of the steps. Most of the remaining stairway has now been restored with Jerusalem stone, but a few of the steps have been left in their original state. Further along the wall to the right you can see a triple gateway, which has been filled in. This also gave access to the Temple precincts.

AUTHORS' COMMENTS

A visit to the excavations is very worthwhile. A detailed plan of the area is provided on admission so that the numbered features can be identified. Three routes are marked out, and it is suggested that about an hour should be allowed to follow the shorter one, which concentrates on the remains of the Second Temple Period and includes the ancient steps. Two hours are recommended to cover the intermediate route, and three for the longest, on which a total of eighteen different features can be visited.

Opening Times: 9:00–4:00 Sunday–Thursday; Friday and holiday eves closes two hours earlier; closed on Saturdays

Souvenir Shop: postcards and books in the ticket office

Toilets: none

Custodian: East Jerusalem Development Ltd.

Telephone: (02) 6254403

MOUNT ZION

Dormition Abbey
Upper Room
Tomb of David

Mount Zion is the high ground outside Zion Gate in the southwest corner of the Old City (see the plan of Jerusalem on page 15). It also extends into the Armenian Quarter inside the city walls.

In our Lord's time the whole of Mount Zion was densely populated and enclosed within the walls. There is a tradition that the Last Supper was celebrated in an "upper room" in this area. It seems likely that in a house on Zion, Jesus appeared on the first

Mount Zion was densely populated in our Lord's time, and tradition holds that he celebrated the Last Supper in an "upper room" in this area. *(George Martin)*

Easter evening—"the doors were locked where the disciples were, because of their fear of the Jews" (John 20:19). It is also probable that on Mount Zion the Holy Spirit descended upon them at Pentecost.

It is thought that a small church, possibly a house church, existed on the mount in the early Christian era. However, it seems likely that this was destroyed by Diocletian in 303. Later in the fourth century it was rebuilt and known as the Upper Church of the Apostles. Reference was made to it in the middle of the fifth century as the "Holy and Glorious Sion, the Mother of all the Churches." It is, therefore, sometimes referred to as "Holy Sion" (Holy Zion).

Dormition Abbey

The conical gray roof with the fine adjacent bell tower is one of the most distinctive landmarks in Jerusalem. The full Latin name of the church is *Dormitio Sanctae Mariae*, "the falling asleep of St. Mary." There is a tradition that the Virgin Mary spent the latter years of her life on Mount Zion.

ACCESS

Refer to the map on page 15. From Zion Gate in the southwest corner of the Old City, cross the road to take the promenade that runs away from the city walls, and after sixty yards bear right. After forty more yards turn right into a narrow passageway leading to the courtyard in front of the church. Within the Benedictine abbey complex is a quality gift shop and a pleasant refectory where refreshments are available.

TOUR

The church was consecrated in 1910 and is in the care of an international community of German-speaking Benedictine monks. Inside, the lofty circular interior has a sense of spaciousness, and a fine golden mosaic of the Virgin and Child dominates the apse. Portrayed below are the eight Old Testament prophets who foretold the coming of the Messiah: Micah, Isaiah, Jeremiah, Ezekiel, Daniel, Haggai, Zechariah, and Malachi.

Tradition holds that the Blessed Virgin Mary spent the latter years of her life on Mount Zion. Shown here, Dormition Abbey commemorates her "falling asleep." *(George Martin)*

On either side of the apse are three chapels. Facing the altar and working clockwise from the left, these are dedicated to St. Boniface, the Benedictine archbishop; St. John the Baptist; St. Joseph; Maternus, the first bishop of Cologne (the present bishop continues to be responsible for the abbey); St. Willibald, born in Wessex and the first known English pilgrim to the Holy Land, who later became bishop of Eichstätt; and St. Benedict, the founder of the monastic order.

The church is often used for concerts, and on these occasions a carpet hides the fine round mosaic in the floor below the rotunda from view. The design, in concentric circles, represents the spreading of the Word through time and space, emanating from the Triune God outward via the Old and New Testaments. The three intersecting circles at the center each contain the Greek word *hagios* (holy) and symbolize the Godhead. The second circle contains the names of the four major prophets, and the third those of the twelve minor prophets. The four evangelists with their appropriate symbols are next depicted, while the fifth circle contains the names of the twelve apostles. It is interesting to note that Paul has replaced Judas. The penultimate circle shows the months of the year together with the signs of the Zodiac—pagan symbols sometimes used by Christians to represent the whole universe. Finally, around the outside is a quotation in Latin from Proverbs 8:23–25: "He formed me from of old, / from eternity, even before the earth. / The abyss did not exist when I was born, / the springs of the sea had not gushed forth, / the mountains were still not set in their place / nor the hills, when I was born...."

On the balcony at the back of the church is a fine modern organ built in the early 1980s by the German firm of Oberlinger Brothers.

To the right of the organ, at ground level, stairs lead down to the crypt, where in the center the prominent feature is a life-size statue of the sleeping Virgin Mary. It is carved from cherry wood and ivory. The cupola above is adorned with mosaics depicting Christ surrounded by six women of the Old Testament: Eve, Miriam, Jael, Judith, Ruth, and Esther.

There are three chapels on either side of the main altar dedicated to the memory of the apostles. From the crypt stairs, working immediately clockwise, these are gifts from the United States, Brazil, Venezuela, Hungary, Austria, and the Ivory Coast.

AUTHORS' COMMENTS

Quite apart from the veneration of the Blessed Virgin Mary, this is a most suitable place in which to remember three primary events in the history of the early Church: the institution of the Last Supper; our Lord's Resurrection appearance to the disciples when they were all together on Easter evening; and the coming of the Holy Spirit at Pentecost, which traditionally has been held to have occurred on Mount Zion.

Opening Times: 8:00–noon, 12:30–6:00; Sundays open at 9:30
Souvenir Shop: within the abbey complex
Toilets: within the abbey complex
Custodian: The German Society for the Holy Land (the abbey is entrusted
to an international community of German-speaking Benedictine monks)
Telephone: (02) 6719927

Upper Room

Known also as the
Cenacle or Coenaculum
(Upper Supper Room),
this room, with its cen-
tral pillars and Gothic
arches, is reminiscent
of many throughout
Europe in medieval ab-
beys and castles. Built
more than a thousand
years after the event it
commemorates—the
Last Supper—it is most
unlikely that any part

This room, of Crusader and earlier origin, commemorates our
Lord's Last Supper and institution of the Eucharist. *(George Martin)*

dates from apostolic times. For Christians there is no focal point for devotion, but one of the walls contains a Muslim *mihrab* (indicating the direction of Mecca).

THE LAST SUPPER

*When it was evening, Jesus arrived with the Twelve. While they were
at table eating, Jesus said, "Truly, I tell you, one of you will betray me,
one who shares my meal." They were deeply distressed at hearing this
and asked him, one after the other, "You don't mean me, do you?" And
Jesus answered, "It is one of you Twelve, one who dips his bread in the
dish with me. The Son of Man is going as the Scriptures say he will. But
alas for that man by whom the Son of Man is betrayed; better for him if
he had never been born."*

*While they were eating, Jesus took bread, blessed and broke it, and
gave it to them. And he said, "Take this, it is my body." Then he took a cup*

*and after he had given thanks, passed it to them and they all drank from
it. And he said, "This is my blood, the blood of the Covenant, which is to
be poured out for many. Truly, I say to you, I will not taste the fruit of the
vine again until the day I drink the new wine in the kingdom of God."*

*After singing psalms of praise, they went out to the Hill of Olives. (Mark
14:17–26)*

> Bread becomes his Flesh from heaven,
> Wine becomes his holy Blood:
> Here, where sight is unavailing,
> Faith may seize with grasp unfailing
> What can ne'er be understood.

ACCESS

See the map on page 15. From Zion Gate in the southwest corner of the
Old City, cross the road to take the promenade that runs away from the city
walls, and after sixty yards bear right in front of the entrance to Terra Sancta
Monastery. Go straight ahead, and about seventy yards, on the left, is a small
archway leading to a flight of stone steps at the back, constructed on the
outside of the building. At the top is a bare room; walk through this and into
the open, then immediately ahead is the entrance to the Upper Room.

DETAILS

It seems likely that the Crusaders had an upper room here, but the present
chamber dates only from the early fourteenth century. At that time the
Franciscans engaged Cypriot architects who designed the building in a typical Gothic style. The central pillars, of a much earlier date, have fine carved
capitals. Of particular interest in the southwest corner is a slender marble
column supporting a stone canopy. Carved on each face of the capital can be
seen two young pelicans feeding on the blood the mother has drawn from
her breast—symbolizing the blood of Christ at the Eucharist.

In 1524 the Turks expelled the Christians from the building. An inscription in Arabic on the wall commemorates the event. Suleiman the Magnificent, who constructed the present walls of the Old City, added the *mihrab*
and adapted the room for Muslim worship. The chamber continued as a
Muslim mosque until 1947 when the Israelites took over the complex and
opened it to all.

The ground floor of the building houses the Tomb of David, and part of
its surrounding walls dates from the Byzantine Period.

AUTHORS' COMMENTS

Given the significance of the upper room for Christians, this could possibly prove to be one of the most disappointing of all the gospel sites in the Holy Land. No one can be certain of the exact position of the original room, and pilgrims should keep in mind that the present chamber was constructed as late as the fourteenth century.

The Syrian Orthodox community also claims that their Church of St. Mark (see page 81) is built over the authentic site of the "upper room." Although it is well within the present city walls, it is nevertheless on the slopes of Mount Zion. Many pilgrims find it more helpful to remember the Last Supper here. The church is not easy to find but is situated roughly between the Cathedral of St. James in the Armenian Quarter in the southwest of the Old City and the rebuilt Jewish Quarter west of the Temple Area.

Opening Times: 8:30–5:00; closed Friday afternoons

Souvenir Shop: none

Toilets: none

Tomb of David

This large sarcophagus covered with a velvet cloth, upon which stand Torah scroll-boxes and crowns, is situated in a narrow room directly below the Crusader Upper Room. The building, therefore, is a place of pilgrimage for Jews, Muslims, and Christians.

ACCESS

Follow the instructions on page 89 for reaching the Upper Room as far as the small archway. Instead of turning through this to reach the Upper Room, continue on up the steps and pass under the tall archway ahead, and after fifteen yards turn left again. The entrance to the tomb complex is through a doorway on the left.

DETAILS

The Jews consider this holy place second in importance to that of the Western Wall of the Temple Area. It is necessary for men to cover their heads, and prayer caps (*kippahs*) are available just inside to the right of the entrance door. From here proceed directly into a smaller room, which serves as an annex to the tomb and is used for prayer.

There is some doubt about the validity of the tomb because the Old Testament clearly states that King David and his ancestors were buried in the City of David (1 Kings 2:10). This was directly south of the Temple platform and is now known as Mount Ophel. Another school of thought places the burials in Bethlehem because this town is mentioned in the New Testament as the City of David (Luke 2:4). However, excavations have not revealed the royal necropolis in either location.

The earliest reference to the tomb in its present position is made by the historian Josephus in the first century. In 1173 Rabbi Benjamin of Tudela describes the tomb as one of Judaism's holiest shrines. In 1859 the Italian engineer Pierotty was granted permission to investigate the tomb, and he reported that underneath was a small, shallow, and empty cave.

AUTHORS' COMMENTS

This is a Jewish holy place of some significance. The wall at the back of the tomb could possibly date from the early Christian "Hagia Zion" Church.

Opening Times: 8:00–sunset

CHURCH OF ST. PETER IN GALLICANTU

This modern church on the eastern slope of Mount Zion is built over a reputed site of the house of the high priest Caiaphas. It commemorates St. Peter's denial of Jesus after his arrest in the Garden of Gethsemane and his subsequent remorse. There are four levels: the Upper Church, the Lower Church, the Guardroom, and the Dungeon.

PETER'S DENIAL

Then they seized him [Jesus] and took him away, bringing him to the High Priest's house. Peter followed at a distance.

A fire was kindled in the middle of the courtyard where people gathered, and Peter sat among them. A maidservant noticed him. Looking at him intently in the light of the fire, she exclaimed, "This man also was with him!" But he denied it, saying, "Woman, I do not know him."

A little later someone who saw him said, "You are also one of them!" Peter replied, "My friend, I am not!" After about an hour another asserted, "Surely this man was with him, for he is a Galilean."

Again Peter denied, "My friend, I don't know what you are talking about."

Built over the reputed site of Caiaphas's house, the Church of St. Peter in Gallicantu commemorates Peter's denial of Jesus and subsequent remorse. *(George Martin)*

He had not finished saying this when a cock crowed. The Lord turned around and looked at Peter and he remembered the word that the Lord had spoken, "Before the cock crows today you will have denied me three times." Peter went outside, weeping bitterly. (Luke 22:54–62)

How many times with faithless word
have we denied his holy name,
How oft forsaken our dear Lord,
and shrunk when trial came.

ACCESS

From the Tomb of David, turn left into a small courtyard. The way out is diagonally opposite. Walk along the cloister toward the museum, but just before reaching it, turn into a rather dark entrance on the left. Immediately opposite, though hidden from view, another door leads out into a small "garden" opening onto the road. Turn right along this road, and at the end bear around to the left to reach the main road. Here turn left again (toward the city walls), and after a short distance take the turn on the right that leads down to the church. Beyond the parking lot is a booth where you can purchase admission tickets.

THE BELVEDERE

Before turning left down to the church, it is well worth going out onto the Belvedere to enjoy the extensive views. The panorama includes the Temple Mount and the southern wall of the Old City, the Mount of Olives, modern-day Silwan, the intersection of the Kidron and Hinnom Valleys, and on a clear day the Mountains of Moab in Jordan. Three panels identify the features. The houses of Silwan tightly packed together afford some idea of how the City of Jerusalem here on Mount Zion might have looked in our Lord's time.

THE MAIN SITE

The validity of this site has sometimes been questioned because it is thought that such an important person as the high priest would have had his residence in a more commanding position at the top of Mount Zion. There is some documentary evidence dating back to the fifth century of a church in the area dedicated to St. Peter, but its exact position is not stated. At the top of Mount Zion, near the Dormition Abbey, is a site owned by the Armenians that has not been extensively excavated. Some believe that this is more likely to have been the position of the house of the high priest.

The French Assumptionists built the church in the 1920s and consecrated it in 1931. In May 1997 a service of reconsecration took place after extensive renovation of the church and the introduction of a number of modern features. There are many artifacts that support their claim that it is on the site of the house of the high priest Caiaphas. These are mentioned here before proceeding further.

Excavations have revealed the remains of a substantial building with its own water cistern, corn mill, and storerooms. More important, a number of artifacts have been discovered, including a complete set of measures for liquids and solids as used by the priests in the Temple. Also a door lintel with the word *korban* (sin offering) inscribed in Hebrew, together with coins, pottery, and glass dating from the Second Temple Period. One of the lower levels contains what could have been a guardroom, and the other what might have been a prisoners' cell. The walls of the latter have been inscribed with crosses, which the Assumptionist Fathers claim are Byzantine and indicate that Christians reverenced the place during this period.

TOUR

Approach the Upper Church through a new entrance porch. Immediately inside on the right of this are two Byzantine mosaics, one of them still in its original position. Ahead, doors lead into the Upper Church, which is extensively decorated with mosaics. The scene above the high altar shows the "trial" before Caiaphas.

From the entrance porch, directly opposite the two Byzantine mosaics, stairs lead down to the lower levels.

The Lower Church has been carefully adapted to provide groups with another place for worship. Three modern icons above the altars depict St. Peter's denial, his repentance, and his reconciliation with his master on the Galilean shore after the Resurrection. The natural rock of Mount Zion forms the west wall of this Lower Church.

In the floor is an ancient shaft giving access to what was possibly a small deep dungeon below. This opening would have been its only entrance, necessitating the prisoners' being raised by means of a rope harness. There is a mosaic depicting Jesus in such a harness outside on the south wall of the church. Three crosses dating from the Byzantine period are cut into the side of the shaft, and these, together with others in the dungeon, confirm an early Christian presence.

The Guardroom is down the stairway at the next level. From the entrance, descend the steps. The entire area has been hewn out of the bedrock; the original chisel marks are clearly visible, and the floor has not been leveled.

It seems most likely that this was indeed a Jewish prison. In such a place there was no need for individual cells, or to pay much attention to the floor, because under the law offenders were not given long terms of imprisonment. They were brought in and shackled to the walls. Corporal punishment, usually in the form of scourging, was swiftly administered. The maximum number of lashes allowed was forty, but to avoid breaking the law by possibly miscounting, thirty-nine were given. The relatively few prisoners actually awaiting trial for serious crimes would have been detained in a more secure communal cell, which in this instance was on a lower level.

Walk across to look between the two central pillars on the right. On one pillar and on the wall at the back are tethering loops cut into the rock, through which the prisoners' chains might have been passed. At the base of the pillars are two basins hewn out of the bedrock. It is suggested that these would have contained salt to clean the wounds after scourging, and vinegar to revive the offender.

It should be remembered that the Jews did not scourge Jesus because the accusation against him was much more serious: that of claiming to be the Son of God. It is suggested, therefore, that he was put in the dungeon overnight before appearing in front of Caiaphas, who was anxious that he should be crucified. Only the Roman procurator, Pontius Pilate, could authorize the death sentence, and it was, therefore, under Roman jurisdiction that Jesus was scourged in the Praetorium.

However, it seems quite likely that St. Peter, and possibly some of the other disciples, may have been scourged in this place because, according to the Acts of the Apostles, after the Resurrection they were accused of "preaching Christ" in the Temple, and this was an offense against the religious authority.

Now proceed to the back of the Guardroom down a step, then turn to the left. In the wall is an opening, and directly below it a stone block that has been carved out of the bedrock. From this elevated position there is a good view through the aperture directly onto the dungeon. Thus it would have been possible for just one man to observe those in the Guardroom and at the same time keep an eye on anyone in the cell below.

To reach this cell, return to the entrance and turn right. Further flights of steps lead down to this lower level.

Above is the shaft into the cell that was visible earlier from the Lower Church. High up in one wall is the opening that allowed the jailer to keep watch from the Guardroom.

Around the walls are some rather faint Byzantine crosses painted in red. There are seven in all, and these, together with the three crosses actually cut into the rock face of the entrance shaft, are said to date from the fifth century. High in the east wall are the remains of a flight of steps of uncertain date. Psalm 88 is especially suitable to read here and also the account of Jeremiah's being cast into a similar pit. The biblical text includes a graphic description of his being raised in a rope harness (Jeremiah 38:6–13).

Leave the dungeon, but before walking through the exit door, look at the modern bronze statue portraying Jesus the Suffering Servant of the Lord held captive and praying for the sins of many. The texts on the wall from Isaiah and St. Paul's letter to the Philippians state its significance. Below the east wall of the church are the excavated remains of the cellars, storerooms, and cistern of what is believed to have been the house of the high priest. It was here that many of the artifacts mentioned earlier were discovered.

Finally, on the north side of the complex are the ancient steps that were part of a main street running between the Kidron Valley and the Upper City at the top of Mount Zion. They date from not later than the Second Temple Period but were only uncovered in 1897. They would undoubtedly have been familiar to Jesus and his disciples, and it is most likely that after arresting him in the Garden of Gethsemane, the Temple Guard would have brought him up by this route for his interrogation before Caiaphas—even if the position of the high priest's house was higher up at the top of Mount Zion.

AUTHORS' COMMENTS

Whether or not one accepts that St. Peter in Gallicantu is built over the true site of the House of Caiaphas, the existence of a possible guardroom and prisoners' cell afford an excellent visual aid to the events of Maundy Thursday night. To recall those events here, and to see the ancient steps of the city of our Lord's time, can indeed be a memorable and rewarding experience.

Opening Times: 8:30–noon, 2:00–5:00 (closed on Sundays)

Souvenir Shop: opposite the west façade of the church on the upper path level; well stocked, containing quality gifts and books; refreshments available

Toilets: in the parking lot and at the top of the stairs inside the gift shop

Custodian: The Assumptionists

Telephone: (02) 6731739

POOL OF SILOAM

$$+\!\!\parallel\!\!+$$
$$+\!\!\parallel\!\!+$$

For the past 2,700 years the waters from the Spring of Gihon have flowed through Hezekiah's Tunnel to supply the Pool of Siloam. Jesus sent the man who had been blind from birth to the pool to bathe his eyes and receive sight. In his time Siloam was an extensive reservoir serving the inhabitants of the densely populated city above, but today all that remains is a narrow watercourse in a cutting between high walls.

JESUS GIVES SIGHT TO A MAN BORN BLIND

As Jesus walked along, he saw a man who had been blind from birth. His disciples asked him, "Master, if he was born blind because of sin, was it his sin or his parents'?"

Jesus answered, "Neither this man nor his parents sinned; he was born blind so that God's power might be shown in him. While it is day we must do the work of the One who sent me; for the night will come when no one can work. As long as I am in the world, I am the light of the world."

As Jesus said this, he made paste with spittle and clay and rubbed it on the eyes of the blind man. Then he said, "Go and wash in the Pool of Siloam." (This name means sent.) So he went and washed and came back able to see.

Jesus sent the man born blind to this, the Pool of Siloam, to bathe his eyes and regain his sight. *(George Martin)*

His neighbors and all the people who used to see him begging, wondered. They said, "Isn't this the beggar who used to sit here?" Some said, "It's the one." Others said, "No, but he looks like him." But the man himself said, "I am the one." Then they asked, "How is it that your eyes were opened?" And he answered, "The man called Jesus made a mud paste, put it on my eyes and said to me: 'Go to Siloam and wash.' So I went, and washed, and I could see." They asked, "Where is he?" and the man answered, "I don't know." (John 9:1–12)

Let thy glorious light
shine ever on my sight,
and clothe me round,
the while my path illumining.

ACCESS

Refer to the map on page 15. The Pool of Siloam (*Shiloah* in Hebrew) lies outside the walls on the south side of the Old City and about a quarter mile from Dung Gate.

ON FOOT

Walk down the road immediately opposite the gate, going around to the left. Descend the steep slope, and almost immediately after it joins another road, look out on the left for a break in the wall where steps lead down to the entrance. The minaret of a mosque directly behind the pool will be clearly visible.

BY CAR

From Jaffa or Damascus Gate drive around the Old City walls in a clockwise direction until reaching the far southeast corner where the massive stones tower above the roadway. Continue on around the walls for a short distance and look for a road on the left beside a parking lot. Descend this road for about a quarter mile, then on the left look for the minaret of a mosque, which is directly behind the pool. Park nearby and walk down some steps to the entrance.

DETAILS

Enter through a doorway in the surrounding wall on the left. Inside on the right is a kiosk selling souvenirs. For a small donation the owner may unlock the iron gates leading down to the pool. Descend the thirty-two stone steps to the water level, and ahead you will see, through an archway, the south end of Hezekiah's Tunnel. The water flowing through it comes from the Spring of Gihon, which wells up at the other end outside the line of the ancient city walls. The tunnel is about 550 yards long and was hewn out of the solid rock in the seventh century B.C. by Hezekiah, king of Judah. He thereby ensured that even when under siege Jerusalem had its own fresh-water supply within the confines of the city. If nobody is walking through the tunnel the water is clear, otherwise it can become very cloudy at the pool end.

Notice in the water some of the remains of the columns from a fifth-century Byzantine church that stood on this site and was destroyed by the

Persians in A.D. 614. Today the pool is a mere channel only fifteen yards long and two yards wide. Immediately above are the walls of a mosque built about a hundred years ago.

In our Lord's time the water from the Pool of Siloam played an important part in the Feast of Tabernacles. On the last day of the festival the high priest ceremonially carried the water to the Temple in a golden ewer and poured it on the great Altar of Sacrifice. It is thought that Jesus had just witnessed this ceremony when he spoke the words recorded in St. John's Gospel (7:37) "If anyone is thirsty, let him come to me; and let him who believes in me drink...."

AUTHORS' COMMENTS

Although there are no accurate records of its shape and size two thousand years ago, the pool was undoubtedly much larger then.

Opening Times: when the custodian is in attendance; a small donation is required to descend the steps to the water

Souvenir Shop: on the site

Toilets: none

Custodian: The Muslims

☩

Hezekiah's Tunnel
Warren's Shaft

The spring is situated in the Kidron Valley three hundred yards due south of the southeast corner of the Temple Area (see the map on page 15). At the time of writing, the road was blocked to vehicles at the Gethsemane end of the valley, and it is unwise to descend to the site on foot unaccompanied.

When approaching from the north, the entrance to the underground spring is on the right of the road running along the bottom of the valley, just beyond a school playground and beneath a fairly modern house. Thirty-three steps lead down to the water, which wells up in a rock cavern. A tunnel dating possibly from 1800 B.C. runs off westward and used to take the water to a point directly under the ancient city. It was then hauled up in buckets via a deep shaft, now known as Warren's Shaft (see page 101). It is thought most likely that, circa 1000 B.C., this was the shaft that King David's men climbed to capture the city (2 Samuel 5:6–8; 1 Chronicles 11:4–9). The spring was the only freshwater source in Jerusalem, and here Zadok the Priest and Nathan the Prophet anointed Solomon king of Israel (1 Kings 1:38–40).

☩

Hezekiah's Tunnel

At the beginning of the eighth century B.C., Hezekiah, king of Judah, accomplished a remarkable feat by extending part of the original tunnel for a distance of a third of a mile (2 Kings 20:20; 2 Chronicles 32:30). Following a natural fissure, the winding conduit was hewn out of solid rock to bring the spring water within the city to the Pool

Hezekiah's Tunnel was hewn out of solid rock to bring spring water within Jerusalem to the Pool of Siloam. *(George Martin)*

of Siloam (see page 97), which then served as a reservoir. The workmen started cutting from both ends, and it is interesting to note that the roof from the Siloam entrance is higher because when the two teams eventually met, the floor had to be lowered at that end to allow the water to flow. The axe and chisel marks can be seen along the entire length, and in some places there are signs that the workmen started to cut slightly off course. After completion of the work, the Gihon end was then hidden from view because it was vulnerable to attack during a siege.

As recently as 1880 an ancient Hebrew inscription was discovered engraved in the rock of the tunnel, commemorating the fact that the workmen had achieved their objective. This chunk of original wall was removed and is now in the Archaeological Museum in Istanbul. A replica has now been placed in the tunnel.

A feature of the Gihon Spring is that it gushes out in great volume for about half an hour and then hardly flows at all for many hours (the name Gihon means "gushing"). Generally, the water level in the tunnel is about knee-high, but when in full flow it can reach the lower part of the body. However, at two points it is even deeper.

Before wading through the tunnel, an entrance fee must be negotiated at either the Gihon or the Siloam end. Candles will probably be supplied, but they are likely to blow out, so a flashlight is essential. You should also wear sturdy shoes or boots. The passage is very narrow, and in places it is just possible to pass another person.

$$\begin{array}{c}+\;\|\;+\\[-4pt]\hline\\[-10pt]+\;\|\;+\end{array}$$

Warren's Shaft

The shaft is named after the English engineer Charles Warren who in 1867 discovered this ancient subterranean access to the spring water. The most recent excavation took place under the direction of the Israeli archaeologist Yigal Shiloh between

Warren's Shaft is an ancient subterranean access to spring water beneath Jerusalem. *(George Martin)*

1978 and 1982, when all the rubble was removed, so that it is now possible to walk down the wide underground approach to the top of the shaft. This is very worthwhile, and one is reminded of the tunnel hewn out of the rock to reach a similar water source at Megiddo in Northern Israel, but the approach is very steep and hazardous toward the end.

ACCESS

Refer to the map on page 15. Very few tourist maps show the location of Warren's Shaft, which is approachable only on foot. It is best to start from Dung Gate in the south wall of the Old City. Cross the main road outside the gate and turn left to walk downhill parallel to the walls. Take the first right into a road running south beside the parking lot. Proceed for about a hundred yards and then look out for a tarmacadam path on the left beside a wall. Walk along this, and turn right at the end, descending a series of steps leading directly to the City of David Archaeological Garden containing the excavated Jebusite walls of the ancient city. Here turn right and descend one series of steps, then left to descend additional steps. Halfway down, descend another flight of steps on the right onto the approach path to Warren's Shaft, which runs parallel to the Kidron Valley but may not be well marked.

There is an admission fee. Descend the steep spiral staircase to a small exhibition area and then follow the signs. Other long flights of steps have to be negotiated to reach the wide tunnel some one hundred feet in length, which itself is fairly steep and rough underfoot in places. The ancient shaft at the end is forty-three feet deep, and you can hear the water below if the Gihon Spring is in full flow.

Opening Times: Sunday to Thursday 8:30–3:00; Friday and holiday eves 8:30–1:00; closed on Saturdays; the admission charge is reduced for groups

Telephone: (02) 6288141

BETHLEHEM

*The Town
Church of the Nativity
Place of the Nativity
Church of St. Catherine
Cave of St. Jerome
Milk Grotto
Shepherds' Fields*

The main feature of this world-famous town is the Church of the Nativity built over the cave where, according to a very strong and unchallenged tradition, Jesus was born. The existing building dates from the latter part of the sixth century and is Christendom's oldest complete church.

THE BIRTH OF JESUS

At that time the emperor issued a decree for a census of the whole empire to be taken. This first census was taken while Quirinus was governor of Syria. Everyone had to be registered in his own town.

So everyone set out for his own city; Joseph too set out from Nazareth of Galilee. As he belonged to the family of David, being a descendant of his, he went to Judea to David's town of Bethlehem to be registered with Mary, his wife, who was with child.

Manger Square, in Bethlehem. The Church of the Nativity (left) was erected over the cave where Jesus was born.

They were in Bethlehem when the time came for her to have her child, and she gave birth to a son, her firstborn. She wrapped him in swaddling clothes and laid him in the manger, because there was no place for them in the living room. (Luke 2:1–7)

> I come, I bring, I offer here
> All Thou to me hast given.
> Take then, dear Lord, my mind and heart,
> My spirit, soul, and every part,
> For all I offer gladly.

ACCESS

Bethlehem lies about five miles south of Jerusalem on the main Hebron/Beersheba road. After about three miles notice on the left the Greek Orthodox Monastery of Mar Elias, where it is claimed the Prophet Elijah rested. From here one has the first view of the "Little Town of Bethlehem"—still quite small by modern standards. Soon after entering the outskirts of the town, look out on the right for Rachel's Tomb, a place of pilgrimage for Jews and Muslims. Be sure to take the left fork at a small traffic circle soon afterward, then remain on this road, ignoring all left turns, to reach the Church of the Nativity and Manger Square.

✠

The Town

Bethlehem is likely to be among the first places visited on a pilgrimage before one has had time to become accustomed to Arab culture and living standards. A word of warning, therefore, to the Christian pilgrim who may have been conditioned from a very early age by children's carols and Christmas scenes. The town can come as quite a shock to those who, perhaps less than twenty-four hours earlier, were still at home in the West:

- It is a relatively poor and untidy place even compared with Jerusalem, and the sharp contrast between the East and the West is very pronounced.
- It is a mecca, not only for Christians, but for millions of tourists who flock here from all over the world. Occasionally, the little town can suddenly be inundated by passengers from a cruise ship calling in at Haifa, the only consolation being that these large parties do not stay very long.
- Pilgrims sometimes feel that there is too much commercialism, but this is only because practically everyone wishes to take home a souvenir of their visit, a desire even stronger among Christians.

Consequently, be prepared for competitive street trading and realize that most of the shops are dependent upon the tourist. There is no trading within the Church of the Nativity.

In addition to the Church of the Nativity, there are many other churches, monasteries, convents, and orphanages in the town. Try to visit the market, which is frequented by Bedouin from the surrounding desert. To reach this, walk due west from the Church of the Nativity, cross Manger Square, and take the street to the right of the Tourist Information Office, then ascend a flight of steps. In this area there are no tourist shops, and the streets nearby have changed very little in two thousand years.

Bethlehem is renowned for its olive-wood carvings and mother-of-pearl souvenirs. Some of these are made by craftsmen in the little shops along Milk Grotto Street, which is to the right of the Church of the Nativity.

Church of the Nativity

HISTORICAL EVIDENCE

Although there is no actual mention in the gospels of Jesus' being born in a cave, even today one can see primitive shepherd dwellings in these Judean hills where families live directly above a cave providing natural shelter for their animals.

Certainly, local people would have remembered the birth—not least the shepherds who must often have been asked by their children, and their grandchildren, to tell the story of how the angels appeared to them on that first Christmas night. Their descendants would have known exactly where the birth took place. The visit of the Magi must also have been a memorable event.

Like a benediction, a shaft of light falls in the ancient Church of the Nativity. The priest is a member of the Greek monastery attached to the church. *(Ewing Galloway)*

The oral tradition was undoubtedly very strong, and in A.D. 135 Roman Emperor Hadrian, perhaps to divert attention from the site, gave orders that a grove, dedicated to the pagan god Adonis, should be planted in the immediate vicinity of the cave. If, as St. Jerome suggests, this really was his intention, in effect he marked the cave's location for the next two hundred years. The Christian missionary Justin Martyr, in A.D. 155, makes the earliest written reference to the Bethlehem cave surrounded by a grove dedicated to Adonis. The writer Origen also confirms the same tradition in A.D. 215.

In 315 Emperor Constantine, having been converted to Christianity by his mother, St. Helena, directed that a magnificent basilica should be erected over the cave. His building stood for two hundred years before being extensively damaged in the Samaritan Revolts during the first half of the sixth century. Later during that same century, Emperor Justinian erected a larger basilica on the site, incorporating parts of Constantine's structure. This building has survived to the present day.

TOUR

It is important to realize that the Greek Orthodox and Armenian Churches today jointly own the sixth-century building; thus the interior reflects the Eastern tradition. In contrast, the comparatively modern Roman Catholic Church of St. Catherine, built adjacent to the north wall of the ancient basilica, is more in keeping with the Western tradition.

Cross the road from Manger Square and pause to identify how the buildings are integrated. Immediately on the right is the Armenian convent with its rather squat modern bell tower. Farther along on the right you can see the top of the much larger tower belonging to the Greek Orthodox convent, while the Roman Catholic tower, from which the bells are sometimes broadcast on Christmas Eve, is on the left. However, from this position it is hidden from view behind the fortresslike west front of the main church.

Before entering the building, pause again to observe the three earlier doorways that have now been filled in. The highest arch dates from the sixth century. Immediately across this is a lintel that was constructed some time later. Much farther down is a twelfth-century Crusader arch, while finally the Turks made the very low doorway in the sixteenth century. These entrances were reduced in size solely for defensive purposes, but for the Christian there is the rather profound thought that everyone, except a child, has to bow the head to enter Jesus' birthplace.

This is the oldest complete church in the world. According to a legend documented as early as A.D. 838, when the Persians destroyed all the Chris-

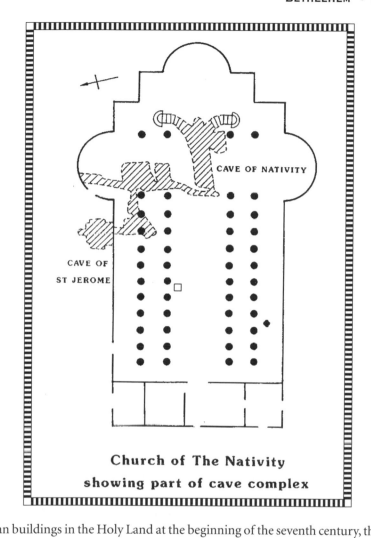

Church of The Nativity
showing part of cave complex

tian buildings in the Holy Land at the beginning of the seventh century, they recognized on this west façade a representation of the Magi in costumes of their own country. Thus in respect and reverence for their ancestors they spared the basilica from destruction.

Now stoop to enter the low doorway, and after passing through a rather dark narthex, stop to survey the interior, which has changed very little since Emperor Justinian constructed it. In accordance with the Eastern Orthodox tradition, the nave is completely devoid of furniture. The fine red limestone columns were quarried locally, while it is said that some of the roof timbers were a gift from King Edward III of England in the fourteenth century. The main altar is hidden from view behind a large wooden screen, known as an iconostasis, ornately carved and adorned with icons. Before moving on, look back to see the heavy wooden entrance door made by an Armenian carpenter in 1227.

Next turn right to examine the ancient Justinian font in the south aisle. Now turn back into the center of the nave to view, about two feet below the present floor level, a section of the exceptionally fine mosaic from the original floor of Constantine's church dating from A.D. 325. Notice also high up on the walls some remains of much later mosaics with which the Crusaders lavishly adorned the church in the twelfth century.

On Christmas day A.D. 1100 the Crusaders' first king, Baldwin I, was crowned here. Godfrey de Bouillon, who had previously been elected king of Jerusalem, refused this title but became "Defender of the Holy Sepulchre," saying, "How can I accept a crown of gold in the place where my Savior was crowned with thorns?"

Before proceeding further, stand in the middle of the nave facing the Greek iconostasis. The Cave of the Nativity is directly below the platform in front of this screen. Originally, Constantine built an octagonal structure over the cave from which it was possible for worshipers to look down directly into the place of birth.

Mount the steps of the platform, and pause to reflect that beneath one's feet is the sacred place where the Son of God was born.

Now turn right into the south transept. The altar against the east wall belongs to the Greek Orthodox Church and commemorates the circumcision. The steps beside the iconostasis lead down to the cave. If there is a line, try to wait until the way is clear, as the majority of groups pass through very quickly. It may also be helpful to have some idea of the layout of the cave before entering:

Place of the Nativity

The cave is rectangular and measures approximately forty feet by ten feet. To the left at the bottom of the steps, at a lower level than the main floor, is a representation of the manger. Between the staircases there is a small apse with an altar built into it. Underneath, set in the floor, is a silver star marking the traditional place of birth. The other steps also lead up into the Church of the Nativity.

The silver star in the floor marks the traditional birthplace of Jesus. This natural cave at one time housed livestock and is believed to have sheltered the Holy Family during their visit to Bethlehem.

Since the sixth century the walls of the cave have been lined with marble to preserve them. This, in turn, was protected by heavy leather drapes backed with asbestos following a serious fire in 1869. The holes in these drapes allow the ceiling lamps to be lowered. Nevertheless, depending upon how elaborately the cave is decorated, it may be possible to see small sections of the natural rock. The roof has been blackened by the burning of candles for over fourteen hundred years.

On feast days the cave is lit by forty-eight hanging lamps, twenty-one of them belonging to the Roman Catholic Church. At Christmas a life-size effigy of the Holy Babe is placed in the manger. The small altar opposite it is dedicated to the Magi.

Pause to reflect that the church is open for twelve hours each day, and during this time the cave is rarely empty. It is probably true to say that more prayers have been offered from this hallowed place than from anywhere else in Christendom.

Leave the cave by ascending the steps to the left of the star; these lead into the north transept of the church. This area belongs to the Armenians. The altar immediately to the right is dedicated to the Three Kings, while the one straight ahead honors the Virgin. Beside the raised platform in front of the Greek iconostasis are trapdoors in the floor, under which can be seen the remains of other fine mosaics from the Constantinian church. Now pass through the north door into the Church of St. Catherine.

The courtyard and façade of the Church of St. Catherine, with the statue of St. Jerome on a pillar. *(George Martin)*

⊹ Church of St. Catherine

This Roman Catholic church, greatly enlarged from the original Crusader building, was constructed in 1882 and further extended in 1949. It is from here that Midnight Mass is sometimes broadcast on Christmas Eve. Notice the design of the nave lighting in the form of Catherine wheels. In the south aisle twenty-nine steps lead down to the Cave of St. Jerome.

⊹ Cave of St. Jerome

This cave is of considerable importance for two reasons. First, it was here that from A.D. 386–404 St. Jerome labored to translate the Bible from Hebrew and Greek into Latin. His version, known as the Vulgate, is still used by the Roman Catholic Church. He was assisted by two pious ladies, St. Paula and her daughter St. Eustochium, who, together with St. Jerome, founded Christian monastic communities around Bethlehem.

Second, the cave is beneath the Church of the Nativity and is also directly connected to the place of birth. The underground caverns were carefully reinstated by the Franciscans in 1964.

TOUR

From the bottom of the narrow steps into the first cavern, look to the left and notice a half-arch that is part of the Constantinian foundation of the Church of the Nativity. Farther around on the left is an altar and a number of first- and second-century sarcophagi, some of which are reputed to be those of the Holy Innocents. The main feature here is a raised altar commemorating St. Joseph's dream in which the angel instructed him to take Mary and the Babe and hasten into Egypt. Immediately to the right of the altar is a narrow passage, reputedly cut by St. Jerome so that he could have direct access to the Cave of the Nativity.

Walk under an archway, close to the entrance steps, which leads into two smaller caverns. In the first, on the right, is an altar dedicated to St. Eusebius, a disciple of St. Jerome, while on the left is an ancient cistern. Notice how the rim has been worn by the rubbing of ropes. A little farther on in the next cavern is an altar dedicated to St. Paula and St. Eustochium, while ahead is the cenotaph of St. Jerome himself.

Finally, walk through another narrow passageway to the Chapel of St. Jerome. In this room he is said to have produced the Vulgate. At the back of the chapel, behind a glass door with an ornate grille, is a flight of steps that leads directly up into the cloister in front of St. Catherine's Church.

Now return to the Church of St. Catherine and go out by the west door into a delightful cloister dedicated to St. Jerome, whose statue, made of terra cotta and mounted on a granite column, provides a fitting centerpiece.

Opening Times:

Church of the Nativity: 5:30 A.M.–6:30 P.M. daily; winter closes 5:00 P.M.

Church of St. Catherine: 5:00–noon, 2:00–6:00 daily; winter closes 5:00 P.M.

Souvenir Shop: none

Toilets: none

Custodians:

Church of the Nativity: The Armenians and the Greek Orthodox

Church of St. Catherine: The Roman Catholics

Telephone:

Church of the Nativity: (02) 741020

St. Catherine's: (02) 742425

Milk Grotto

The Armenian and Greek Orthodox convents adjoin the Church of the Nativity. The Greek Orthodox convent is reached through the door in the south transept. The Armenian convent can be approached by going through the south door of the dark entrance-narthex of the church.

Nearby in Milk Grotto Street, which runs east from Manger Square, is the church built over the shrine of the Milk Grotto. The entrance is 250 yards along on the right. It is so called because, according to a sixth-century legend, when the Virgin Mary was suckling the baby Jesus, here a drop of her milk fell onto the ground, and the rock immediately turned white. Pieces of the rock can be seen as relics in many churches throughout the world because it is claimed to have therapeutic qualities.

Even today some young women come here to pray to the Holy Mother for a plentiful supply of milk for their babies. The Franciscans built the present shrine in 1871, and parts of it are lavishly decorated with mother-of-pearl.

Opening Times:

Milk Grotto: 8:00–11:45, 2:00–6:00 daily; winter closes 5:00 P.M.; ring the bell

Telephone: (02) 743867

Shepherds' Fields

There are two principal sites commemorating the appearance of the angels to the shepherds on that first Christmas night. Where precisely this event occurred is unknown, but the exact location is quite unimportant because anywhere down here at the bottom of the hill from the little town, it is easy to imagine the shepherds tending their sheep. Although many of the fields are now cultivated, you can still see sheep nibbling the scanty pasture by the roadside.

The older site of the two is near the distinctive modern red-domed Greek Orthodox church, which was finally completed in 1989. Here there are the remains of a fourth-century church, the crypt of which was regularly used by the Orthodox community prior to the opening of the new building. The latter contains a beautiful iconostasis and many other fine examples of modern art and craftsmanship. If time permits it is well worth a visit.

A view of the countryside outside Bethlehem. In fields such as these the shepherds wondered at the angels' announcement of Jesus' birth. *(George Martin)*

The Franciscans own the alternative site, and the view from it is probably more in keeping with the Western idea of what the fields would have looked like two thousand years ago. There is a pleasant garden that provides an ideal setting in which to meditate upon the Christmas story. This location is described in detail below.

THE STORY OF THE SHEPHERDS

There were shepherds camping in the countryside, taking turns to watch over their flocks by night. Suddenly an angel of the Lord appeared to them, with the Glory of the Lord shining around them.

As they were terrified, the angel said to them, "Don't be afraid; I am here to give you good news, great joy for all the people. Today a Savior has been born to you in David's town; he is the Messiah and the Lord. Let this be a sign to you: you will find a baby wrapped in swaddling clothes and lying in a manger."

Suddenly the angel was surrounded by many more angels, praising God and saying, "Glory to God in the highest; peace on earth for God is blessing humankind."

When the angels had left and gone back to heaven, the shepherds said to one another, "Let us go as far as Bethlehem and see what the Lord has made known to us." So they came hurriedly and found Mary and Joseph with the baby lying in the manger. On seeing this they related what they had been told about the child, and all were astonished on hearing the shepherds.

As for Mary, she treasured all these messages and continually pondered over them.

The shepherds then returned giving glory and praise to God for all they had heard and seen, just as the angels had told them. (Luke 2:8–20)

> While the angels in the sky
> Sang praise above the silent field,
> To shepherds poor the Lord most high,
> The one great Shepherd, was revealed.

ACCESS

To reach the Franciscan compound, which is about a mile and a half from the town, depart from Manger Square by the main road. After fifty yards turn right, at the sign "Shepherds' Fields." Descend the steep hill for a half mile and turn left at the sign "Welcome to the Shepherds' Fields," then keep to the left down the hill. On reaching the crossroads, go straight ahead. Ahead, among the trees, is the Franciscan compound.

To visit the Greek Orthodox site continue on past the Franciscan compound for another 250 yards. Turn right onto the main road, and on the left you can see the red domes of the modern church. To reach it, take the first left off the main road, then the first left again.

TOUR OF THE FRANCISCAN SITE

From the entrance gate there is a pleasant walk of about 150 yards to the main compound. At the end on the left are the remains of a Byzantine agricultural monastery. From here there is a fine view across the barren countryside. In the distance are the modern suburbs of Jerusalem, but in the foreground one can see caves where the shepherds still shelter. Of particular interest is a track winding around the hillside because it is probable that Joseph and Mary used this if, as St. Luke suggests, they journeyed from Nazareth. The track bypasses Jerusalem on the way up from the Jordan Valley. Although the Jordan route was longer than going through Samaria, the journey would have been easier for Mary in her condition, and the road less prone to attack from brigands.

Shepherds traditionally still lead their sheep, rather than driving them from behind as in the West. Each man has a distinctive call that his flock recognizes. Jesus said, "The keeper opens the gate to him and the sheep hear his voice; he calls each of his sheep by name and leads them out. When he has brought out all his own, he goes before them and the sheep follow him for they know his voice….I am the good shepherd. I know my own and my own know me" (John 10:3–4, 14).

Follow the boundary railing around, and on the left is a gate leading down to a secluded area where an altar has been erected among the Byzantine ruins. Ahead are the remains of a tower that has been converted into the custodian's residence. In the foreground is a cave containing an altar, and a little farther to the right is a larger one, now protected by an entrance door, which has also been set out as a chapel. Notice within how the ceiling has been blackened by the shepherds' fires since time immemorial.

Finally, follow a path that leads up to the Chapel of the Angel. This expressive building designed by the Italian architect Antonio Barluzzi represents a Bedouin tent. The foundation stone was laid on Christmas 1953, and the chapel was consecrated exactly a year later. There is a fine bronze casting of an angel above the entrance door. Inside, four figures support the central altar, while the light floods through the dome, symbolizing the heavenly light that surrounded the angels on that first Christmas night. Three small apses contain delightful paintings depicting the scenes.

Opening Times: 8:00–noon, 2:00–6:00 daily (winter closes 5:30)
Souvenir Shop: none (beware of persistent traders outside the gate)
Toilets: on the left at the end of the entrance path
Custodian: The Franciscans
Telephone: (02) 6472413

HERODION

Herod the Great adapted the summit of a mountain in the barren Judean hills to create another of his private fortified palaces. This particular loca-tion, however, must have been rather special to him as he named it after himself and ex-pressed the wish that upon his death he should be buried there. Today it resembles an extinct volcano and can be seen in the distance to the left of the Jerusa-lem/Bethlehem road. At the foot of the moun-tain, he also had con-structed a number of

A view from the Herodion of the ruins of Herod's guest palace and pool. Herod built this complex on the summit of a mountain as another of his private fortified palaces. *(George Martin)*

other buildings, including a separate palace for the reception and accommo-dation of guests. The complex also comprised a large rectangular pool sur-rounded by attractive gardens.

ACCESS

FROM JERUSALEM

The Herodion is about twelve miles from Jerusalem. From Jaffa Gate take the main road to Bethlehem, but after three miles look on the left for the prominent Mar Elias Monastery. Soon after passing this, turn left just *before* the traffic lights, then almost immediately right. Go one mile and at the junction turn right, then drive for three miles until reaching the crossroads that are at the summit of a hill (*) [see page 116]. Here continue straight ahead to the next T-junction and turn left.

Soon afterward at the bottom of the hill take the right fork uphill. Go about two miles and bear right by a mosque. The Herodion is about a mile from here and is clearly visible to the left. When almost parallel to the moun-tain, look for a number of reerected Roman pillars beside the road, then almost immediately take the road to the left. The parking lot, toilets, and ticket office are near the top of the mountain.

FROM BETHLEHEM

Depart from Manger Square and after fifty yards turn right at the sign "Shepherds' Fields." Go straight ahead down this road for a half mile and take the left fork. After another half mile take the left fork again at the sign "Jericho." Continue for about a mile, and at the crossroads turn right. Then follow the access instructions from Jerusalem after the (*) on page 115.

HISTORY

Around 25 B.C. Herod began the construction of this mountain fortress by creating an artificial mound on the top of a natural peak. He then surmounted the earthworks with a circular defensive wall, into which were built four towers. Three of them were low and semicircular, while the fourth on the north face rose several stories above the wall and acted as a watchtower. Within the enclosure was the small but luxurious accommodation for himself and his family. Two hundred white marble steps led up to the summit, where a drawbridge gave access to the interior. The superstructure has disappeared over the years, so all that can now be seen from the outside is the conical earthwork.

At the base of the mountain, he had a separate palace constructed for the reception of his guests. Nearby, a large artificial pool was created with a circular pavilion in the center. This had the dual purpose of serving as a reservoir for the water that was channeled into it from a source near Bethlehem, as well as providing an attractive place for swimming and relaxation. A formal garden surrounded the area. The Jewish historian Flavius Josephus records that Agrippa, son-in law of Emperor Augustus, stayed in the palace as a guest of Herod in 15 B.C. He also records that Herod died at Jericho and gives a detailed account of his funeral cortege on its way to the Herodion, but in spite of extensive excavations since 1962 no trace of his tomb has been found.

In A.D. 70, during the First Jewish Revolt against the Romans, the insurgents used the fortress as a refuge. Later, in the Second Revolt from 132–135, the Zealot leader Bar Kokhba developed the fortress as his headquarters. The Herodion water cisterns were extended to form a complicated underground network of tunnels from which surprise attacks could be made. A synagogue and *mikve* (ritual cleansing bath) were also constructed within the walls.

After the defeat of the Zealots, the Herodion remained unoccupied for some three hundred years. Between the fifth and the seventh centuries, monks, possibly of Egyptian origin, inhabited the site, and there are many Christian symbols on the walls. A chapel was built among the remains at the top, and another at the foot of the mountain. There is no evidence of any particular habitation after the seventh century.

TOUR

The approach is via a modern road at the foot of the mountain, passing beside the remains of the Herodion pool, which is partially flanked by re-erected pillars. You can gain a better idea of the extensive layout from the top of the mountain, which is over 350 feet higher than its surroundings. Half-way up are a parking lot, toilets, and a ticket booth. From here there is a fairly steep two hundred–yard path to the top, including fifty-five shallow steps.

At the summit the impression is of standing on the rim of a volcano whose crater surprisingly contains the remains of a compact royal residence. You can see the foundations of the original entrance to the fortress, which was approached by two hundred marble steps, below the modern footbridge on the left. Looking down into the palace ruins, and also on the left, is the base of the large circular watchtower. Immediately in front of it, you can see the extent of Herod's colonnaded courtyard.

Walk around to the right, passing the foundations of the north semicircular defensive tower, and proceed to a position between the head of the stairway leading down into the interior and the foundations of the west defensive tower. From here other features of the site are identifiable. Immediately below are the remains of the fifth/seventh-century chapel built within part of Herod's residential accommodation. To the left of the foot of the stairway, and immediately below the north tower, are the remains of his bathhouse in typical Roman layout. The monks subsequently occupied the roofed complex and used Herod's caldarium (hot room) as a bakery. On the extreme right of the ruins is a rectangular area, originally the dining hall, which the Zealots later adapted for use as a synagogue. They added the stone slab seating on three sides.

Before descending the steps, enjoy the panoramic views of the Judean hills and the wilderness beyond. To the northwest in the far distance you can see the taller buildings of Jerusalem, while much nearer lies Bethlehem.

If time permits, make a closer inspection of the ruins, the main features of which are clearly marked. You can reach the entrance to the Bar Kokhba underground defense network via a stairway in the corner of the colonnaded courtyard. If the door is locked, you may obtain the key from the ticket office.

On the way down to the parking lot (either from the top or from the exit from the Bar Kokhba tunnels) there are good views of part of the lower palace complex at the foot of the mountain. The outline of the rectangular pool with its circular central feature is very clear, as is the surrounding leveled area where Herod laid out his formal garden. Excavations between the garden and the mountain foot have revealed another building, the purpose of which has not been established.

Opening Times: April to September 8:00–5:00; October to March 8:00–4:00; on eve of Shabbat and holidays closes one hour earlier; closed on Yom Kippur; the tourist "green card" is accepted

Souvenir Shop: only a few postcards at the ticket office

Toilets: beside the parking lot

Custodian: The National Parks Authority

BETHANY

Franciscan Church
Tomb of Lazarus

Bethany was a "home away from home" for the Galileans, and it was here that Jesus often stayed when visiting Jerusalem. A modern Franciscan church has been built over the traditional home of Lazarus, Martha, and Mary. There is a mosque above the reputed tomb where Jesus raised Lazarus from the dead. Close to a modern Greek Orthodox church are the ruins of a Crusader tower. Simon the Leper also lived in the village, although the site of his home has not been identified.

THE ANOINTING OF JESUS BY MARY

Six days before the Passover, Jesus came to Bethany where he had raised Lazarus, the dead man, to life. Now they gave a dinner for him, and while Martha waited on them, Lazarus sat at the table with Jesus.

Then Mary took a pound of costly perfume made from genuine nard and anointed the feet of Jesus, wiping them with her hair. And the whole house was filled with the fragrance of the perfume.

Judas, son of Simon Iscariot—the disciple who was to betray Jesus—remarked, "This perfume could have been sold for three hundred silver coins and turned over to the poor." Judas, indeed, had no concern for the poor; he was a thief and as he held the common purse, he used to help himself to the funds.

But Jesus spoke up, "Leave her alone. Was she not keeping it for the day of my burial? (The poor you always have with you, but you will not always have me.)" (John 12:1–8)

> Take my love; my Lord, I pour
> at thy feet its treasure-store;
> take myself, and I will be
> ever, only, all for thee.

ACCESS

BY CAR

The straggling village is on the Jericho road about two and a half miles from Jerusalem. The slender bell tower and the cupola of the Franciscan church are on the left of the road at the end of the second double bend.

Here there is a bus stop and a small parking space. You may reach the site either by going through a gate leading into a walled garden between the road and the church or by following the wall around, keeping to the left and walking up the narrow road.

ON FOOT

It is possible to walk from Jerusalem via the top of the Mount of Olives (refer to the map on page 18). From the top of Olivet take the road running east between the high walls and then fork right. After a short distance there is a magnificent view of the village of Bethphage and Upper Bethany, with the Judean wilderness beyond. On a clear day it is possible to see the Mountains of Moab on the other side of the Jordan Valley. Walk down the road to the walled Franciscan monastery, which marks the place where "the two ways meet" (see "Bethphage," page 123 for details of this church). Follow the boundary walls around on the right-hand side and on to the ancient track to Bethany. Continue south, and be sure to go straight ahead at the crossroads. The village will eventually come into view. The track is very steep, and one should allow at least forty-five minutes from the top of the Mount of Olives.

Franciscan Church

The building was completed in 1954 and is dedicated to St. Lazarus. It stands among the ruins of three earlier churches. The Italian architect Barluzzi, who always tried to make his buildings expressive of the events they commemorate, has contrasted the rather dark interior, resembling a mausoleum, with the light flooding from the dome to remind Christians of the Resurrection. The earliest church was erected in the middle of the fourth century soon after Emperor Constantine built his great basilicas in Bethlehem and Jerusalem. Some of the lower courses of masonry among the ruins surrounding the modern church date from this period.

An earthquake damaged the first church; a larger one replace it in the fifth/sixth centuries. The Persians destroyed it in A.D. 614. You can see some fine mosaics from these two Byzantine churches a few inches below the level of the courtyard in front of the church; they are also incorporated in the floor to the right of the nave.

In the twelfth century the Crusaders built a very large Benedictine convent encompassing the whole area of the earlier churches, the Tomb of Lazarus farther along the road, and stretching as far as the modern Greek Orthodox church. The tower, now in ruins, marked the west boundary of the convent.

TOUR

The present church is designed in the form of a Greek cross. Notice, inside, the mosaics high up on the four walls: on the left Jesus is depicted with Martha and Mary; above the main altar the theme is "I am the Resurrection and the Life"; on the right Jesus raises Lazarus from the dead; and above the entrance door Jesus dines with Simon the Leper.

Around the cupola is an inscription in Latin from John 11:25: "Whoever believes in me, though he die, shall live. Whoever is alive by believing in me will never die." Portrayed in the mosaics of the dome are blossoms, with flames and doves symbolizing faithful souls taking flight to heaven.

Upon leaving the church, walk diagonally across to the far left corner of the courtyard and mount the steps to see into a building open to the skies, where a roof arch stands aloft over these ancient walls. The stones on the left were part of the Crusader Benedictine convent, while those at the end and on the right are Byzantine and date from the fifth/sixth centuries.

On the left are a series of rooms that were once part of the convent. In one long room is a millstone together with an ancient, deeply cut wooden screw that was part of an olive press. The largest of the rooms has been converted for use as a chapel.

Tomb of Lazarus

Leave the church courtyard and walk farther up the road where, on the left, is the reputed Tomb of Lazarus. Entry is by way of twenty-six steps down a steep shaft. At the bottom, another three shallow steps connect the vestibule with the inner chamber, and it is necessary to crouch low under a stone slab to enter the tomb. According to tradition, it was in the vestibule that Jesus stood when he called Lazarus from the dead. The tomb is lined with ancient stone blocks for protection.

In the fourth century there was a Byzantine shrine over the site. During the Crusader Period the entrance to the tomb was from within the Benedictine convent, and after this was destroyed, access was from the mosque now above it. The Muslims also venerate St. Lazarus. They constructed the present steps leading from the road in the sixteenth century.

On leaving the tomb, walk farther up the road where, on the left, is the modern Greek Orthodox church dedicated to Simon the Leper and completed in 1964. Behind it you can clearly see the ruins of the west tower of the twelfth-century Benedictine convent. This was built upon much earlier foundations, and it is interesting to note that the base contains some massive Herodian stone blocks. To follow the traditional "Palm Sunday Walk," turn right at the junction by the church.

AUTHORS' COMMENTS

Many guided tours allow insufficient time at Bethany, using it only as a short break in a long day visiting Jericho, the Dead Sea, and Masada. The village deserves much more attention because it was a favored resting place of Jesus and as such is referred to a number of times in each of the four gospels. More important, it was here that in calling forth Lazarus from the tomb, our Lord demonstrated so vividly his power to raise the dead.

Opening Times:

Franciscan Church: 8:00–11:30, 2:00–5:00 daily (winter closes 4:30)

Tomb of Lazarus: admission on request at the shop across the street; a small fee is charged

Souvenir Shop: opposite the Tomb of Lazarus; refreshments available

Toilets: at the far end of the church courtyard; also to the left of the souvenir shop

Custodians:

The Church: The Franciscans

The Tomb: The Muslims

Telephone:

The Church: (02) 749291

BETHPHAGE

$$+\!\!\parallel\!\!+ \atop +\!\!\parallel\!\!+$$

The Franciscan monastery stands within high walls at a place where "the two ways meet." According to tradition, it was here that Jesus mounted the donkey to make his triumphal entry into Jerusalem on the first Palm Sunday.

THE TRIUMPHAL ENTRY INTO JERUSALEM

When they drew near to Jerusalem and arrived at Bethphage and Bethany, at the Mount of Olives, Jesus sent two of his disciples with these instructions, "Go to the village on the other side and, as you enter it, you will find there a colt tied up that no one has ridden. Untie it and bring it here. If anyone says to you: 'What are you doing?' give this answer: 'The Lord needs it, but he will send it back immediately.'"

They went off and found the colt out in the street tied at the door. As they were untying it, some of the bystanders asked, "Why are you untying that colt?" They answered as Jesus had told them, and the people allowed them to continue.

They brought the colt to Jesus, threw their cloaks on its back, and Jesus sat upon it. Many people also spread their cloaks on the road, while others spread leafy branches from the fields. Then the people who walked ahead and those who followed behind Jesus began to shout, "Hosannah! Blessed is he who comes in the name of the Lord! Blessed is the kingdom of our father David which comes! Hosannah in the highest!" (Mark 11:1–10)

> The people of the Hebrews
> with palms before thee went:
> our praise and prayer and anthems
> before thee we present.

ACCESS

BY CAR OR ON FOOT

From Gethsemane, follow the instructions to reach the Place of the Ascension (see page 18), but continue on past the shrine for about a hundred yards until reaching the wall ahead surrounding the Church of the Pater Noster. Turn left here. Continue east between the high walls and take the right fork. After a short distance there is a magnificent view of the village of

123

Bethphage and Upper Bethany with the Judean Wilderness beyond. On a clear day it is possible to see the Mountains of Moab on the other side of the Jordan Valley. Proceed down the road, and straight ahead is the walled Franciscan monastery. Allow twelve minutes walking from the top of Olivet.

DETAILS

The monastery was built in 1883 on a twelfth-century Crusader site. Ring the bell for admission, and once inside walk across the courtyard to the church. On the left of the nave, protected by a wrought-iron grille, is an ancient stone cube measuring about a yard on each side. There is a tradition that our Lord mounted the donkey from this stone. The early paintings on each face were restored in 1950. They portray, on the north side, the disciples collecting the donkey; on the east, the crowd receiving palms; on the south, Jesus calling Lazarus from the tomb; and on the west, Jesus with Martha and Mary.

Above the altar is a mural of Jesus riding on the donkey, receiving the acclaim of the crowds. Around the walls are scenes from the Palm Sunday story, while the ceiling of the church is attractively painted with tiny sprays of flowers.

It is worthwhile seeking permission to visit the first-century tombs in the olive grove at the rear of the monastery. Descend the path, and on the right-hand side is a fine example of a tomb with its rolling stone still intact. There are a number of other burial chambers in the vicinity, and it is here that the Galileans who died while visiting Jerusalem were laid to rest.

Opening Times: 8:00–11:30, 2:00–5:00 daily (winter closes at 4:30); ring the bell

Souvenir Shop: none

Toilets: to the right of the entrance courtyard

Custodian: The Franciscans; the gatekeeper appreciates a small gratuity

Telephone: (02) 284352

EIN KEREM

$$\frac{+\|+}{+\|+}$$

Church of the Visitation
Church of St. John the Baptist

A pleasant village about four miles west of Jerusalem, Ein Kerem is the traditional home of the priest Zechariah and his wife, Elizabeth. The Virgin Mary visited her cousin here, and it was the birthplace and home of St. John the Baptist.

ACCESS

BY CAR

From the northwest corner of the Old City, take the main Tel Aviv road named Jaffa Street for about a mile, then turn left at the junction, and bear left into Herzl Boulevard after a quarter mile. Continue along this main thoroughfare for another mile until reaching the Military Cemetery and Herzl Memorial Park on the right. (Behind this is Yad Vashem.) Turn right at the traffic lights by a modern steel sculpture. This road leads down to the village, which is about a mile farther on. Parking space is available on the left opposite the village police station.

$$\frac{+\|+}{+\|+}$$

Church of the Visitation

THE VISITATION OF MARY TO ELIZABETH

Mary then set out for a town in the Hills of Judah. She entered the house of Zechariah and greeted Elizabeth. When Elizabeth heard Mary's greeting, the baby leapt in her womb. Elizabeth was filled with holy spirit, and giving a loud cry, said, "You are most blessed among women and blessed is the fruit of your womb! How is it that the mother of my Lord comes to me? The moment your greeting sounded in my ears, the baby within me suddenly leapt for joy. Blessed are you who believed that the Lord's word would come true!"

And Mary said:

"My soul proclaims the greatness of the Lord,
my spirit exults in God my savior!
He has looked upon his servant in her lowliness,
and people forever will call me blessed.
The Mighty One has done great things for me,
Holy is his Name!
From age to age his mercy extends
to those who live in his presence.
He has acted with power and done wonders,
and scattered the proud with their plans.
He has put down the mighty from their thrones
and lifted up those who are downtrodden.
He has filled the hungry with good things
but he has sent the rich away empty.
He held out his hand to Israel, his servant,
for he remembered his mercy,
even as he promised our fathers,
Abraham and his descendants forever."
Mary remained with Elizabeth about three months and then returned
home. *(Luke 1:39–56)*

> *Still to the lowly soul*
> *he doth himself impart,*
> *and for his dwelling and his throne*
> *chooseth the pure in heart.*

ACCESS

From the center of the village you reach the church by walking down the road to the left. Go about three hundred yards, then notice the old village spring, which has the minaret of a mosque above it. The spring is interesting because here is a natural water source that must have been familiar to the Virgin Mary when she stayed in this "hill country of Judea" with her cousin Elizabeth. Walk along the path opposite for another 450 yards to reach the church, but be careful to keep to the right to avoid taking an alternative track that leads up to the Convent of the Russian White Sisters. Farther along, climb the steep slope and series of steps to the church.

TOUR

First notice the fine wrought-iron screen at the entrance to the courtyard. Then look at the mosaic on the west façade of the church depicting the Blessed Virgin Mary, mounted on a donkey, meeting her cousin Elizabeth. The church, completed in 1955, was erected over the remains of earlier Byzantine and Crusader buildings.

Proceed to the Lower Chapel by walking through the cloister arches directly below the mosaic. This area dates from the sixth century. Standing at the entrance, notice ahead a tunnel leading to an old well. There is an ancient tradition that the waters joyfully sprang out of the rock here when the Virgin Mary greeted her cousin. The three large paintings on the walls of the chapel portray Zechariah performing his priestly duties in the Temple; the Visitation; and the slaughtering of the innocent babes by King Herod's soldiers. Below this is a rock set in a niche known as the Stone of Hiding, which, according to the second-century "Testimony of James," is reputed to have concealed St. John the Baptist from the perils of the sword.

After leaving the chapel, cross the courtyard to examine the attractive ceramic plaques on the wall opposite. The Blessed Virgin's Magnificat is displayed here in forty-five different languages.

To reach the Upper Church, ascend the steps to the left of the cloister arches. The interior is decorated with paintings depicting the glorification of the Virgin through the centuries, and also holy women of the Old and New Testaments. Notice the large stone blocks in the wall of the apse forming part of the Crusader church. Some of the paintings above illustrate incidents from the life of Mary, while the one in the center depicts the dedication of the building by the Roman Catholic patriarch and the Custos of the Holy Land.

Five large paintings adorn the south wall. Looking at them from the apse you will see the Council of Ephesus when the Blessed Virgin was proclaimed the Mother of God; the protection of the Church by Mary; the miracle of turning the water into wine at Cana in Galilee; the Battle of Lepoto, which was won through the intercession of Mary; and on the far right John Duns Scotus defending the Immaculate Conception before the Sorbonne. The mosaic floor of the church is particularly attractive and depicts Nature's tribute to Mary.

Before returning to the village, pause outside the wrought-iron screen to look down upon Ein Kerem, which is dominated by the spire of the Church of the Nativity of St. John the Baptist. Notice how the buildings of modern Jerusalem are just beginning to encroach into this area. Nevertheless, the view across these Judean hills is still comparatively unspoiled and delightfully rural.

AUTHORS' COMMENTS

The Church of the Visitation is probably one of the most beautiful of all the gospel sites in the Holy Land. This peaceful setting is an excellent place for meditation.

Opening Times: 8:00–11:45, 2:30–6:00; winter closes at 5:00; closed on Saturdays

Souvenir Shop: sometimes open

Toilets: in the courtyard

Custodian: The Franciscans

Telephone: (02) 6417291

Church of St. John the Baptist

THE BIRTH AND NAMING OF JOHN THE BAPTIST

When the time came for Elizabeth, she gave birth to a son. Her neighbors and relatives heard that the merciful Lord had done a wonderful thing for her and they rejoiced with her.

When on the eighth day they came to attend the circumcision of the child, they wanted to name him Zechariah after his father. But his mother said, "Not so; he shall be called John." They said to her, "No one in your family has that name"; and they asked the father by means of signs for the name he wanted to give. Zechariah asked for a writing tablet and wrote on it, "His name is John," and they were very surprised. Immediately Zechariah could speak again and his first words were in praise of God.

A holy fear came on all in the neighborhood, and throughout the Hills of Judea the people talked about these events. All who heard of it pondered in their minds and wondered, "What will this child be?" For they understood that the hand of the Lord was with him. (Luke 1:57–66)

> *The great forerunner of the morn,*
> *The herald of the Word, is born;*
> *And faithful hearts shall never fail*
> *With thanks and praise his light to hail.*

ACCESS

From the center of the village you can reach the church by walking up the road to the right for about a hundred yards, passing through an archway.

TOUR

The façade has a fortresslike appearance, although it was rebuilt as recently as the seventeenth century on the lines of an earlier Crusader building. However, remnants of two chapels belonging to a fifth-century church have been found under the substantial west porch of the present structure.

From the courtyard, ascend the steps to reach this porch and enter the church. The interior is rather dark, and adjusting to the dim light takes some time. Of particular interest is a high dado of blue and white tiles on the massive central pillars and walls. These were brought from Valencia in Spain. A large Crusader mosaic has been relaid in the center of the nave, and another under the dome.

The main feature of the church is the Grotto of the Benedictus, which is reputed to be part of the home of Zechariah and Elizabeth and thus the birthplace of St. John the Baptist. To reach it, descend the flight of steps at the east end of the north aisle. The floor and apse date from the twelfth century. A medallion under the altar marks the traditional place of birth.

AUTHORS' COMMENTS

The site dates from the fifth century and is the only one to be reverenced as the birthplace of St. John the Baptist.

Opening Times: summer 8:00–noon, 2:30–6:00 (winter closes 5:00); closed on Saturdays; Sundays 9:00–noon, 2:30–5:00

Souvenir Shop: to the right of the entrance portico

Toilets: none

Custodian: The Franciscans

Telephone: (02) 6413639

EMMAUS

```
+ ‖ +
══╬══
+ ‖ +
```

Amwas
Abu Gosh
El Qubeibah
Qalunieh

St. Luke records that, on the day of his Resurrection, Jesus joined two disciples as they journeyed on the road to the village of Emmaus about seven miles from Jerusalem. At first they thought he was a stranger and did not recognize him. When they reached their destination, they persuaded him to stay with them, and it was there during the meal that he revealed himself in the breaking of bread. The location of the gospel Emmaus is unknown, but over the years four possible sites have been suggested.

```
+ ‖ +
══╬══
+ ‖ +
```

Amwas

Here within a walled compound are the extensive ruins of a substantial fifth-century Byzantine church and some evidence of later Crusader occupation. Unfortunately, the entrance gate is often locked, and it is then possible to view the ruins only from a distance.

ACCESS

Sometimes known today as Latrun, Amwas is about nineteen miles from Jerusalem off the main Tel Aviv highway. When the coastal plain comes into view, take the first right turn to Ramallah at the Latrun junction. The site is almost immediately on the right behind an iron gate, but you might miss it because the ruins are not easily visible from the road.

DETAILS

This site is the oldest of the four. The historian Josephus in the first century mentioned it several times, and as did both St. Jerome and Eusebius in the fourth century when the town had the Roman name Nicopolis. The first church here was built in the fifth century, but like so many others in the land was vandalized by the Persians after A.D. 614. The name Amwas is an Arab corruption of the word *emmaus* (hot spring).

In the twelfth century the Crusaders erected a smaller church within the nave of the Byzantine basilica. Today the ruins are deserted but are most impressive, and the three Byzantine apses still rise to a height of about twenty feet. There are a number of floor mosaics, which, sadly, are rapidly deteriorating. The Byzantine baptismal place to the north of the ruins is particularly interesting because the ceremony involved total immersion by the priest who stood in a higher section where only his feet were in the water.

During the Crusader Period doubts were cast as to the validity of the site when greater credence was given to the earlier manuscripts of St. Luke. These gave the distance of Emmaus from Jerusalem as only 60 stadia (7 miles). In later transcriptions the figure 160 stadia (19 miles) was mentioned, but many considered it unlikely that the two disciples could have walked the 38-mile double journey in the same day. Alternative sites 60 stadia from Jerusalem were, therefore, sought, and apparently two were chosen: Abu Gosh and El Qubeibah.

$$+\|+$$
$$+\|+$$

Abu Gosh

This is the site of a well-preserved Crusader church in a tranquil setting adjoining a Benedictine monastery.

ACCESS

The village is also off the main highway to Tel Aviv about seven miles from Jerusalem. From the large traffic circle (connecting the north ring-road and other main roads in the northwest of the modern city), drive toward Tel Aviv, and after about four miles you'll pass under a road bridge. After another mile and a half, bear off to the right, at the sign "Qiryat Yearim." Go about a mile and a half, then turn left toward the Benedictine monastery, which is situated in a cluster of trees. The high walls of its compound are clearly visible, as is the minaret of a nearby mosque. Ring the bell for admission.

DETAILS

Within the peaceful grounds and adjoining the monastery is an impressive Crusader church very similar to St. Anne's in Jerusalem. In the crypt is a spring dating from Neolithic times used by the Roman Tenth Legion when it camped here in A.D. 70. An original plaque commemorating the event has been inserted in the wall to the left of the door leading into the crypt.

Throughout the Middle Ages the building was used as a hostelry. At the beginning of the nineteenth century the brigand Abu Gosh, after whom the village has now been named, robbed travelers as they journeyed from the coast to Jerusalem. Those who refused to pay found themselves prisoners here.

After the Crimean War, the Turkish sultan presented the ruins to Napoleon III, who in turn entrusted them to the French Benedictine Lazarus fathers. Restoration was carried out at the beginning of this century. Since 1976 monks and nuns from the Benedictine community in Bec, Normandy, have occupied the monastery. The church is dedicated to the Resurrection and is a most suitable place in which to recall our Lord's appearance to the two disciples.

Towering above the village is a huge statue of the Madonna and Child surmounting the Church of Our Lady of the Ark of the Covenant. The building was constructed in the 1920s on the foundations of a Byzantine church and commemorates the fact that the Ark of the Covenant rested here for twenty years before King David had it taken to Jerusalem, circa 1000 B.C.

Opening Times: 8:30–11:00, 2:30–5:30; closed Sundays and Thursdays

Souvenir Shop: to the left of the main building

Toilets: beside the souvenir shop

Custodian: The Benedictines

Telephone: (02) 5342798

El Qubeibah

The present twentieth-century church follows the lines of an earlier one constructed by the Crusaders. Within the grounds is a section of Roman road believed by the Franciscans to be the one mentioned in the gospel narrative.

ACCESS

Like Abu Gosh, the site is also approximately seven miles from Jerusalem. Join the main highway between Damascus and New Gates by the palm plantation. After leaving the traffic lights by the palms, go straight ahead through the next two sets of lights and turn left at the third (at the sign "Ramot Alon") into Shemuel Ha'navi Street. Stay on this route for about four and a half miles to the highest point. On the right at the top of the hill, and surmounted by a minaret, is Nabi Samwil, the traditional site of the tomb of the prophet Samuel. Shortly afterward, and before descending the hill, turn left into an unmarked road that leads into the Arab village of El Qubeibah. At a junction in the center of the village, go straight ahead, and the compound is a half mile on the right behind a stone wall.

TOUR

This peaceful location standing about 2,400 feet above sea level affords fine views across the surrounding countryside. Within the compound a section of Roman road has been excavated. It is claimed that this was part of the route that linked Jerusalem with Caesarea and that the two disciples walked along it with the risen Jesus on the first Easter Day.

The church, dedicated to the one named Cleophas, was consecrated in 1902. It is built upon the lines of an earlier Crusader church, the foundations of which are visible in the lower courses of the sanctuary. To the left of the nave, protected by a glass-and-wood panel in the floor, are the remains of what is claimed to be the house of Cleophas.

On Easter Monday there is a large public pilgrimage to El Qubeibah, and the Franciscan "custodian" of the Holy Land blesses the bread.

Opening Times: 8:00–6:00 daily (winter closes 5:00); ring the bell
Shop: none
Toilets: in the garden
Custodian: The Franciscans
Telephone: (050) 200417

Qalunieh

This fourth possible site of Emmaus is mentioned here only because it appears in a number of guidebooks and therefore requires an explanation.

The Arab village four miles from Jerusalem, earlier known as Colonia, was totally destroyed in 1948. It was situated just off the modern highway to Tel Aviv. Josephus mentions this other "Emmaous" as a refuge for eight hundred veterans of the Jewish-Roman War after Titus's sacking of Jerusalem in A.D. 70. The only factor in its favor is that it was sufficiently near the city for the two disciples to have made the journey there and back comfortably in the same day. Modern houses have been built on the site of the old village, and there is now nothing to view.

Resurrection Appearance on the Road to Emmaus

That same day, two of them were going to Emmaus, a village seven miles from Jerusalem, and they talked about what had happened. While they were talking and wondering, Jesus came up and walked with them, but their eyes were held and they did not recognize him.

He asked, "What is this you are talking about?" The two stood still, looking sad. Then one named Cleophas answered, "Why, it seems you are the only traveller in Jerusalem who doesn't know what has happened there these past few days." And he asked, "What is it?"

They replied, "It is about Jesus of Nazareth. He was a prophet, you know, mighty in word and deed before God and the people. But the chief priests and our rulers sentenced him to death. They handed him over to be crucified. We had hoped that he would redeem Israel.

"It is now the third day since all this took place. It is true that some women of our group have disturbed us. When they went to the tomb at dawn, they did not find his body; they came to tell us that they had seen a vision of angels who told them that Jesus was alive. Some friends of our group went to the tomb and found everything just as the women had said, but they did not see him."

He said to them, "How dull you are, how slow of understanding! You fail to believe the message of the prophets. Is it not written that the Christ should suffer all this and then enter his glory?" Then starting with Moses and going through the prophets, he explained to them everything in Scripture concerning himself.

As they drew near the village they were heading for, Jesus made as if to go farther. But they prevailed upon him, "Stay with us, for night comes quickly. The day is now almost over." So he went in to stay with them. When they were at table, he took the bread, said a blessing, broke it and gave each a piece.

Then their eyes were opened, and they recognized him; but he vanished out of their sight. And they said to each other, "Were not our hearts filled with ardent yearning when he was talking to us on the road and explaining the Scriptures?"

They immediately set out and returned to Jerusalem. There they found the Eleven and their companions gathered together. They were greeted by these words: "Yes, it is true, the Lord is risen! He has appeared to Simon!" Then the two told what had happened on the road and how Jesus made himself known when he broke bread with them. (Luke 24:13–35)

He is risen, he is risen!
Tell it with a joyful voice;
He has burst his three days' prison;
Let the whole wide earth rejoice.

JERICHO

Inn of the Good Samaritan
Jericho Town

This view of the road to Jericho gives the pilgrim a good idea of the desolate setting for Jesus' Parable of the Good Samaritan.
(Ewing Galloway)

Jericho means "City of Palms," aptly named because of its setting in a green fertile oasis at the lowest inhabited place on earth 1,300 feet below sea level. Here Jesus healed Bartimaeus, the blind beggar, and dined with Zaccheus, the rich tax collector, who had climbed a sycamore tree to gain a better view of him. Our Lord also chose the road to Jericho as the setting for his Parable of the Good Samaritan. He was undoubtedly very familiar with the area as he must often have passed through it when taking the route from Galilee to Jerusalem along the Jordan Valley.

ACCESS FROM JERUSALEM

Jericho is about twenty-five miles away along the main road. From the northeast corner of the Old City, follow the Jericho road, passing the Garden of Gethsemane; continue on through Bethany and into the open country. Shortly afterward a modern highway joins the road from the left. The Inn of the Good Samaritan is about five miles away from here. It lies on the right at the top of a fairly steep ascent.

Inn of the Good Samaritan

It should be remembered that Jesus merely used an inn as part of the setting for his Parable of the Good Samaritan, which he told in response to the question "Who is my neighbor?" It seems likely, however, that there has been some sort of travelers' rest at this point for thousands of years, bearing in mind that Jericho itself is the oldest known inhabited place on earth, and travelers to Jerusalem coming up from the Jordan Valley would have gained their first view of the Mount of Olives and Mount Scopus from here. There is ample evidence of earlier buildings on either side of the road.

In 1903 the Turks constructed a police post on the traditional site of the inn, but the British partially destroyed it in 1917. In more recent times the ruins have been converted into an Israeli gift shop.

THE PARABLE OF THE GOOD SAMARITAN

Jesus then said, "There was a man going down from Jerusalem to Jericho, and he fell into the hands of robbers. They stripped him, beat him and went off leaving him half dead.

"It happened that a priest was going along that road and saw the man, but passed by on the other side. Likewise a Levite saw the man and passed by on the other side. But a Samaritan, too, was going that way, and when he came upon the man, he was moved with compassion. He went over to him and treated his wounds with oil and wine and wrapped them with bandages. Then he put him on his own mount and brought him to an inn where he took care of him.

"The next day he had to set off, but he gave two silver coins to the innkeeper and told him, 'Take care of him and whatever you spend on him, I will repay when I come back.'"

Jesus then asked, "Which of these three, do you think, made himself neighbor to the man who fell into the hands of robbers?" The teacher of the Law answered, "The one who had mercy on him." And Jesus said, "Go then and do the same." (Luke 10:30–37)

When I needed a neighbor, were you there, were you there?
And the creed and the color and the name won't matter, were you there?

ACCESS

Drive on for about a mile and a half and look for a left turnoff with the sign "Nahal Perat." Here decide whether to continue along the main road or take the left turn to pick up the very narrow and twisting Wadi Kelt road.

ROUTE 1: THE MAIN ROAD

Proceed for another two and a half miles and look on the right for a fairly large stone inscribed "Sea Level." In the tourist season there is often an enterprising Bedouin near it with his camel to attract photographers.

Shortly after this the Jordan Valley and the Dead Sea come into view. In the distance you can see the Mountains of Moab and Mount Nebo from where Moses, having led the tribes of Israel out of Egypt, had a view of the Promised Land before his death. On entering the valley, look for the first turn on the left, which leads to Jericho. The distance from here to the town is about five miles.

ROUTE 2: VIA THE WADI KELT ROAD

Turn left off the main Jericho road, then almost immediately turn left again and continue until reaching another road rising sharply back to the right. Take this road, which becomes very narrow and twisting with little room in places to pass another car. After about two and a half miles you'll come to a small parking space on the left with a cross on the hill above it. From the cross, there is a view of St. George's Monastery, which literally clings to the ravine edge on the other side of the Wadi Kelt Valley.

John of Thebes, who for a time became bishop of Caesarea, founded the monastery in A.D. 480. St. George of Koziba lived here in the sixth century, and subsequently the foundation was named after him. Much of the present building dates from Crusader times, and the Greek Orthodox Church restored it toward the end of the nineteenth century.

Continue along the twisting road from which later on there are fine views of the Jericho oasis. A little farther along still, notice on the left that the Wadi Kelt runs parallel to the road and eventually crosses it. At this point there is a good view across the valley to the archaeologic excavations of Herod's Palace and the first-century town around it. This is known as "New Testament Jericho," although it seems likely that the present town, within the oasis, was also inhabited in our Lord's time.

Descend into the Jordan Valley. You will join the main road near a police station on the outskirts of the town.

Jericho Town

No church has yet been built to specifically commemorate either of the two gospel events that took place here. However, there are Roman Catholic and Greek Orthodox churches that serve the local population. It is a very untidy and scruffy town, although prior to 1948 there were some fine houses belonging to wealthy Palestinians. In the center you can see a large sycamore tree reminiscent of the one Zaccheus climbed to have a better view of Jesus.

THE STORY OF ZACCHEUS

When Jesus entered Jericho and was going through the city, a man named Zaccheus was there. He was a tax collector and a wealthy man. He wanted to see what Jesus was like, but he was a short man and could not see because of the crowd. So he ran ahead and climbed up a sycamore tree. From there he would be able to see Jesus who had to pass that way. When Jesus came to the place, he looked up and said to him, "Zaccheus, come down quickly for I must stay at your house today." So Zaccheus hurried down and received him joyfully.

All the people who saw it began to grumble and said, "He has gone to the house of a sinner as a guest." But Zaccheus spoke to Jesus, "The half of my goods, Lord, I give to the poor, and if I have cheated anyone, I will pay him back four times as much." Looking at him Jesus said, "Salvation has come to this house today, for he is also a true son of Abraham. The Son of Man has come to seek and to save the lost." (Luke 19:1–10)

Blest be the Lord, who comes to men
With messages of grace;
Who comes, in God his Father's name,
To save our sinful race.

OLD TESTAMENT JERICHO (TEL ES–SULTAN)

The earliest known inhabited place on earth is situated about one and a quarter miles north of the modern town, to the left of the main road leading up the Jordan Valley. The word *tel* is the name for an ancient mound formed through the centuries as the result of a city's being razed to the ground many times, and on each occasion rebuilt on top of the rubble. In this instance, evidence of over twenty-one previous civilizations has been unearthed, and at its highest point the mound is forty-five feet above the road.

Considering its antiquity and importance, the first view of the Tel from the road is not particularly impressive, and the total area is surprisingly small, only five acres. The first inhabitants settled here about ten thousand years ago, but the site has not been occupied since the Babylonian exile. It had, therefore, already been in a state of ruin for over five hundred years before the birth of Christ.

The outstanding feature is a substantial watchtower, which the British archaeologist the late Dr. Kathleen Kenyon uncovered in a deep trench in the mid-1950s. This stands as a monument to the incredible achievements of an unknown Stone Age people who lived here around 8000 B.C. Even more remarkable is the fact that within the tower there is still a perfectly formed staircase.

At some points toward the perimeter of the Tel you can see the remnants of the ancient mud-brick walls similar in style to those made famous by the story recorded in Joshua 6:1–21. At the blowing of the trumpets the walls came tumbling down.

Looking west from the Tel, notice the Greek Orthodox Monastery of the Temptation, which clings to the cliff edge in a way similar to that of St. George's Monastery in the Wadi Kelt Valley.

At the foot of the Tel, on the other side of the road, is a water source known as Elisha's Spring, which not only supplied the early inhabitants but has been one of the main sources of irrigation for the fertile oasis for thousands of years. Pumping gear has now been installed; consequently, it is not possible to view the spring itself.

Opening Times:

The Tel: April to September 8:00–5:00, Fridays 8:00–4:00; October to March 8:00–4:00, Fridays 9:00–3:00; closed on Yom Kippur; the tourist "green card" is accepted

Souvenir Shop: none

Toilets: inside the entrance on either side

Custodian: The National Parks Authority

Telephone: (02) 922909

MASADA

The Masada story must surely be one of the most dramatic and moving in the history of humankind. Here in A.D. 73 on this tabletop mountain overlooking the Dead Sea, 960 men, women, and children, having withstood a prolonged siege, chose to die by their own swords rather than submit to Roman slavery.

ACCESS

Masada lies to the south of Jerusalem about sixty miles by road via the west shore of the Dead Sea. Allow about two hours. Follow the access instructions for Qumran on page 151 as far as the bus stop where there is a turnoff to the right, at the sign "Qumran." From here continue south on the main road

Masada, as seen from the east. Atop this plateau, 960 men, women, and children chose to die by their own swords rather than submit to Roman slavery. *(George Martin)*

for twenty-two and a half miles to pass through the oasis of En Gedi, where there is a public bathing beach. About eight and a half miles farther on, start looking on the right for the rocky mass of Masada. When almost opposite the mountain, turn off onto the approach road by a bus stop. In two and a half miles you'll come to a large parking lot. To get to the top of Masada, take the cable car (a two-and-half-minute ride) or, if you're very fit, hike up the "Snake Path" (allow at least forty minutes for the steep climb).

If ascending by cable car, visitors should be warned that on leaving the terminal at the top it is necessary to climb an external wooden stairway to reach the admission booth. There are sixty-six fairly shallow steps, but the ground below can be seen between each one.

The price of the cable car ticket normally includes admission to the site. However, visitors possessing the National Parks Authority tourist "green card" need pay for only the cable car.

History

Flavius Josephus, the first century A.D. historian, in his book *Jewish War* provides a detailed record of the sequence of events that occurred here. Around the end of the first century B.C. Alexander Jannaeus built a fortress on the summit. Later in 40 B.C. the young Herod was forced to leave Jerusalem and used Masada as a safe refuge for his family. He left them with a garrison of eight hundred men while he made his way to Rome, where he was nominated King of Judea by Mark Anthony. While he was away, Masada proved its value as a stronghold capable of withstanding siege. Being encircled on all sides by its own steep cliffs rising over 1,400 feet above the Dead Sea, it was a natural fortress. During the early part of his reign, Herod lived in fear of being deposed by Mark Anthony and later of being overthrown by the Jews. He, therefore, set about developing the mountain as a last stronghold for himself should the need ever arise.

Around the top he constructed an eighteen-foot-high defensive casemate wall two-thirds of a mile long with thirty-eight watchtowers, which totally enclosed the summit.

On the cooler north face he built his own private palace on three terraces with a most luxurious bath and sauna complex nearby. A series of storerooms was constructed adjacent to the palace and filled with enormous reserves of weapons, food, wine, and oil. In addition he designed another palace for public ceremonies near the west wall. To ensure an adequate water supply a number of large cisterns capable of holding more than 1.5 million cubic feet of water were carved out of the bedrock. By an ingenious system of aqueducts, water from flash floods in the winter was channeled into reservoirs quarried low in the northwest of the mountain. From here it was transferred mainly via the water gates to other parts of the fortress.

After Herod's death in 4 B.C. the mountain remained in Roman hands and was manned by a small garrison. In A.D. 66 Jewish Zealots captured it, set up their own community, and converted some of the buildings for religious use, including a synagogue and two *mikves* (ritual immersion pools). The population of Masada grew as freedom fighters joined them from the sacked Holy City.

The Masada Story

According to Flavius Josephus, following the fall of Jerusalem in A.D. 70 the Romans turned their attention to the few remaining pockets of Jewish resistance, and the last to be dealt with was Masada. In A.D. 72 General Flavius Silva himself took command of the Tenth Legion and set out with fifteen thousand men, including his soldiers, auxiliaries, and many prisoners, to overthrow the stronghold. He first built eight camps around the base of the mountain, together with a siege wall over two miles in length to prevent anyone from escaping. You can still see the lines of these fortifications today.

He then began constructing a ramp against the west face of the mountain from which to storm the walls, using a mobile siege-tower equipped with catapults, arrow launchers, and a giant battering ram. The ramp itself was over two hundred yards in length and is still in place today.

In the spring of A.D. 73 General Silva's mobile siege-tower was drawn up the ramp so that the top of it appeared above the casemate wall, forcing the Zealots to take cover. The battering ram was then brought into action and eventually breached the outer wall, but the defenders had hastily constructed an inner wall of timber and earth. The Romans next threw blazing torches down onto this new structure, but unexpectedly the wind blew the flames back against their wooden siege-tower, which caught fire. For a short while the Zealots felt they had been successful in warding off this first attack, but unhappily for them the wind changed again, and by nightfall it became clear that their position was hopeless. The 960 men, women, and children on Masada were faced with an agonizing decision. They had to choose between surrendering to the Romans and submitting themselves to abuse and slavery or committing mass suicide.

According to Josephus, the Zealot leader Eleazar Ben Yair called his bravest together and delivered a powerful and moving oration, persuading them that death by their own hands was a more honorable choice than slavery. The speech has been recorded for posterity, and the following text is an abridged version of Whiston's translation·

Since we, long ago, my generous friends, resolved never to be servants to the Romans, nor to any other than to God himself, who alone is the true and just Lord of mankind, the time is now come that obliges us to make that resolution true in practice.

It is very plain that we shall be taken within a day's time; but it is still an eligible thing to die after a glorious manner, together with our dearest friends. This is what our enemies themselves cannot by any means hinder, although they be very desirous to take us alive. Nor can we propose to ourselves any more to fight them and beat them.

Let our wives die before they are abused, and our children before they have tasted of slavery; and after we have slain them, let us bestow that glorious benefit upon one another mutually, and preserve ourselves in freedom, as an excellent funeral monument for us. But first

*let us destroy our money and the fortress by fire; for I am well assured
that this will be a great grief to the Romans, that they shall not be able
to seize upon our bodies, and shall fail of our wealth also: and let us
spare nothing but our provisions; for they will be a testimonial when
we are dead that we were not subdued for want of necessaries; but that
we have preferred death before slavery.*

*We revolted from the Romans with great pretensions to courage;
and when at the very last they invited us to preserve ourselves, we
would not comply with them. Who will not, therefore, believe that
they will certainly be in a rage at us, in case they can take us alive?
Miserable will then be the young men, who will be strong enough in
their bodies to sustain many torments! Miserable also will be those of
elder years, who will not be able to bear those calamities which young
men might sustain! One man will be obliged to hear the voice of his
son imploring help of his father, when his hands are bound: but certainly our hands are still at liberty, and have a sword in them: let
them then be subservient to us in our glorious design; let us die before
we become slaves under our enemies, and let us go out of the world,
together with our children and our wives, in a state of freedom.* (Flavius
Josephus, Jewish War)

Josephus records that the head of each family, thus persuaded, killed his
own wife and children. The remaining men subsequently drew lots to choose
ten of their number to slay the rest. After this horrendous task was completed, a further lot was drawn to select one man to put to death the other
nine. Finally, having satisfied himself that no one had survived, the last man
set fire to their personal possessions and himself committed suicide.

When the Roman soldiers broke into the fortress at daybreak they met no
resistance. They must have been amazed to discover the bodies of the 960
men, women, and children lying together in their family groups. Theirs was
indeed a hollow victory.

Two women and five children evaded the carnage by hiding themselves in
a cavern and were thus able to recount the details of that fateful night.

A small garrison from the Tenth Legion remained in occupation for a
further forty years before the Romans finally abandoned the mountain. Later,
at some time during the fifth/sixth centuries, a group of Byzantine monks
occupied Masada and built a church on the summit. You can still see the
remains of this building with its distinctive wall decoration today.

There then followed a gap of about 1,400 years when the mountain was
forgotten. Over the centuries the precise location of Masada was lost—some

scholars were of the opinion that Josephus may even have made up the story—until Edward Robinson and his companion E. Smith identified the site in 1838. During the next century various expeditions to Masada were undertaken.

Between October 1963 and April 1965 during the two winter seasons, hundreds of volunteers from twenty-eight countries took part in the world's most ambitious archaeological dig under the direction of Professor Yigael Yadin. The rubble from the collapsed walls and roofs had to be removed before the lines of the original Herodian buildings were discovered. Many of the rooms and walls have been partially rebuilt to afford a better idea of the first-century layout.

TOUR

On arriving at the top cable car station, follow the arrows under the covered way and climb the stone steps, but before mounting the external wooden stairway notice ahead an opening in the mountain face, where it is possible to look down into one of the massive water cisterns quarried by Herod's engineers. Sometimes the water level almost reached the roof. This cistern is one of a number cut into the mountain but is not the largest. Now return to the stairway and mount the sixty-six steps to the admission booth.

Masada is 1,900 feet long and 650 feet wide, and there is a great deal to see. If time is limited, follow the numbers on the plan on page 146, as these offer a logical sequence for viewing. Allow a minimum of two hours to visit the more important features asterisked below.

The black line painted on various walls indicates the level below which archaeologists found the original stone blocks still in place. Above this everything has been painstakingly reconstructed.

1. Casemate Wall Room*: There were originally 110 similar chambers within the defensive walls and towers that were later used to house the Zealots and their families. Notice how a wide stretch of land, exposed in recent decades by a dramatic reduction in the water level, divides the Dead Sea. Millions of gallons are being drawn off from its only source, the Jordan River, and this concerns environmentalists. From this vantage you can also see in the plain below the position of three of the Roman camps that guarded the east approaches to Masada and the lines of the siege wall. Within these protective squares the soldiers lived in tents. Various sections of the Snake Path are visible winding to the top.

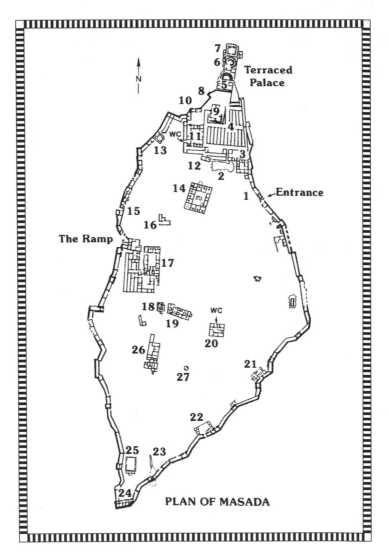

PLAN OF MASADA

2. Quarry: The stone from here provided Herod's workmen with some of their building material. All the blocks used in his massive construction program were quarried from the mountain itself.

3. Herodian Villa (designated Building VIII): One of five erected on the summit, in addition to the two palaces. These were probably intended for the use of Herod's wives or brothers. The three south rooms here contain some original decoration.

4. Storerooms*: There are no fewer than fifteen of these huge rectangular areas within this complex, where grain, oil, wine, dates, and pulses were kept in their distinctively shaped jars, in addition to a large arsenal of weapons. Originally, each room held one particular commodity. Not all the storeroom walls have been reconstructed to their original height of eleven feet. A number have been deliberately left in a ruined state to give visitors an idea of the magnitude of the task that faced the archaeologists.

5/6/7. Herod's Terraced Palace Villa*: The villa was built on three separate levels, the top and two lower terraces, to take advantage of the cooler north aspect. The main living accommodation (5) included the area now covered by the viewing platform. The curved line of this modern structure follows precisely the outer bay of the porch of Herod's private palace with its impressive panoramic views. Adjacent to the porch were four ornately decorated dwelling rooms with mosaic floors. This entire palace complex, demanding considerable effort and resources to construct, was designed solely for Herod's personal pleasure and relaxation. It was not intended to accommodate many people.

On the middle terrace (6) stood a circular colonnaded pavilion, while at the lowest level was an elegant rectangular structure (7) also designed for relaxation. This was erected on a human-made platform supported by walls over eighty feet high because the natural rock is only a few yards wide at this point. Preserved here is a fine example of plaster painted to resemble marble. Josephus records that the columns were made in one piece, but time has exposed the deception because each is made up of a number of circular stone drums that were then covered in plaster. At this level a small Roman bathhouse was also discovered.

It is possible to descend to these terraces via a series of metal stairways, the top of which is marked at (8) on the plan. There are 170 steps. Originally, internal staircases linked the three levels.

From the viewing platform you can see the outer walls of the most northern of General Silva's encircling camps.

8. Modern Stairway leading down to the two lower terraces of Herod's north palace.

9. Bathhouse*: This is a most impressive complex in typical Roman style. Note the original painted plaster on the walls of the first room (apoditorium), which was used for disrobing. The next

room (tepidarium) was kept warm. Adjacent to this, on the right and at a lower level, was a cold bath (frigidarium). At the end of the wooden walkway is the largest of the chambers, which was the hot room (caldarium). This was heated by air circulating under the floor, which itself was supported by more than two hundred pedestals. Air from the same source venting through the rows of vertical clay pipes that lined the room heated the six-foot-thick walls. The furnace was located immediately outside the wall opposite the viewing platform. High temperatures could be achieved, and a considerable amount of steam produced by splashing the floor and walls with water. Bathers probably wore clogs.

10. Water Gate: A path led from here to the reservoirs below.

11. Administration Building used by the Roman garrison: Within its courtyard is a *mikve* (ritual immersion bath) constructed later by the Zealots. It consisted of a series of three pools for Jewish purification and is one of two found on the mountain.

12. Herodian Lookout Tower.

13. Synagogue*: Built by Herod for the Jewish members of his entourage and modified by the Zealots, it, therefore, dates from the Second Temple Period and is the oldest yet discovered in Israel. Beneath the floor of the adjacent room were found two parchments inscribed with parts of the books of Deuteronomy and Ezekiel, which are believed to have been buried by the Zealots. Today some young Jewish boys come to Masada to celebrate their bar mitzvah.

14. Garrison Building: This consists of an open central courtyard with apartments leading off it. It is thought that Roman officers and their families occupied it during the Herodian Period. Later the leaders of the Zealot community with their families certainly occupied it. Beneath the floor of one of the dwellings was found a hoard of silver shekels from the period of the Jewish revolt.

15. Casemate Rooms*: From these rooms along the west wall there is a good view of the Roman assault ramp. Directly across the valley you can see the seating for the *son et lumière* presentation. Between the two are modern replicas of the siege tower, catapult, and battering ram, which were used in the epic film on Masada. On the right are two more of the Roman Tenth Legion's camps. The largest was General Silva's headquarters.

16. Byzantine Church*: This church dates from the fifth century. A small community of monks, the last known inhabitants of Masada, established themselves here after the earthquake that destroyed many of the buildings. Notice in particular in the nave the original patterned wall decorations of pottery shards and small stones set in the plaster. In one of the rooms on the north side are some fine floor mosaics.

17. Western Palace*: Herod's official residence designed for grand ceremonial occasions, audiences, and receptions, this was the largest building on Masada. It consisted of three main wings: In the southeast were the royal quarters, including the throne room and its entrance hall with a beautiful colored mosaic floor. Adjacent to this was a small private bathhouse with its approach corridor, both of which also have fine mosaics. The service wing lay to the north, while the west area contained the administrative block and storerooms. The entire complex was designed to be self-sufficient, even to having its own water reservoir. Visitors should not miss the opportunity to climb to the covered viewing platform to look down upon the royal mosaics.

18. Bathing Pool or Public Bath*: The recesses around the upper walls were used to store the bathers' clothes. Steps led right down to the bottom of the pool to enable bathing even when the water was fairly shallow. All the water had to be carried here.

19. Herodian Villa was for the use of Herod's family.

20. A Royal Residence: Another villa erected specifically for a member of the royal family.

21. Zealot Quarters: This is a good example of how the Zealots partitioned off the Roman structures to form small simple living units. They made niches in the walls to house their few personal belongings and constructed very basic domestic ovens. Their lifestyle was one of extreme austerity and strict religious observance, in contrast to the affluence and luxury of the Romans.

22. Casemate Rooms: Immediately adjacent to the "bakery" is another room also converted by the Zealots, in which can be seen the other *mikve,* a series of three adjacent pools: one for collecting the rainwater (probably as it drained from the roof) to be used for cleansing; a small bath for washing hands and feet before immersion; and the actual *mikve.* Periodic ritual immersion was an essential part of Orthodox Jewish life.

23. Water Cistern: You can view this largest of twelve cut into the mountain by descending thirty-six steep steps hewn out of the bedrock.
24. Southern Citadel for the defense of this end of the mountain.
25. "Great Pool": There is some doubt about its purpose because it is hardly designed to contain water.
26. Southern Villa: A Herodian construction, never completed but converted by the Zealots for their use.
27. Columbarium: There are varying opinions about the purpose of this unusual circular structure with its many niches and dividing central wall. Three theories are (a) pigeon roost, (b) pagan shrine, (c) resting place for cremated human remains. Professor Yadin favored the last as the most likely explanation.

Opening Times for Masada: 8:00–4:00 daily (Fridays 8:00–2:00); last cable car down at 5:00 (Fridays 3:00)

Souvenir Shops: adjacent to the large air-conditioned restaurant near the parking lot; beside the lower cable car station, where light refreshments are also available; water fountains underneath the cable car station and at numerous positions on the mountaintop

Toilets: adjoining the large restaurant near the parking lot; beside the lower cable car station; on the top of the mountain (marked "WC" on the plan on page 146)

Custodian: The National Parks Authority

Telephone: (07) 6584207 (cable car)

(07) 6584208 (site office)

QUMRAN MONASTERY AND CAVES

Shrine of the Book in Jerusalem

Situated on a sandy plateau at the foot of towering cliffs overlooking the northwest shore of the Dead Sea are the excavated remains of the monastery of the Essenes—a strict religious sect. Here they inscribed their now world-famous "Dead Sea Scrolls" nearly two thousand years ago. In 1947 some of the hidden manuscripts were accidentally discovered after a young Bedouin goatherd threw a stone into a cave in the escarpment not far from the site. Many scholars are of the opinion that St. John the Baptist may have had close connections with the Essenes.

ACCESS

The site is about twenty-seven miles due east of Jerusalem. Follow the access instructions for Jericho (see page 136) as far as the Inn of the Good Samaritan. From there, descend through the increasingly barren mountains, and after four miles look on the right for a fairly large milestone inscribed "Sea Level." In the tourist season there is sometimes an enterprising Bedouin near it with his camel to attract photographers. Drive on to reach the wide basin of the Jordan Valley; then continue, passing the first turn off to the left leading to Jericho town and the second too, at the sign "Jericho By-Pass," until arriving at the shore of the Dead Sea. Here turn right at the T-junction and proceed along the coastal road for another four miles until reaching a bus stop where there is a turnoff to the right, with the sign "Qumran." Take this road, and the site is straight ahead.

In this cave at Qumran in 1947, a Bedouin goatherd accidentally discovered the world-famous Dead Sea Scrolls. *(Allan Weinert)*

HISTORY

There was an Israelite fort here in the eighth century B.C., but it was abandoned long before a group of Essenes came to the site in the middle of the second century B.C.

They had broken away from the Temple worship in Jerusalem to embrace a more strict and ascetic way of life. By about 100 B.C. most of the building had been completed, and their numbers had grown to some two hundred. The monastery itself was used as a center for worship, study, and meals, but it is thought that most of the community lived in caves, shelters, or tents nearby.

In 31 B.C. a major earthquake forced them to abandon the site for thirty years, but at the beginning of the Christian era members of the sect returned, repaired the damage, and remained in occupation until A.D. 68. During this year, fearing the imminent approach of the conquering Roman soldiers, the community packed their precious parchments into jars and hid them in the nearby caves. It is thought that some of the Essenes joined up with the Zealots at the top of Masada and no doubt perished there.

Prior to 1950 when archaeologists began to excavate the site following the discovery of the scrolls, the only part of the monastery visible above the sand had been the stub of a watchtower, which was locally assumed to be Roman.

The story of how the scrolls were found in the spring of 1947 is worth briefly recalling: Mohammed Edib, a young Bedouin, was searching for one of his lost goats and threw a stone into the opening of a cave, thinking that the animal might possibly have strayed inside. The stone made such a strange noise when it hit something that he ran away frightened. The next day he returned with his cousin, and the two scrambled down into the cave. They saw eight large earthenware pots, and they hoped these might contain gold.

Some of the jars were complete with their sealed lids, and it was discovered that they contained in total seven rolls of inscribed parchment. The young Bedouins had no idea of the significance of their find, but when they were next visiting Bethlehem they were able to sell them. Subsequently, Professor Elazar Sukenik, who held the chair of Archaeology at the Hebrew University in Jerusalem, purchased three, and Archbishop Samuel of the Syrian Church of St. Mark bought the other four. Two years later the archbishop took his scrolls to America, where he had been advised he would obtain a better price. It transpired that by chance the son of Professor Sukenik, who had adopted the name Yigael Yadin, was visiting the United States and was able to anonymously purchase all four scrolls for $250,000. He immediately returned them to Israel. During further searches of the Dead Sea caves another scroll was found, which Yadin was able to acquire in 1967. In all, over nine hundred pieces of manuscript were discovered.

Two of the scrolls are inscribed on copper, the remainder are parchment or papyrus. They include all the books of the Old Testament, except Esther, but the most famous document is the complete text of Isaiah, which is one foot wide and twenty-four feet long. It proved to be one thousand years older than any other known copy. When comparisons were made with two other later documents of the ninth/tenth centuries, they were found to be almost identical, testifying to the accuracy of the scribes throughout the centuries between. A facsimile of this script can be seen in the "Shrine of the Book" in Jerusalem, which is part of the Israeli National Museum not far from the Knesset Parliament building. Also on view are the "Thanksgiving Scroll," the scroll of "The Battle of the Sons of Light against the Sons of Darkness," and the "Manual of Discipline" setting out in detail the rules of the Qumran community.

TOUR

From the ticket office walk across to the ruins and ascend to the wooden observation platform erected over the original watchtower. All the main features are clearly identified on touring the site, but it is helpful to gain an idea of the layout from this position.

To the south (facing away from the ticket office) and below the tower was a complex of rooms including the Council Chamber—a feature indicating that the community was run on democratic lines. Immediately to the left of this is a rectangular room where archaeologists discovered the remains of a plastered table five yards long and some benches, all of which had fallen from the room above known as the "Scriptorium," where it is thought the scrolls may have been written. They also identified two inkwells, one made of clay and the other of bronze.

Descend the exit steps and follow the arrows around the site. Notice in particular on the left the Assembly Hall and Refectory. Running away from this at right angles is a smaller room that served as a pantry. Here hundreds of bowls stacked in dozens, over two hundred plates, a large number of beakers, and many other vessels were discovered. Crockery for the everyday use of the community was made on the site.

The Essenes depended for their water upon the rain that drained from the mountains during the winter months. It was channeled via an aqueduct into at least seven storage cisterns within the monastery complex. Some of the reservoirs were probably used as baths for ritual cleansing, which was a feature of the religious life of the community.

Archaeologists discovered outside the east wall a large burial ground consisting of over 1,100 graves in neat lines. Most contain the remains of men, although a few women were also interred.

Continue walking south across the sand to the end of the plateau, where on the right you will see one of the human-made caves in which some fifteen thousand fragments of parchment were found.

Return to the site to complete the circular tour.

Opening Times: April to September 8:00–4:00; October to March 9:00–4:00; on the eve of Shabbat and holidays closes one hour earlier; closed on Yom Kippur; the tourist "green card" is accepted

Souvenir Shop: up the steps from the parking lot before reaching the ticket office; large and well stocked; there is an excellent restaurant

Toilets: near the ticket office

Custodian: The National Parks Authority

Telephone: (02) 6942235

$$\begin{array}{c} + \| + \\ \hline + \| + \end{array}$$

Shrine of the Book in Jerusalem

Opening Times: Sunday, Monday, Wednesday, Thursday 10:00–5:00; Tuesday 10:00–10:00: Friday and eve of holidays 10:00–2:00; Saturday and holidays 10:00–4:00

Telephone: (02) 6708811

JACOB'S WELL

A view of the unfinished church above Jacob's Well, with the two entrances to the crypt. Here, Jesus spoke at length to the Samaritan woman about the "living water" he offers to all people.
(George Martin)

There can be no doubt about the authenticity of this well, which Jacob dug 3,700 years ago. Here Jesus met the Samaritan woman and spoke to her at length about the "living water." Since the fourth century the well has been enclosed within the crypt of a series of churches. The site is situated on the south approach to the town of Shechem (Nablus), thirty-eight miles north of Jerusalem.

MEETING WITH THE SAMARITAN WOMAN

He [Jesus] came to a Samaritan town called Sychar, near the land that Jacob had given to his son Joseph. Jacob's well is there. Tired from his journey, Jesus sat down by the well; it was about noon. Now a Samaritan woman came to draw water and Jesus said to her, "Give me a drink." His disciples had just gone into town to buy some food.

The Samaritan woman said to him, "How is it that you, a Jew, ask me, a Samaritan and a woman, for a drink?" (For Jews, in fact, have no dealings with Samaritans.) Jesus replied, "If you only knew the Gift of God! If you knew who it is that asks you for a drink, you yourself would have asked me and I would have given you living water."

The woman answered, "Sir, you have no bucket and this well is deep; where is your living water? Are you greater than our ancestor Jacob, who gave us this well after he drank from it himself, together with his sons and his cattle?"

Jesus said to her, "Whoever drinks of this water will be thirsty again; but whoever drinks of the water that I shall give will never be thirsty; for the water that I shall give will become in him a spring of water welling up to eternal life."

The woman said to him, "Give me this water, that I may never be thirsty and never have to come here to draw water." Jesus said, "Go, call your husband and come back here." The woman answered, "I have no husband." And Jesus replied, "You are right to say: 'I have no husband'; for you have had five husbands and the one you have now is not your husband. What you said is true."

The woman then said to him, "I see you are a prophet; tell me this: Our fathers used to come to this mountain to worship God; but you Jews, do you not claim that Jerusalem is the only place to worship God?"

Jesus said to her, "Believe me, woman, the hour is coming when you shall worship the Father, but that will not be on this mountain or in Jerusalem. You Samaritans worship without knowledge, while we Jews worship with knowledge, for salvation comes from the Jews. But the hour is coming and is even now here, when the true worshipers will worship the Father in spirit and truth; for that is the kind of worship the Father wants. God is spirit and those who worship God must worship in spirit and truth."

The woman said to him, "I know that the Messiah, that is the Christ, is coming; when he comes, he will tell us everything." And Jesus said, "I who am talking to you, I am he."

At this point the disciples returned and were surprised that Jesus was speaking with a woman; however, no one said, "What do you want?" or: "Why are you talking with her?" So the woman left her water jar and ran to the town. There she said to the people, "Come and see a man who told me everything I did! Could he not be the Christ?" So they left the town and went to meet him. (John 4:5–30)

He feeds the hungry with the Bread of heaven,
And living streams to those who thirst are given.

ACCESS

From Jerusalem take the main road north for about thirty-six miles and look for a sign on the left to Shekem and Jenin. Take this road and continue on it for almost two miles, then turn sharply right at the green sign for Jiftliq, Jordan Valley, and Alon More. The entrance gates are two hundred yards on the left in a high stone wall.

DETAILS

In A.D. 404 St. Jerome mentioned the earliest church erected here during the latter part of the fourth century. The original building was in the shape of a Latin cross with the ancient well in a crypt under the high altar. This structure was damaged during the Samaritan revolts of the fifth and early sixth centuries but was completely restored soon afterward on the orders of Emperor Justinian. The Persians destroyed it in 614, as other Christian shrines in the Holy Land. In the twelfth century the Crusaders constructed a three-aisled church on part of the Byzantine foundations. After their defeat the building was left to decay.

In the sixteenth century it is recorded that the Franciscans celebrated an annual Mass within the ruins, and a century later the Greek Orthodox from Sebaste occasionally conducted their liturgy at the site. Finally, in 1860 the Greeks acquired the property and immediately set about restoring the crypt. It was not until 1914, however, that work commenced on the construction of a substantial church above it with funds provided by the Pravoslav Church of Czarist Russia, but the Revolution of 1917 brought the project to an abrupt halt.

It is this impressive but incomplete building that the pilgrim sees today. The massive nave pillars and unfinished walls stand unroofed and remain open to the skies. Entrance to the crypt containing Jacob's Well is via one of two staircases temporarily protected by wooden structures resembling sentry boxes. The well has an exceptional depth of more than a hundred feet and is the only one in the area. The Greek Orthodox priest on duty will be happy to let down the bucket by means of a simple metal winch to draw up the cool clear drinking water.

From the site, look to the left for an excellent view of Mount Gerizim, which is the Holiest Place for the ancient Samaritan sect, which still worships on its summit rather than in Jerusalem. To the right is Mount Ebal.

Opening Times: 8:00–5:00 daily (winter closes 4:00); ring the bell
Souvenir Shop: in the crypt
Toilets: near the entrance gate
Custodian: The Greek Orthodox
Telephone: (09) 8375123

SEA OF GALILEE

General Description

The tranquility of this beautiful lake cannot fail to delight the pilgrim and provide a store of lifetime memories. It is still a very special place for the Christian despite modern developments, and the outline of the surrounding hills has changed little since our Lord walked upon these Galilean shores.

The lake, which lies 660 feet below the level of the Mediterranean Sea, is approximately fifteen miles long by eight miles wide. Its maximum depth is 165 feet.

The fact that it is referred to by so many different names causes some initial confusion. To Christians it is generally known as the Sea of Galilee, but road signs direct travelers to Lake Kinnereth (derived from the Hebrew word for a harp). St. Matthew, St. Mark, and St. John all mention the Sea of Galilee, although St. John also calls it the Sea of Tiberias. St. Luke refers to Lake Gennesaret.

Jesus spent much of his ministry along the shores of the Sea of Galilee. Its tranquillity still inspires pilgrims.
(Allan Weinert)

Most of our Lord's lakeside ministry—as recorded in the four gospels—was confined to the north half. In his day the area was densely populated, with possibly as many as seven large towns and a thriving fishing industry.

It was also on one of the major trade routes between the East and the West. The pilgrim today is reminded of so many incidents in the Gospel story:

- Fishermen still stand in the shallow waters near the shore, casting their nets in the traditional fashion, while others set off in boats at sunset to fish at night.

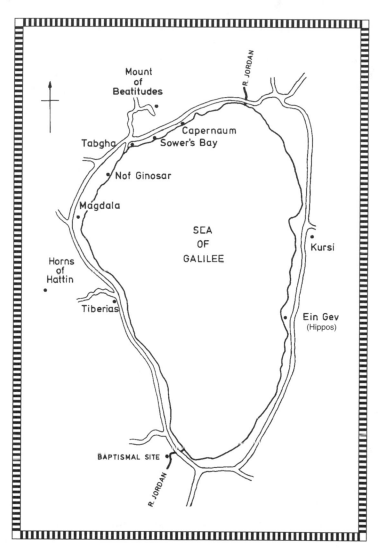

- Violent storms sometimes develop in the midafternoon as the cooler air rushes down from the surrounding mountains and whips up the water to produce enormous waves. Then in a relatively short time there is a great calm again.
- The wheat and the tares still grow together in fields around the lake, and in springtime there is a profusion of wildflowers to remind the pilgrim of our Lord's words: "Even Solomon in all his glory was not arrayed like one of these."

- The twinkling lights from the medieval city of Safed, high up in the north mountains, are an illustration of our Lord's comment "A city that is set on a hill cannot be hid."
- The dawn chorus in the trees surrounding the lake and the truly unforgettable pink hue across the water just before the sun rises are all wonders that Jesus himself experienced in this very place.

Around the shores are many places of interest to the Christian pilgrim. Looking at the map and reading clockwise from Tiberias, these are

HORNS OF HATTIN

The name given to a long low hill with a hump on either end resembling horns (when seen from the main road, traveling west from Tiberias). Here Saladin inexorably defeated the Crusaders in a horrendous battle on July 4, 1187.

MAGDALA

According to tradition the birthplace of Mary Magdalene. About three miles north of Tiberias between the main road and the sea are some excavations. The Franciscans own the fenced compound, which is not open to the public. In our Lord's time there was an important fishing port here. Indeed, both the Hebrew and Greek names for the town made reference to the fish. Toward the end of the first century, the historian Flavius Josephus mentions a population of 40,000 with a fleet of 230 boats.

NOF GINOSAR

Within the grounds of a modern hotel and kibbutz are preserved the remains of a first-century fishing boat that was discovered in 1986 when the water of the lake was particularly low. This prosperous establishment is possibly on the site of another important fishing port, Gennesaret, from which the lake took one of its names in New Testament times.

TABGHA

The traditional site of the Feeding of the Five Thousand and of Jesus' Resurrection appearance to the disciples when he cooked breakfast for them on the seashore after they had been fishing all night. (See details on page 168.)

MOUNT OF BEATITUDES

Almost directly behind Tabgha on higher ground is the place where the Sermon on the Mount is commemorated. (See details on page 166.)

CHORAZIN

Two miles due north of the Mount of Beatitudes. One of the three towns Jesus condemned for failing to repent. Archaeological excavations have revealed the remains of a synagogue. The site is open to the public.

SOWER'S BAY

About a half mile east of Tabgha. A possible site of our Lord's Parable of the Sower and other teachings. (See details on page 173.)

CAPERNAUM

Our Lord's adopted hometown, it has more gospel references than any other place in the Holy Land. (See details on page 174.)

JORDAN RIVER

Two and a half miles to the east of Capernaum, you can see the river passing under a road bridge. Here it flows on to enter the Sea of Galilee about a half mile farther south. The Jordan continues its course from the south end of the lake, where there is a modern baptismal site. (See details on page 164.)

BETHSAIDA

The other town, in addition to Chorazin and Capernaum, Jesus condemned for failing to repent. It seems likely that this town was situated to the east of the point where the Jordan River joins the lake. The site is covered by water and a swamp; consequently, excavations have still to be carried out. (For Jesus' healing of the blind man in Bethsaida, see Mark 8:22–26.)

KURSI

On the eastern side of the lake, almost opposite Magdala, and inland of the main road are the impressive remains of a fine Byzantine church and monastery dating from the fifth century. The site is open to the public. Traditionally, this area is associated with the story of the Gadarene swine. Jesus, having cleansed a tormented man of evil spirits, transferred them to a large herd of swine grazing nearby. Being thus possessed, they ran headlong down the hillside into the sea and were drowned (Matthew 8:28–33; Mark 5:1–20; Luke 8:26–39).

HIPPOS

Three miles farther south of Kursi, on the summit of a hill directly behind the kibbutz at Ein Gev, is the site of this ancient fortified town dating from 332 B.C. Although it is now overgrown, you can just identify the outline of its foundations from the road. The site is of particular significance to the Christian pilgrim because it seems quite probable that this is the place that our Lord had in mind when he said, "A city that is set on a hill cannot be hid."

STILLING THE STORM

Jesus got into the boat and his disciples followed him. Without warning a fierce storm hit the lake, with waves sweeping the boat. But Jesus was asleep.

They woke him and cried, "Lord save us! We are lost!" But Jesus answered, "Why are you so afraid, you of little faith?" Then he stood up and ordered the wind and sea; and it became completely calm.

The people were astonished. They said, "What kind of man is he? Even the winds and the sea obey him." (Matthew 8:23–27)

> When fears appal and faith is failing,
> Make thy voice heard o'er wind and wave;
> And in thy perfect love prevailing
> Put forth thy hand to help and save.

DETAILS

Opening Times of Chorazin and Kursi: summer 8:00–5:00 (Fridays close at 4:00); winter 8:00–4:00 (Fridays 9:00–3:00); closed on Yom Kippur; the tourist "green card" is accepted

Souvenir Shops: none

Toilets: in the parking lots

Custodian: The National Parks Authority

Telephone: Chorazin (06) 6934982

Kursi (06) 6731983

JORDAN RIVER

There are five different locations where, according to various traditions, Jesus was baptized. At the time of writing most of them are in forbidden military zones, but a modern site commemorating the event has been built on the riverside at the south end of the Sea of Galilee.

THE BAPTISM OF JESUS

So John began to baptize in the desert; he preached a baptism of repentance for the forgiveness of sins. All Judea and all the people from the city of Jerusalem went out to John to confess their sins and be baptized by him in the river Jordan.

John was clothed in camel's hair and wore a leather garment around his waist. His food was locusts and honey. He preached to the people saying, "After me comes one who is more powerful than I am; I have baptized you with water, but he will baptize you in the Holy Spirit. As for me, I am not worthy to bend down and untie his sandals."

Many pilgrims travel to the River Jordan to experience baptism in the place where our Lord began his active ministry.
(Allan Weinert)

At that time Jesus came from Nazareth, a town of Galilee, and was baptized by John in the Jordan. And the moment he came up out of the water, Heaven opened before him and he saw the Spirit coming down on him like a dove. And these words were heard from Heaven, "You are my Son, the Beloved, the One I have chosen." (Mark 1:4–11)

So when the Dove descended
on him, The Son of Man,
the hidden years had ended,
the age of grace began.

163

ACCESS FROM TIBERIAS

Refer to the map on page 159. Travel south on the lakeside road, and after almost five miles look for a sign on the right to the Baptismal Place. The turn is just before the bridge over the Jordan River (Gesher Yarden), and the site is about two hundred yards from the main road.

DETAILS

An extensive baptismal place has been constructed on the riverbank adjoining purpose-built facilities consisting of a large parking lot, snack bar, souvenir shop, changing rooms, and toilets.

If the place is too crowded, it is possible as an alternative to scramble down to the river from the roadway beyond the Jordan Bridge, but devotions can be interrupted by traffic noise.

A quieter location is at the north end of the lake eleven and a half miles from Tiberias. Follow the access instructions for Capernaum on page 174 as far as the beach resort, but instead of turning right at this point go straight for another two and a half miles. Turn right at the sign "Arique Bridge." Here the banks are in a natural setting, but there is a steep and rather difficult approach to the water.

AUTHORS' COMMENTS

The site in the south is conveniently near Tiberias, but it is run as a commercial enterprise. Nevertheless, on a quiet day, it can be a pleasant place set amidst the prolific vegetation of the riverbank. The north alternative, although much farther away, is totally unspoiled.

Opening Times: southern site 8:00–5:00 daily

Souvenir Shop: large and well stocked

Toilets: changing rooms also available

Custodian: The State Tourism Corporation

Telephone: (06) 6759486

MOUNT OF BEATITUDES

In a delightful setting overlooking the Sea of Galilee from its north shore, our Lord's Sermon on the Mount is commemorated. The colonnaded terrace of the distinctive twentieth-century Italian church, built on the brow of a hill, affords magnificent panoramic views across the lake.

THE BEATITUDES

When Jesus saw the crowds, he went up the mountain. He sat down and his disciples gathered around him. Then he spoke and began to teach them:

Fortunate are those who have the spirit of the poor, for theirs is the kingdom of Heaven.

Fortunate are those who mourn, they shall be comforted.

Fortunate are the gentle, they shall possess the land.

Fortunate are those who hunger and thirst for justice, for they shall be satisfied.

Fortunate are the merciful, for they shall find mercy.

Fortunate are those with a pure heart, for they shall see God.

Fortunate are those who work for peace, they shall be called children of God.

This church, built on the traditional site of the Sermon on the Mount, provides a magnificent panorama of the Sea of Galilee. *(Allan Weinert)*

Fortunate are those who are persecuted for the cause of justice, for theirs is the kingdom of Heaven.

Fortunate are you, when people insult you and persecute you and speak all kinds of evil against you because you are my followers. Be glad and joyful, for a great reward is kept for you in God. This is how this people persecuted the prophets who lived before you. (Matthew 5:1–12)

> *Lord, we thy presence seek;*
> *may ours this blessing be;*
> *give us a pure and lowly heart,*
> *a temple meet for thee.*

ACCESS FROM TIBERIAS

Refer to the map on page 159. The site is about ten miles from the town. Drive north on the lake ring road. After six and a half miles ascend the hill, passing an electricity grid station. Go straight at the Kefar Nahum junction; and in a mile, climb another hill, negotiating three sharp bends. Shortly afterward look for a sign on the right to the Hospice of Beatitudes. The site is about a half mile from here. Parking space is available in front of the main gates.

DETAILS

The National Association for Aid to Italian Missionaries acquired the land in 1926. This organization built a hospice here to enable pilgrims to spend time in contemplation and prayer.

The church was constructed in 1937 to a design by the Italian architect Antonio Barluzzi, who was responsible for so many expressive buildings in the Holy Land. The style is typically Italian, and the interior is symbolically octagonal. A slender arch of alabaster and onyx surmounts the centrally placed altar. There are fine views of the surrounding countryside through the narrow horizontal windows in the lower walls, while in the upper windows are written the Eight Beatitudes from our Lord's sermon. The mosaics in the floor represent the seven virtues he mentioned. In the landscaped garden outside are a number of altars for group worship.

AUTHORS' COMMENTS

This is undoubtedly one of the most beautiful gospel sites in the Holy Land, and a visit here should not be rushed.

Opening Times: 8:00–noon, 2:30–5:00 daily (winter closes 4:00)

Souvenir Shop: just inside the church on the right

Toilets: in the garden to the right of the hostel

Custodian: The Franciscan Missionary Sisters of the Immaculate Heart of Mary

Telephone: (06) 6790978

TABGHA

$$\frac{+\ \|\ +}{+\ \|\ +}$$

Church of the Multiplication
Church of Mensa Christi

The word *tabgha* is a corruption of the Greek words *hepta pegon* (seven springs), and these still exist in the area. There are two major sites in this small fertile oasis on the northwest shore of the Sea of Galilee.

1. The modern Church of the Multiplication commemorates the place where, according to tradition, Jesus fed the five thousand with five loaves and two small fishes. Incorporated into the floor of the church are some particularly fine fifth-century mosaics considered to be among the loveliest in the Holy Land.
2. Nearby is the little Church of Mensa Christi (Table of Christ), also known as "Peter's Primacy," built upon a rock at the water's edge. Traditionally, this is held to be where Jesus appeared to the disciples on the lakeside after his Resurrection.

ACCESS FROM TIBERIAS

Refer to the map on page 159. Tabgha is about eight miles from Tiberias and is situated at the top of the Sea of Galilee. Drive north on the lake ring road. After six and a half miles ascend the hill, passing by an electricity grid station. Turn right at the Kefar Nahum junction, and in about a hundred yards, at a smaller junction, keep to the left. Ahead on the right among some trees is the Church of the Multiplication, where ample parking space is available.

The Church of Mensa Christi is another two hundred yards along the road on the right. There is a small parking area opposite. The two buildings are not directly linked by any footpath.

Church of the Multiplication
Feeding of the Five Thousand

HISTORY

The first church on the site was very small and built circa A.D. 350. A much larger basilica with a central nave and two side aisles superseded it 130 years later. After the Persian invasion in 614 and the subsequent occupation of Palestine by Arabs, this church fell into ruins. There is no record of any Crusader building here in the twelfth century, and it was not until 1932 that the area was excavated. Shortly afterward the Benedictines erected a fairly plain church, and this in turn

This mosaic, found in the Church of the Multiplication, commemorates our Lord's miraculous feeding of the five thousand with five loaves of bread and two fish. *(George Martin)*

was demolished to make way for the present building, which was completed in 1984.

FEEDING OF THE FIVE THOUSAND

After this Jesus went to the other side of the Sea of Galilee, near Tiberias, and large crowds followed him because of the miraculous signs they saw when he healed the sick. So he went up into the hills and sat down there with his disciples. Now the Passover, the feast of the Jews, was at hand.

Then lifting up his eyes, Jesus saw the crowds that were coming to him and said to Philip, "Where shall we buy bread so that these people may eat?" He said this to test Philip, for he himself knew what he was going to do. Philip answered him, "Two hundred silver coins would not buy enough bread for each of them to have a piece."

Then one of Jesus' disciples, Andrew, Simon Peter's brother, said, "There is a boy here who has five barley loaves and two fish; but what good are these for so many?"

Jesus said, "Make the people sit down." There was plenty of grass there so the people, about five thousand men, sat down to rest. Jesus then took the loaves, gave thanks and distributed them to those who were seated. He did the same with the fish and gave them as much as they wanted. And when they had eaten enough, he told his disciples, "Gather up the pieces left over, that nothing may be lost."

So they gathered them up and filled twelve baskets with bread, that is with pieces of the five barley loaves left by those who had eaten. (John 6:1–13)

> Thou who dost give us earthly bread,
> Give us the Bread eternal.

TOUR

Walk across the pleasant courtyard into the cloister where, on the wall that faces the church, is displayed an archaeological diagram showing the positions of the three previous buildings and the history of the site. Notice that the small original church was set at a different angle from that of the other two. The fine bronze west doors depict various events in the ministry of Jesus, and to the right of this is a casting, also in bronze, delineating the positions of the three earlier churches.

The principal feature of the present building is the famous fifth-century mosaic, in front of the main altar, depicting a basket of loaves flanked by two fishes. The ancient stone under the altar is reputed to be part of the one upon which Jesus placed the loaves and fishes.

On either side of the altar in the floor of the two side aisles and to the left of the nave are extensive areas of beautiful mosaics depicting numerous birds among the flora and water vegetation. It is possible to identify herons, cranes, ducks, geese, cormorants, peacocks, a flamingo, and a swan. There are also a number of geometric designs, copies of those that covered the remaining floor area of the fifth-century building.

On the south side of the church is a Benedictine monastery built in 1956. Here the monks specialize in caring for disabled young people by providing them with an opportunity for a holiday beside the lake during the summer months.

AUTHORS' COMMENTS

The modern church and cloister are a very pleasant setting in which to reflect upon one of our Lord's best-known miracles.

Opening Times: 8:30–5:00 daily (Sundays opens at 10:00)
Souvenir Shop: in the cloister
Toilets: in the parking lot
Custodian: German Benedictine Catholic community
Telephone: (06) 6721061

Church of Mensa Christi, or "Peter's Primacy"

The Table of Christ or the Commissioning of Peter

This is a small Franciscan chapel built over an area of rock at the water's edge, commemorating the Resurrection appearance of Jesus to his disciples. They had been fishing all night and had caught nothing. There is an ancient tradition that this was the rock upon which our Lord prepared breakfast for them. After the meal Jesus commissioned Peter with the words "Feed my sheep."

ACCESS

From the entrance to the Church of the Multiplication, continue along the main road for about two hundred yards. The gates are on the right.

HISTORY

Although the Franciscans have discovered the remains of an early building on the rock, there is no documentary evidence of a church here until the ninth century. Nevertheless, in A.D. 383 the nun Egeria mentions some steps upon which the Lord stood. There are some ancient steps cut into the south face of the rock close to the water's edge.

In the twelfth century there was certainly a church here, but like other Christian buildings on the shores of Galilee, it appears to have fallen into ruins after the defeat of the Crusaders. In 1933 the Franciscans built the present chapel, using the dark basalt rock that is so plentiful in the area.

BREAKFAST ON THE SEASHORE

After this Jesus revealed himself to the disciples by the Lake of Tiberias.
He appeared to them in this way. Simon Peter, Thomas who was called
the Twin, Nathanael of Cana in Galilee, the sons of Zebedee and two
other disciples were together; and Simon Peter said to them, "I'm going
fishing." They replied, "We will come with you" and they went out and
got into the boat. But they caught nothing that night.

When day had already broken, Jesus was standing on the shore, but
the disciples did not know that it was Jesus. Jesus called them, "Children,
have you anything to eat?" They answered, "Nothing." Then he said to
them, "Throw the net on the right side of the boat and you will find
some." When they had lowered the net, they were not able to pull it in
because of the great number of fish.

Then the disciple Jesus loved said to Peter, "It's the Lord!" At these
words, "It's the Lord," Simon Peter put on his clothes, for he was stripped
for work, and jumped into the water. The other disciples came in the boat
dragging the net full of fish; they were not far from land, about a hundred
meters.

When they landed, they saw a charcoal fire with fish on it, and some
bread. Jesus said to them, "Bring some of the fish you've just caught." So
Simon Peter climbed into the boat and pulled the net to shore. It was full
of big fish—one hundred and fifty-three—but, in spite of this, the net
was not torn.

Jesus said to them, "Come and have breakfast," and not one of the
disciples dared ask him, "Who are you?" for they knew it was the Lord.
Jesus then came and took the bread and gave it to them, and he did the
same with the fish.

This was the third time that Jesus revealed himself to his disciples af-
ter rising from the dead. (John 21:1–14)

> In simple trust like theirs who heard,
> beside the Syrian sea,
> the gracious calling of the Lord,
> let us, like them, without a word
> rise up and follow thee.

DETAILS

On the right just inside the entrance to the site you can see the ruins of a
Byzantine water tower, one of a number in the area. Continue along the path
through the garden to the little chapel. Opposite the west door is an area

designed for group worship, and between this and the lake is a modern bronze statue of Jesus symbolically commissioning Peter with his shepherd's crook.

Inside the simple chapel, the striking feature is the extensive granite rock running across its entire width. According to tradition it was here that Jesus made his Resurrection appearance to his disciples at the lakeside.

AUTHORS' COMMENTS

A truly delightful site at the water's edge, it lends itself well to meditation and prayer.

Opening Times: 8:00–noon; 2:00–5:00 daily

Souvenir Shop: none

Toilets: to the left of the garden

Custodian: The Franciscans

Telephone: (06) 6724767

SOWER'S BAY

About a half mile due east of Mensa Christi is a bay that possesses all the characteristics of a natural amphitheater. On a fine day—when there is no wind and little traffic—it is possible to stand at the water's edge and read the Parable of the Sower, which can be heard quite clearly from the roadside. This parable and a number of others were preached from a boat, and from such a place, therefore, Jesus would have addressed the multitude.

THE PARABLE OF THE SOWER

Again Jesus began to teach by the lake, but such a large crowd gathered about him that he got into a boat and sat in it on the lake while the crowd stood on the shore. He taught them many things through stories or parables. In his teaching he said,

"Listen! The sower went out to sow. As he sowed, some of the seed fell along a path and the birds came and ate it up. Some of the seed fell on rocky ground where it had little soil; it sprang up immediately because it had no depth; but when the sun rose and burned it, it withered because it had no roots. Other seed fell among thornbushes and the thorns grew and choked it, so it didn't produce any grain. But some seed fell on good soil, grew and increased and yielded grain; some produced thirty times as much, others sixty and others one hundred times as much." And Jesus added, "Listen then, if you have ears." (Mark 4:1–9)

Speak to us, O Lord, believing,
as we hear, the sower sows;
may our hearts, your word receiving,
be the good ground where it grows.

Capernaum

This partially excavated archaeological site is of major importance to Christians because Jesus adopted Capernaum as his "hometown" after he was driven out of Nazareth. Here he called Peter, Andrew, James, John, and Matthew to follow him and performed a number of miracles. He worshiped and taught in the synagogue. From this busy fishing port and frontier post on the main route to Damascus, he chose to carry out the major part of his ministry.

Today its two main features are the partly reconstructed late-fourth-century synagogue, built upon the foundations of the one in which our Lord preached, and the contrasting late-twentieth-century church erected over the site of a house claimed by the Franciscans to have been the home of St. Peter.

ACCESS FROM TIBERIAS

Refer to the map on page 159. Capernaum is about nine miles from Tiberias and is situated at the top of the Sea of Galilee in the middle of its north shore. Drive north on the lake ring road. After six and a half miles ascend the hill, passing by an electricity grid station. Turn right at the Kefar Nahum junction, and after a hundred yards at a smaller junction keep to the left. Ahead on the right are the two churches at Tabgha, and a half mile beyond them is Sower's Bay. If not stopping at the bay, continue along the lakeside road for another half mile, then look for a turnoff to the right, by a beach resort, which leads directly to Capernaum, where ample parking facilities are available. The parking lot is beyond the bus stop.

GENERAL

Capernaum fell into disuse over a thousand years ago. During the nineteenth century scholars began to take some interest in the scattered ruins, and in 1894 the Franciscans purchased part of the site. A number of different excavations took place at the beginning of the twentieth century, centered on the synagogue and the remains of a fifth-century octagonal church, but it was not until 1968 that more intensive work commenced. Archaeologists then discovered the "Peter House" under the octagonal church, and the remains of shops and other dwellings undoubtedly familiar to our Lord. To date only a comparatively small part of the town, which had a lakeside frontage of about a quarter mile, has been excavated.

The area is relatively small and rather like the Church of the Holy Sepulchre or the Place of the Nativity in Bethlehem. Capernaum is on the main tourist route. At peak times it is not unusual to see a dozen or more buses parked, and the site can become somewhat overcrowded. In the high season try to arrive early or at lunchtime.

To the east of the walled compound is a small Greek Orthodox church, identified by its red domes. However, you can reach it only by a rough track from the main road.

THE HEALING OF THE PARALYTIC

After some days Jesus returned to Capernaum. As the news spread that he was at home, so many people gathered that there was no longer room even outside the door. While Jesus was preaching the Word to them, some people brought a paralyzed man to him.

The four men who carried him couldn't get near Jesus because of the crowd, so they opened the roof above the room where Jesus was and, through the hole, lowered the man on his mat. When Jesus saw the faith of these people, he said to the paralytic, "My son, your sins are forgiven."

Now, some teachers of the Law who were sitting there wondered within themselves, "How can he speak like this insulting God? Who can forgive sins except God?"

At once Jesus knew through his spirit what they were thinking and asked, "Why do you wonder? Is it easier to say to this paralyzed man: 'Your sins are forgiven,' or to say: 'Rise, take up your mat and walk?' But now you shall know that the Son of Man has authority on earth to forgive sins."

And he said to the paralytic, "Stand up, take up your mat and go home." The man rose and, in the sight of all those people, he took up his mat and went out. All of them were astonished and praised God saying, "We have never seen anything like this!" (Mark 2:1–12)

Manifest in making whole
Palsied limbs and fainting soul;
Anthems be to thee addressed,
God in Man made manifest.

TOUR

Inside the first entrance gate and on the left is a small garden in which there is a bronze statue of St. Francis. To the right of the pathway is a building that at one time the Franciscans inhabited. Inside the second archway and on the right is an office where entrance tickets and a limited number of souvenirs are sold. From here, walk diagonally across to the remains of the old synagogue.

In 1923 an effort was made to reconstruct the building from the profusion of material on the site. It is thought that this synagogue was probably the most ornate in the whole of Galilee. The white limestone came from a local quarry. Some fine carved pieces are displayed featuring flowers, grapes, pomegranates, and particularly the date palm, which is a symbol of the land. There are also a number of geometric designs, including the Star of David.

Before ascending the steps into the main prayer hall, notice on the left the black basalt volcanic rock foundations upon which this late-fourth-century "White Synagogue" was built. It is now almost certain that these earlier remains are part of the building that Jesus knew so well.

Ascend the steps and enter the rectangular prayer hall. It is thought that there may have been a gallery supported by a row of columns running down either side and across the far end. Adjoining the right side of the main hall are the remains of an open courtyard that was added a century later. Pass through the archway into this area. A colonnaded cloister enclosed the courtyard on three sides. Walk across to the far side from where you can see the outline of a first-century street with a number of shops.

Before finally leaving the synagogue, walk through one of the reconstructed portals and notice immediately below the excavated walls of houses built from the dark basalt volcanic rocks that are so plentiful in the region. These simple dwellings date from the beginning of the first century and would also have been familiar to Jesus.

It is interesting to note that many of the houses follow a standard pattern in which a number of low-roofed rooms with windows facing inward surrounded an open courtyard. Some of the door and window lintels have now been reconstructed, albeit nearer the ground, to give an idea of the layout. The fairly primitive roofs would have been made of wooden beams covered with a mixture of beaten earth and straw. One is reminded of the story of the sick man being let down through the roof to be healed by Jesus. Access was via a flight of stone steps, and some of the lower ones are still visible.

The courtyard itself played a very important part in the life of the family. Here they cooked, ate their meals, and worked at their crafts. During the hot summer months when there was no rain, they probably slept on mats laid out on the compressed soil. The small rooms were used for storage, although in the rainy season or in case of sickness these provided shelter.

Between the synagogue and the sea stands the modern Roman Catholic church completed in June 1990 and dedicated to St. Peter. It was designed by the Italian architect Ildo Avetta of Rome, whose objective was twofold: first, to provide a place of worship within this important gospel site; and second, to protect the excavated remains of a fifth-century church and "Peter House."

The Franciscan archaeologists, mainly Fathers Virgilio Corbo and Stanislao Loffreda, who have carried out a very thorough study of the site, believe that this Byzantine church was built over the family home of Peter and that here Jesus often stayed. The archaeologists claim that the house dates from before the birth of Christ. In the late first century A.D. the early Judeo-Christians apparently used the courtyard as a *domus ecclesia* (house church). This is borne out by the fact that, unlike other buildings so far uncovered in the town, the floor was relaid in lime several times during the first to fourth centuries, and the walls were replastered on a number of occasions. The archaeologists discovered over one hundred inscriptions in Greek, Aramaic, and Hebrew, and the words *Jesus, Lord,* and *Christ* appeared several times. The name *Peter* occurred at least twice, and at the lowest level some fish hooks were unearthed.

The excavated remains of "Peter House," in Capernaum, are found beneath a modern Roman Catholic church dedicated to St. Peter. *(Allan Weinert)*

In the fourth century this *domus ecclesia* was enlarged and enclosed within a wall. Finally, in the latter half of the fifth century an octagonal church was built over the whole area with the center exactly above the foundations of the original courtyard. The new church faithfully follows the outline of this ancient octagon.

The present ultramodern structure rests upon eight sturdy pillars to avoid damage to the excavated Byzantine foundations below. Reinforced concrete has been used to withstand earthquakes and, in an attempt to blend it with its surroundings, has been faced with local basalt. For the same reason the roof has been covered in lead.

At the time of writing, visitors are not permitted to enter the church, apart from Roman Catholic groups who may celebrate Mass here by prior arrangement with the Franciscan authorities. Nevertheless, it is possible to view the foundations of the octagonal church and the "Peter House" without entering the building.

Before leaving Capernaum, take the opportunity to examine the exhibits laid out in the area between the synagogue and the ticket office. Of particular interest are an oil press and grinding stones made of black basalt rock. There are also some fine carvings in white limestone along the south boundary. To the left of the central feature in this display is an interesting carving of the Ark of the Covenant looking rather like a traditional gypsy caravan. It is a unique representation showing how the tribes of Israel transported the Tablets of the Law before they finally came to rest in the Temple in Jerusalem.

AUTHORS' COMMENTS

The fourth-century synagogue is impressive, and the excavated remains on the site are also interesting because here one is seeing many objects that were familiar to Jesus. When the area is free of tourists, it is possible to capture a little of the atmosphere of this very special place.

Opening Times: 8:30–4:15 daily; there is a charge for admission

Souvenir Shop: mainly postcards in the ticket office

Toilets: in the parking lot

Custodian: The Franciscans

Telephone: (06) 6721059

CAESAREA PHILIPPI
Modern name: Banias

The area is at the extreme north tip of Israel and is of Christian significance because the gospels of St. Matthew and St. Mark record that Jesus came here with his disciples. The site is now within a National Nature Park and includes one of the three main sources of the Jordan River, which flows out below a rugged cliff. There is a tradition that it was here that Jesus referred to St. Peter as "Rock."

PETER'S COMMISSIONING

After that Jesus came to Caesarea Philippi. He asked his disciples, "What do people say of the Son of Man? Who do they say I am?" They said, "For some of them you are John the Baptist, for others Elijah or Jeremiah or one of the prophets."

Jesus asked them, "But you, who do you say I am?" Peter answered, "You are the Christ, the Son of the living God." Jesus replied, "It is well for you, Simon Barjona, for it is not flesh or blood that has revealed this to you but my Father in heaven.

"And now I say to you: You are Peter (or Rock) and on this rock I will build my Church; and never will the powers of death overcome it.

"I will give you the keys of the kingdom of Heaven: whatever you bind on earth shall be bound in Heaven, and what you unbind on earth shall be unbound in Heaven."

Then he ordered his disciples not to tell anyone that he was the Christ. (Matthew 16:13–20)

> O Rock of ages, one Foundation
> On which the living Church doth rest
> Thy name be blest.

ACCESS FROM TIBERIAS

Caesarea Philippi is about thirty-six miles due north of the town. Make for Qiryat Shemona (twenty-seven miles), passing the town on the left, and soon afterward take the road to the right. The site is another seven miles on the left.

HISTORY

The area is now called Banias, which is an Arab corruption of the earlier name Panias. There was a city here in the first century B.C. dedicated to the pagan god Pan, who in ancient Greece was reputed to protect flocks and herds. Roman Emperor Augustus gave the city to Herod the Great, who built an elaborate palace in his honor. After Herod's death his youngest son, Philip, who became tetrarch of Galilee, renamed the city Caesarea Philippi, to distinguish it from Caesarea on the coast, and made his headquarters here. Later, a Christian community in the city suffered much persecution in a predominantly pagan environment. Nevertheless, it is recorded that their bishops attended councils of the Church in the fourth and fifth centuries. Even after the Persian conquest in the seventh century, it remained a prosperous place on account of its position on the road to Damascus. Later, the Crusaders improved the fortifications. Very little has so far been excavated, although there is much carved stone lying around.

About two miles to the west are the remains of the city of Dan, which is archaeologically more interesting. "Dan to Beersheba" was how the length of the land was described in the Old Testament.

DETAILS

The region is in the southern foothills of Mount Hermon, whose tall peak rises 9,232 feet above sea level. The Israeli authorities own the site of Banias, which is well preserved as a nature park. There is a fairly expensive entrance fee, and the "green card" used by tourists to gain admission to archaeological sites is not accepted. Within the pleasant compound is a restaurant and also a gift shop specializing in posters and postcards of the local flora and fauna. There are a number of signposted walks beside the fast-flowing waters, which at this point are known as the Hermon River.

The main feature is a massive rockface below which the extremely cold water emerges, having started its journey as the melting snows of Mount Hermon. Take the steep path leading up to the base of the escarpment and notice that cut into it are some ornamental niches, which originally contained statues of the pagan god Pan. It seems most likely that Jesus and his disciples would have been familiar with these shrines. The water originally flowed out of the cave to the left, but an earthquake has caused a landslide to block the entrance, and it now emerges at a lower level.

There is a tradition that this rock is the one that prompted Jesus to say to St. Peter, "You are Peter and on this rock I will build my Church."

AUTHORS' COMMENTS

There are no Christian churches in the region, but if the weather is fine a visit is well worthwhile to enjoy the unspoiled countryside and see one of the three main sources of the Jordan River.

Opening Times: 8:00–5:00; winter closes at 4:00; closes one hour earlier on the eve of Shabbat and holidays; closed on Yom Kippur

Souvenir Shop: near the parking lot; about one hundred yards on the left is a snack bar and restaurant

Toilets: opposite the restaurant

Custodian: The Nature Reserve Authority of Israel

Telephone: (06) 6950272

Mount Tabor

Since the fourth century this dome-shaped mountain rising 1,500 feet above the Plain of Jezreel has been venerated as the traditional site of the Transfiguration.

THE TRANSFIGURATION

About eight days after Jesus had said all this, he took Peter, John and James and went up the mountain to pray. And while he was praying, the

This church, one of the largest in the Holy Land, is atop Mount Tabor, the traditional site of Jesus' Transfiguration. *(Allan Weinert)*

aspect of his face was changed and his clothing became dazzling white. Two men were talking with Jesus: Moses and Elijah. They had just appeared in heavenly glory and were telling him about his departure that had to take place in Jerusalem.

Peter and his companions had fallen asleep, but they awoke suddenly and saw Jesus' Glory and the two men standing with him. As Moses and Elijah were about to leave, Peter said to him, "Master, how good it is for us to be here for we can make three tents, one for you, one for Moses and one for Elijah." For Peter didn't know what to say. And no sooner had he spoken than a cloud appeared and covered them; and the disciples were afraid as they entered the cloud. Then these words came from the cloud, "This is my Son, my Chosen one, listen to him." And after the voice had spoken, Jesus was there alone.

The disciples kept this to themselves at the time, telling no one of anything they had seen. (Luke 9:28–36)

'Tis good, Lord, to be here,
Yet we may not remain;
but since thou bidst us leave the mount,
come with us to the plain.

182

ACCESS

Mount Tabor lies east of Nazareth about a mile off the main Afula-to-Tiberias road. It is possible to climb to the top via a steep footpath from the village of Dabburiyah on its west face. There is also a road, involving fifteen sharp hairpin bends, rising from the parking lot at the foot of its north face. You can hire taxis from this point.

FROM NAZARETH

Approximately seventeen miles to the parking lot. After six and a half miles, on approaching the outskirts of Afula, turn left at the traffic lights, then keep to the left, heading toward Tiberias. In another seven miles take the road on the left toward the mountain. The parking lot is about three miles from this point. Circumvent the mountain on its west face, driving through Dabburiyah, until reaching the parking lot.

FROM TIBERIAS

Approximately eighteen miles to the parking lot. Leave on the main road, heading west out of the town, and in nine miles turn left at the Golani junction traffic lights. After another six miles pass through the outskirts of Kfar Tavor, then, in about a mile, take the right turn at the bottom of the hill at the sign "Mount Tabor." The parking lot is about two miles from this point.

HISTORY

The mountain has played an important part in the history of the land since very early times because of its strategic position on the main trade route between East and West. Many battles have been fought at its foot on the Plain of Jezreel (also known as Esdraelon). As early as 2000 B.C., the Canaanites set up a place of worship to Baal on its summit. In Psalm 89 we read, "Tabor and Hermon rejoice at your [God's] name." During the time of the Judges, Deborah the Prophetess and Barak the General assembled their armies here to rout the Canaanite chariots of Sisera. The Arab village of Dabburiyah at its west foot is still named after the prophetess. There is also a tradition that Jesus healed the epileptic boy in this village.

In the sixth century the Anonymous Pilgrim of Piacenza records that there were three churches on the mount. The Persians destroyed these in A.D. 614. In 1099 Tancred, the Crusader knight, built a fortress and a monastery that the Benedictine monks occupied until the defeat of the Crusader Kingdom in 1187. In the thirteenth century the Saracens constructed a defensive wall with twelve watchtowers around the summit.

TOUR

At the top of the twisting ascent road is a stone archway, appropriately named "Gate of the Winds." There was once a drawbridge here, and to the right you can see remnants of a wall built by Flavius Josephus in the first century A.D. Continue along the driveway toward the Franciscan church. Through the trees, on the left, you can see the small red dome of the Greek Orthodox church, which was built in 1911 on Crusader and Byzantine remains. It is dedicated to the prophet Elijah and contains some fine icons and mosaics; unfortunately, the church is often closed to visitors. Ahead on the right is a public parking lot, while farther on taxis unload their passengers in front of the wrought-iron gates leading to the Franciscan church.

Within the gates, the path is flanked by the ruins of the twelfth-century Benedictine monastery, which itself was built upon earlier Byzantine foundations. Notice halfway along on the left of the path the outline of a small chapel, clearly identified by its east apse, which dates from the sixth century and was later adapted for use by the Crusaders. On both sides of the path, you can see other remains of the Benedictine monastery, including, on the left, the central hall and the refectory.

In 1924 Spanish Franciscans erected the present church, which is one of the largest in the Holy Land—a major achievement, bearing in mind that all the building material had to be carried to the top of the mountain. The style is typical of Byzantine basilicas. The Italian architect was Antonio Barluzzi, who designed many of the churches built in the Holy Land this century. A bronze bas-relief commemorating his life is set into the wall opposite the west door.

The interior of the church is most impressive, and an unusual feature is that the nave is at a middle level between the main altar and the crypt. Notice the fine mosaic on the oven vaulting of the apse depicting our Lord's Transfiguration. On the left is St. Peter, while on the right are St. James and St. John. In the background, standing upon clouds, are Moses and the prophet Elijah. The open crypt below is full of color and is greatly enhanced by the brilliant stained-glass east window depicting two peacocks (symbols of eternity) flanking a chalice. The plain stone blocks of the Crusader altar, and the three lower courses of the apse from the same period, fittingly complement the modern decorations. In the floor in front of the altar, below wooden trapdoors, are Byzantine and Canaanite remains.

Before leaving the church, visit the two chapels under the west towers. The one on the north side is dedicated to Moses, who is portrayed in a painting inside, directly above the entrance door. In a similar position in the other chapel, on the south side, dedicated to Elijah, is a painting of this prophet.

On leaving the church, turn immediately left and ascend a flight of steps to a higher level. From here there is a magnificent view across the Plain of Jezreel, which today is regarded as the "breadbasket of Israel." Notice how some fields are being sown, some reaped, and others plowed. The ground is so fertile that it is possible to grow three crops each year. On the horizon are the Gilboa Mountains of King Saul fame, while on the left is the village of Endor, where he consulted the witch, as related in 1 Samuel 28:7. Look half right and notice, beyond the main road, the village of Nain, where Jesus brought to life again the only son of a widow.

Return to the wrought-iron gates. On the left is the Franciscan monastery and convent where the nuns sometimes offer for sale a small selection of souvenirs.

AUTHORS' COMMENTS

Although the gospels do not specify where the Transfiguration took place—and modern scholars now feel that the much higher Mount Hermon is a more likely location—Tabor is nevertheless the only mountain upon which churches have been erected to commemorate the event. Quite apart from the magnificent views from the summit, it is surrounded in mystique and atmosphere. In particular, you should see it in the early morning from the main Tiberias-to-Afula road when sometimes, and quite suddenly, low clouds hide the summit from sight just as described in the gospel story.

Opening Times: 8:00–noon, 2:00–5:00; closed on Saturdays

Souvenir Shop: a small selection of gifts in the refectory

Toilets: near the parking lot and on the right of the entrance inside the refectory

Custodians:

    Church of the Transfiguration: Franciscans

    Church of Elijah: Greek Orthodox

Telephone: (06) 6767489 (Franciscan monastery)

CANA

Franciscan Church of the Wedding Feast
Greek Orthodox Church of the Wedding Feast

Since early Christian times many have believed that this Arab village of Kafr Kanna is where Jesus performed his first miracle by turning water into wine at a wedding feast. There were Byzantine and Crusader churches here, although the present Roman Catholic and Greek Orthodox buildings commemorating the event date only from the nineteenth century. Cana was also the home of Nathaniel, an early disciple of our Lord.

THE WEDDING FEAST

Three days later there was a wedding at Cana in Galilee and the mother of Jesus was there. Jesus was also invited to the wedding with his disciples. When all the wine provided for the celebration had been served and they had run out of wine, the mother of Jesus said to him, "They have no wine." Jesus replied, "Woman, your thoughts are not mine! My hour has not yet come."

However his mother said to the servants, "Do whatever he tells you."

Nearby were six stone water jars meant for the ritual washing as practiced by the Jews; each jar could hold twenty or thirty gallons. Jesus said to the servants, "Fill the jars with water." And they filled them to the brim. Then Jesus said, "Now draw some out and take it to the steward." So they did.

The steward tasted the water that had become wine, without knowing from where it had come; for only the servants who had drawn the water knew. So, he immediately called the bridegroom to tell him, "Everyone serves the best wine first and when people have drunk enough, he serves that which is ordinary. Instead you have kept the best wine until the end."

This miraculous sign was the first, and Jesus performed it at Cana in Galilee. In this way he let his Glory appear and his disciples believed in him. (John 2:1–11)

> The Gospel story has recorded
> how your glory was afforded
> to a wedding day;
> be our guest, we pray.

ACCESS

Kafr Kanna lies northeast of Nazareth on the road to Tiberias. Both churches are situated in the center of the village about two hundred yards off the main road.

FROM NAZARETH

The village is six and a half miles from the town. On approaching, look for the Kafr Kanna village sign, and in another eight hundred yards for a domed church on the right. One hundred yards beyond this (just past the bus stop) a narrow road leads up to the wedding churches. It is advisable to park at a convenient place on the main road. You'll come to the Greek Orthodox church first in about a hundred yards. To visit the Franciscan church, bear right and continue for another fifty yards.

FROM TIBERIAS

The village is about fourteen miles from the town. Take the Tel Aviv road, and at the nine-mile mark go straight ahead at the Golani junction traffic lights. In another four miles turn left, at the sign "Nazareth." In about eight hundred yards look out for the "Kafr Kanna" sign; and in another half mile, opposite the large electricity transformer, a narrow road leads up to the wedding churches. It is advisable to park at a convenient place on the main road. Walk up to the Franciscan church, a distance of about two hundred yards. The Greek Orthodox church is fifty yards farther along on the right.

Franciscan Church
of the Wedding Feast

TOUR

The present church, easily identified by its two western towers and a red dome, was built in 1879. However, there are remains of earlier Crusader and Byzantine buildings in the crypt. Of particular significance is the fact that in the fourth century St. Paula and St. Eustochium, disciples of St. Jerome, recorded in a letter that they "saw Cana, not far from Nazareth, where the water was changed into wine."

Look around the church. The interior is typical of its period, and there is little of particular interest at ground level, although an unusual feature is that the east end is elevated to accommodate the ancient remains in the crypt below. Before descending into the crypt, notice that in the floor nearby, under a metal grille, there is a third/fourth-century mosaic written in Aramaic. A translation can be found on the south wall: "Honoured be the memory of Yosef, son of Tanham, son of Buta and his sons who made this, may it be a blessing to them. Amen." It is claimed that the inscription was originally part of a synagogue bench and that the Yosef referred to may have been Joseph of Tiberias, who was converted to Christianity during the Constantinian Period and founded many churches in Galilee.

Descend the stairs into the crypt. In the center, protected by railings and standing on Byzantine foundations, is a commemorative water pot. Those mentioned in St. John's Gospel were much larger and held twenty–thirty gallons. It should be remembered that it was not unusual for wedding celebrations to last for a whole week.

From a passageway to the right of the altar you can see the remains of an ancient cistern, while on the left are some more water jars. In a room on the left of the crypt are remnants from Crusader, Byzantine, and earlier periods.

Opening Times: 8:00–noon, 2:00–6:00 daily (winter closes at 5:00)

Souvenir Shop: opposite the main entrance

Toilets: none

Custodian: The Franciscans

Telephone: (06) 6517011

Greek Orthodox Church of the Wedding Feast

Standing within its own compound, this church built in the shape of a Greek cross is surmounted by a distinctive dome. The interior contains a number of icons and holy pictures.

Opening Times: 8:30–6:30

AUTHORS' COMMENTS

An alternative site for Cana in Galilee is Khirbet Cana, which is about eight and a half miles north of Nazareth. Apparently, it was favored in the Middle Ages, although today there is nothing to be seen but a mound of ruins. Certainly, Kafr Kanna has more to offer.

Aesthetically, neither the churches nor the village are particularly attractive. Nevertheless, Cana in Galilee has always held a very special place in the affections of those who have been blessed with a happy Christian marriage.

Nazareth

The Town
Basilica of the Annunciation
St. Joseph's Church
Church of St. Gabriel (Mary's Well)
The Old Synagogue

The words *Jesus of Nazareth* highlight for Christians the importance of this otherwise relatively insignificant town. There are four places of primary importance: the Basilica of the Annunciation; St. Joseph's Church ("the Church of the Carpenter's Shop"); the Church of St. Gabriel ("Mary's Well"); and the Greek Catholic church built over the traditional site of the synagogue of our Lord's time.

The Town

The old town nestles in a valley and should not be confused with Nazareth Ilit, the modern Israeli suburb two and a half miles to the east and easily identified by its profusion of tall buildings.

Nazareth is the largest Arab town in northern Israel and the commercial center for the many surrounding villages. It is a bustling, traffic-congested place and in the summer can be both hot and dusty. As in Bethlehem the population is predominantly Christian, and there are a number of church schools and religious foundations.

You should visit the principal sites on foot as they are all within a fairly small area. Car parking can be difficult, especially on Saturday when there is a market. The modern Basilica of the Annunciation is in the center of the town, and its cupola surmounted by a lantern is the distinctive feature.

Basilica of the Annunciation

This imposing modern basilica was erected over what is claimed to be part of the home of the Blessed Virgin Mary and is the fifth building for Christian worship on this site. Funded by Roman Catholic communities throughout the world, work commenced in 1955 on the largest church erected in the Holy Land for nearly eight hundred years. It was completed in 1969.

THE ANNUNCIATION

In the sixth month, the angel Gabriel was sent from God to a town of Galilee called Nazareth. He was sent to a young virgin who was betrothed

The Basilica of the Annunciation, a modern structure completed in 1969, is the fifth on the site of the reputed home of the Blessed Virgin Mary in Nazareth. *(Allan Weinert)*

to a man named Joseph, of the family of David; and the virgin's name was Mary.

The angel came to her and said, "Rejoice, full of grace, the Lord is with you." Mary was troubled at these words, wondering what this greeting could mean.

But the angel said, "Do not fear, Mary, for God has looked kindly on you. You shall conceive and bear a son and you shall call him Jesus. He will be great and shall rightly be called Son of the Most High. The Lord God will give him the kingdom of David, his ancestor; he will rule over the people of Jacob forever and his reign shall have no end."

Then Mary said to the angel, "How can this be if I am a virgin?" And the angel said to her, "The Holy Spirit will come upon you and the power of the Most High will over-

shadow you; therefore, the holy child to be born shall be called Son of God. Even your relative Elizabeth is expecting a son in her old age, although she was unable to have a child, and she is now in her sixth month. With God nothing is impossible."

Then Mary said, "I am the handmaid of the Lord, let it be done to me as you have said." And the angel left her. (Luke 1:26–38)

Love divine, all loves excelling,
joy of heaven, to earth come down,
fix in us thy humble dwelling,
all thy faithful mercies crown.

TOUR

From inside the entrance gates, stop to view the west façade, which is dedicated to the Mystery of the Incarnation. At the apex is a statue of Jesus, and immediately below, in bas-relief, is depicted the angel of the Lord bringing the news to Mary, with the appropriate inscription in Latin underneath. Below are the four evangelists—Matthew, Mark, Luke, and John—with their traditional symbols: man, lion, bull, and eagle. To the left is part of a quotation from Genesis 3:14–15: "The Lord God said unto the serpent...And I will put enmity between thee and the woman, and between thy seed and her seed; it shall bruise thy head, and thou shall bruise his heel." To the right is another quotation from Isaiah 7:14: "Behold, a virgin shall conceive, and bear a son, and shall call his name Immanuel." Finally, above the triple doorway is a quotation from John 1:14: "The Word was made flesh, and dwelt among us."

Before entering the church, turn right to see the colorful wall mosaics along the cloisters, which are gifts from Roman Catholic communities throughout the world. The one nearest the entrance gate commemorates the visit of Pope Paul VI to the town in January 1964.

While standing on this side of the basilica, stop to view the south façade, across which are inscribed the words of the Roman Catholic devotion *"Salve Regina."* In the center above the doorway is a bronze statue of the young Mary extending a welcome to all who come into her house. On the door, depicted in bronze, are twelve scenes from the life of the Blessed Virgin.

Return to the west façade and look at the three doors. On the massive central door, boldly depicted in bronze, are six events in the life of Christ. Viewing them counterclockwise from the top left, they are the Nativity in Bethlehem, the flight into Egypt, life in the carpenter's shop here in Nazareth, baptism in the Jordan River, teaching by the Galilean lakeside, and the Crucifixion. In addition to these central portrayals are also depicted in copper ten other incidents recorded in the gospels. Turning to the door on the left, the scenes here show the fall of humankind and its consequences. The door on the right depicts three prophesies of redemption from the books of the Old Testament: 2 Samuel 7:16, Isaiah 7:14, and Ezekiel 9:4.

Now enter the basilica. It has two levels, and this is the lower church.

Walk across to the balustrade surrounding the most sacred area, which is ten feet below the modern floor. The main feature is the remains of an exposed cavern venerated as the place where the angel Gabriel appeared to Mary. Move around to stand in a position directly opposite this Grotto of the Annunciation. It is flanked by the remnants of earlier Byzantine and Crusader churches. The sixteen-foot-high wall constructed of columns and large stone blocks acts as a backdrop to this scene and also formed part of the Crusaders' building. The altar within the grotto is from the Franciscan church built on a fairly modest scale in 1730, enlarged in 1877, and finally demolished in 1954 to make way for the present basilica.

Lean over the balustrade to discern immediately below two parallel strips of mosaic. The one nearest the railings could possibly have been part of the floor of the earliest known religious building on this site—a second/third-century "synagogue-church." The other dates from the fifth century, and on the right you can clearly see two remaining wall-courses from the apse of this Byzantine church. Before leaving the area, look up at an octagonal opening, which affords a view of this venerated site from the upper church.

Returning toward the entrance, ascend the spiral staircase on the left, passing the brilliantly colored windows of encrusted glass. The steps lead to the upper floor, which serves as the parish church for the Roman Catholic community in Nazareth.

Walk down the right aisle to view on the south wall the impressive decorative panels. These adorn both aisles and are gifts from twenty countries. They portray in a variety of materials the veneration of the Blessed Virgin. Now turn to notice the fine stained-glass window at the back of the nave.

Stand centrally in front of the railings, facing the high altar, and look up to the magnificent cupola 180 feet high and 53 feet in circumference. The name *Nazareth* is a Semitic word that means "a flower," and the cupola represents an inverted lily rooted in heaven opening its petals to the shrine below to crown the place of the Annunciation.

The Italian mosaic above the altar is one of the largest in the world and portrays Jesus with his arms outstretched beside St. Peter surrounded by numerous representatives of Christendom. At our Lord's right hand is the crowned Virgin seated in glory, while overhead is the dove of the Holy Spirit and the all-seeing eye of the Father.

The chapel to the left of the high altar is dedicated to St. Francis, while the one to the right is consecrated to the Holy Spirit. From this central position it is also of interest to note that the full-length wall mosaic nearest to the

Franciscan chapel is a gift from England and depicts Our Lady of Walsingham. The "Slipper Chapel" is featured in the mosaic.

Observe the other plaques on the north wall, then leave the building through the door on this side. Ahead is the baptistery, which, in accordance with an early Christian custom, is separated from the main building because the unbaptized were not allowed to enter the church. The panels of amethyst and green glass represent the flowing baptismal water. The font itself is cast in bronze, and on it you can see a modern representation of Jesus being baptized by John. This entire structure was a gift from Germany.

On the north side of the baptistery, and well below the level of the present courtyard, you can see some of the passages, stores, silos, and water cisterns that existed under the simple dwellings of our Lord's time. Here one is looking on features that were familiar to Jesus and his family. This system of underground caverns is a continuation of the Grotto of the Annunciation. Further examples are also visible in the crypt of St. Joseph's Church, the next place to visit.

Before leaving this particular area turn back to view the impressive cupola of the basilica, which is topped by a lantern symbolizing the Light of the World.

Opening Times: 8:00–11:45, 2:00–6:00; winter closes daily at 5:00
Souvenir Shop: none
Toilets: inside the main gates and turn to the left
Custodian: The Franciscans
Telephone: (06) 6572501

St. Joseph's Church
Church of the Carpenter's Shop

ACCESS

From the Basilica of the Annunciation, ascend the steps beyond the baptistery and turn right. Ahead is the main entrance to the Franciscan monastery built in 1930. On the second floor is the Terra Sancta High School, which provides education for about seven hundred pupils. On the lawn in front of the monastery are remains from the four earlier churches. Continue past the main entrance and ascend additional steps leading to St. Joseph's Church, also known as the Church of the Carpenter's Shop. Turn left at the top, and enter by the west door because the other in the south wall is used as an exit.

TOUR

This church built in 1914 follows the lines of an earlier Crusader building, the foundations of which were discovered in 1895. Now proceed to the aisle on the left, and before descending the stairway into the crypt notice the well-known painting by the French artist François Lafond on the north wall.

There are five main features in the crypt. Stand in front of the altar and notice the eight stone courses of the apse, which remain from the Crusader building. In the floor, slightly to the left, is a metal grille through which there is a view of the caverns below. These probably date from about 1000 B.C. Originally, they were grain silos but later were adapted as living accommodation and were used for domestic purposes until the end of the last century. Next, move to the back of the crypt and look over the wrought-iron guard to view a pit about three yards square with a mosaic floor and seven steps leading down to it. The Franciscans claim this was a baptismal pool dating from the Judeo-Christian era circa first–third centuries.

Leave the crypt by the other side. On ascending the stairway, notice on the right another flight of ancient steps leading down to the complex of caverns underneath the whole area. On the left of the stairway, you can also see an old water cistern. Leave the church by the south door. The exit from the compound is opposite the main entrance to the monastery.

Opening Times: see hours for the Church of the Annunciation
Souvenir Shop: a small booth beside the church
Toilets: same as for the Church of the Annunciation
Custodian: The Franciscans
Telephone: (06) 6572501

AUTHORS' COMMENTS

No one can really be certain of the exact location of the home of the Holy Family or of the carpenter's shop. It is hardly surprising that today nothing remains of the simple houses that Jesus knew, but there is ample evidence that these two Christian sites have been venerated from an early period. The caverns hewn out of the bedrock below the dwellings are clearly visible, and undoubtedly some would have been used for domestic purposes because they were warm in winter and cool in summer. This area owned by the Franciscans makes a pleasing haven from the hustle and bustle outside, and here there are many opportunities for devotion and reflection.

$$\frac{+\|+}{+\|+}$$

Church of St. Gabriel
Church of Mary's Well

The church is built over Nazareth's only freshwater spring, which the Holy Family would have visited daily.

ACCESS

FROM THE EXIT OF THE FRANCISCAN COMPOUND OF THE CHURCH OF THE ANNUNCIATION AND ST. JOSEPH'S CHURCH

Turn immediately right and follow the boundary wall around. Then go straight ahead for about 450 yards until reaching the Church of St. Gabriel.

FROM TIBERIAS

When approaching Nazareth from Tiberias, it is better to call here first before proceeding to the Basilica of the Annunciation. On completing the steep and twisting descent into the Arab town, look on the right for the solid-looking modern stone structure with a circular recess facing the main road. This is known as Mary's Well and until fairly recently was a public washhouse. St. Gabriel's Church is about seventy-five yards behind it.

TOUR

St. Gabriel's is surrounded by a high wall and is approached through a central gateway. Walk across the courtyard and descend the steps under the portico, which lead directly into the south aisle of this Greek Orthodox church. However, before examining it in detail, continue straight ahead and descend additional steps leading into a low vaulted cavern built by the Crusaders in the twelfth century.

At the end is a metal balustrade, below which you can see the clear spring water. It is not possible to date this particular outlet of the spring, but certainly the Holy Family and the inhabitants of Nazareth depended upon its waters two thousand years ago. The Greek Orthodox believe that the Archangel Gabriel first appeared to Mary at the spring, as related in the apocryphal Gospel of St. James.

Before returning to look around the church, notice the ancient Armenian tiles with which the Crusaders decorated the walls. There is a small recess in the wall with a shaft where it is possible to let down a metal cup and draw up the water.

Now move up to view the church, which was built in 1769. The walls and ceiling are lavishly decorated with modern murals. The main altar is hidden from view behind a screen known as the iconostasis, which is decorated with icons and other holy pictures. Within the nave on the right is the bishop's throne, while high up on the left is the tall pulpit. Against the north wall you can see the tomb of the founder of the church.

AUTHORS' COMMENTS

There is no doubt about the authenticity of this freshwater spring, and with a little imagination one can picture a small boy coming to draw water—perhaps twice daily—with his young mother.

Opening Times: 8:00–5:00; Sundays noon–2:00 only

Toilets: within the courtyard

Custodian: The Greek Orthodox Church; in the box by the door a small donation is expected

Telephone: (06) 6576437

The Old Synagogue

There is a tradition that this simple building stands on the site of the synagogue of our Lord's time.

TEACHING IN THE SYNAGOGUE

When Jesus came to Nazareth where he had been brought up, he entered the synagogue on the sabbath as he usually did. He stood up to read and they handed him the book of the prophet Isaiah.

Jesus then unrolled the scroll and found the place where it is written: "The Spirit of the Lord is upon me. He has anointed me to bring good news to the poor, to proclaim liberty to captives and new sight to the blind; to free the oppressed and announce the Lord's year of mercy."

Jesus then rolled up the scroll, gave it to the attendant and sat down, while the eyes of all in the synagogue were fixed on him. Then he said to them, "Today these prophetic words come true even as you listen." (Luke 4:16–21)

Lord, thy word abideth,
and our footsteps guideth;
who its truth believeth
light and joy receiveth.

ACCESS

From the exit of the Franciscan compound of the Basilica of the Annunciation and St. Joseph's Church, walk down the road opposite the gates for about a hundred yards, then turn up to the right into the paved shopping mall. Keep ascending this street, turning first to the left, then to the right. After that in about twenty yards, on the right, look for a doorway by the remains of an ancient pillar (ring the bell if the door is closed) and enter a small courtyard leading into the Old Synagogue.

DETAILS

The interior of this little Crusader building, owned by the Greek Catholic Church, is devoid of any furniture except for a few wooden stalls around the walls and the plain altar at the end. It is claimed that the floor dates from a much earlier period.

AUTHORS' COMMENTS

This is an appropriate place in which to reflect that in the synagogue at Nazareth Jesus was taught and learned to read. Here he read aloud the Scriptures—and here he proclaimed their fulfillment.

Opening Times: 8:00–noon; 2:00–5:00; Sundays 10:00–noon only (ring the bell)

Souvenir Shop: none

Toilets: none

Custodian: The Greek Catholic Church; a small donation is expected

Telephone: (06) 6568488

If time permits, it is well worth ascending the numerous flights of steps to the top of the hill overlooking the town. From here there is a good view over Nazareth. In the middle distance is a hill on which there is a cluster of trees close to a small chapel. This is known as the Mount of Precipitation, from which, according to tradition, the Nazarenes intended to throw Jesus down when he was driven out of the city.

Near this viewpoint is the Silesian Secondary School, which has a fine chapel dedicated to the adolescence of Jesus. In a niche high above the altar is an impressive statue depicting him as a young boy.

While you are in Nazareth, it is also worth exploring the streets in the vicinity of the Old Synagogue because here are a number of modern carpenters' shops.

ACRE

$$\frac{+\|+}{+\|+}$$

Situated on the north sweep of the Bay of Haifa, this picturesque walled town with its fishing harbor gives the impression today of being entirely medieval. In fact, most of it was rebuilt at the end of the eighteenth century, having been totally destroyed on the defeat of the Crusaders in 1291. It is they who in less than two centuries left the greatest impression upon its long and checkered history. Within the walls are the substantial remains of their headquarters—

A picturesque town on the Bay of Haifa, Acre was an important Crusader port. *(George Martin)*

often referred to as the Underground City. Also of particular interest are three merchants' *khans* (trading stations), a network of narrow streets, and the impressive Mosque of Ahmed el-Jazzar.

ACCESS

Acre (spelled on some maps as Akko or Acco) by road is 13 miles north of Haifa, 33 miles from Tiberias, and 109 miles from Jerusalem. Although you can clearly see the skyline of the Old City from the coastal road when driving from the south, it is not visible when approaching from the east (Tiberias or Safed). In both instances it is first necessary to drive through the modern town to reach the Old City.

FROM TIBERIAS

On reaching the outskirts of Acre, go straight at the first two traffic lights. Immediately beyond the second light, on the left, is a large mound (*tel*) that is the site of the ancient city. Soon after this is a railway level crossing, then shortly afterward at the traffic circle go straight ahead toward the center of the town until reaching the pedestrian district. Here turn right. Take the first left, then proceed over the first crossroads and turn left at the second. Drive through two further crossroads, then go straight to pass through the Crusader defensive walls. Watch for the parking signs to the left. From the parking lot entrance, the slim round minaret and dome of the Mosque of Ahmed el-Jazzar where our tour commences are clearly visible.

FROM HAIFA

On approaching Acre at the north end of Haifa Bay, look to the left for the Palm Beach Hotel, and at the traffic circle turn immediately right. In eight hundred yards turn left at the next traffic circle toward the center of town until reaching the pedestrian district. Here turn right. Take the first left, then proceed over the first crossroad and turn left at the second. Drive through two additional crossroads, then go straight to pass through the Crusader defensive walls. Look for the parking signs to the left. From the parking lot entrance, the slim round minaret and dome of the Mosque of Ahmed el-Jazzar where our tour commences are clearly visible.

HISTORY

The large mound (*tel*) marking the site of the ancient city is a mile inland and is one of the oldest recorded settlements in the Holy Land. It was an important Canaanite city long before being mentioned in Egyptian writings of the eighteenth century B.C. At the time of David and Solomon, around 1000 B.C., it was a substantial Phoenician town under the control of Tyre, but little is known about its development during this period because it lay outside ancient Israel.

During the reign of Alexander the Great (356–323 B.C.) the town was of particular importance and even had its own mint, which remained in use for another six hundred years. In the middle of the third century B.C., Acre came under the rule of the Ptolemies of Egypt. The city was renamed Ptolemais after that dynasty, its prosperity grew even further, and the inhabitants spread beyond the bounds of the ancient mound toward the sea.

During the Roman Period, from 63 B.C., a colony was established within its walls for war veterans, and Julius Caesar himself visited in 47 B.C.

St. Paul spent a day with the Christian community in Ptolemais upon returning from his third missionary journey (Acts of the Apostles 21:7). By A.D. 190 Acre had its first bishop. Byzantine influence remained until 636, when the Arabs captured the city and further developed the harbor.

Acre's heyday was during the historical period known as the Crusades. In A.D. 1095 Pope Urban II, in response to an appeal from the emperor of Constantinople, persuaded some of the more powerful nations in Europe to recruit armies to rescue the Eastern Christians from the Muslims. The pope's ultimate objective was to free the Holy Land, and in particular the Tomb of

Christ, from Islamic control. Thousands enthusiastically took up such a worthwhile cause, and it was thought that the campaign would be relatively short-lived. Jerusalem was captured in 1099, and Acre fell in 1104, when the Crusaders used it immediately for the landing of vital supplies and arms. The port also became an important trading link between the West and the East because its natural harbor was one of the best on the Eastern Mediterranean coast.

During the early part of the twelfth century, two great military orders were founded. The first, the chivalrous Hospitalers of St. John of Jerusalem, concerned themselves with the health and spiritual well-being of pilgrims. They built their substantial headquarters in Acre. You can still see much of this, known as the Underground City, today (details follow under "Tour"). They also founded a number of hospitals and built a cathedral on the site now occupied by the Mosque of Ahmed el-Jazzar.

The second order of knights, the Templars, were responsible for the defense of Jerusalem, and they used the El Aqsa Mosque on the Temple Mount as their headquarters. The Crusaders also set about an ambitious building program restoring Acre's city walls. At that time the enclosed area was three times larger than it is now.

One of the inherent weaknesses of the Crusades was that the forces lacked overall command, and the various armies pursued their own objectives. In Acre itself rich merchants from the Italian city-states such as Genoa, Pisa, and Venice developed their separate quarters, but much rivalry soon grew between them.

There was also some discord among the knights of the nations involved, and these factors undoubtedly contributed to the eventual downfall of the Latin Kingdom, as it was then known because the Mass and other offices of the Church were in Latin. Even today the Roman Catholic community in the Holy Land is known by the Eastern Churches as the Latins.

In 1187 Saladin defeated the Crusaders at the Horns of Hattin, and Acre subsequently was taken, but only four years later soldiers under the command of King Philip of France and King of England Richard the Lionheart recaptured it.

In 1219 following a decision by the General Chapter of the Franciscan Order to extend its mission throughout the world, St. Francis of Assisi visited Acre, and as a result the first Franciscan monastery in the East was established. The city remained in Crusader hands as all that was left of the Latin Kingdom until the final expulsion in 1291 by the Egyptian Marmelukes.

To ensure that the port was no longer used for trade, Acre was razed to the ground and lay in ruins for the next 450 years.

In 1750 during a decadent period of the Ottoman Empire an Arab sheik, Daher el-Omar, created his own kingdom in Galilee, and his influence spread as far as the coast. He commenced the redevelopment of Acre as a trading port especially for use between Syria and the west Mediterranean. Daher el-Omar was assassinated in 1775 but was succeeded by the Albanian soldier Ahmed el-Jazzar, nicknamed "the Butcher" because of his extreme cruelty. The Turks appointed him governor of Acre, and with great determination he rebuilt the city on the same pattern as that of Constantinople. Trade once again flourished, and among his many achievements was the building of one of the finest mosques in Palestine, which was named after him. He also restored the walls, erected many public buildings, including the three great khans, and further developed the harbor. Most of the old city buildings seen today date from the period of el-Jazzar.

In 1799 Napoleon, in a bid to extend his empire east, laid siege to Acre for two months. However, el-Jazzar, assisted by the British fleet under the command of Sir Sydney Smith and with the help of Turkish soldiers from Damascus, forced Napoleon to retreat. This proved to be a turning point in Napoleon's ambitions; consequently, he had to abandon any thought of extending his empire as far as India.

Apart from a short period of only eight years from 1832 when Ibrahim Pasha of Egypt drove the Turks out, Acre remained under Turkish control until it fell to the British in 1918. Finally, in 1948, at the instigation of the United Nations, Acre came under the jurisdiction of the State of Israel; since then there has been extensive development of the adjacent modern town.

TOUR

You should explore the Old City on foot. Our tour commences at the Mosque of Ahmed el-Jazzar (see "Access" for details from the nearest parking lot on page 199). Because it is so easy to lose one's way in the bewildering network of narrow streets, the following is a suggested route covering most of the features normally included in a guided tour.

MOSQUE OF AHMED EL-JAZZAR

A small entrance fee is payable to the custodian at the gate. Built by el-Jazzar in 1781, it is one of the most attractive mosques in Israel, and its pleasant courtyard provides an oasis of tranquillity from the bustle outside. The slender minaret and much of the interior had to be reconstructed at the end of the nineteenth century following an earthquake.

In the center of the courtyard stands a ritual cleansing fountain. The entire area is surrounded by a colonnaded cloister, behind which are small rooms designed for use by Muslim students and pilgrims. Most of the granite and marble columns, together with those in the mosque itself, are Roman and date from the first century B.C. They were removed from Caesarea thirty miles farther down the coast. To the right of the mosque is a small mausoleum containing the tombs of Ahmed el-Jazzar and his successor, Suleiman Pasha.

Beneath the courtyard is the original crypt of the Crusader cathedral that once stood on this site. It is now used as a water cistern, and a flight of steps giving access to it is found in the far left-hand corner of the courtyard diagonally across from the street entrance.

The interior of the mosque is of typical Muslim design, which tourists are allowed to view only from just inside the main entrance. Ahead in the far wall is a niche known as a *mihrab*, indicating the direction of Mecca toward which worshipers are required to face. To the right of this is the pulpit, with steps leading up to it from the front. The area beneath the balcony on the right is reserved for Muslim women, as is the balcony itself, where they are segregated from the men. Notice the strings running across the Persian carpets to assist the men in lining up for public worship.

CRUSADER HEADQUARTERS

The extensive remains of the twelfth-century headquarters of the Knights Hospitalers are sometimes referred to as the Underground City because today they lie well below street level.

The entrance and ticket booth are opposite the Mosque of Ahmed el-Jazzar. The walls of the courtyard beyond the ticket booth bear witness to the substantial way in which the European knights constructed their buildings. At the far end is the entrance to the Knights' Halls. Originally, there were seven, and the knights from different parts of Europe—England, France, Germany, Italy, Spain, Provence, and Auvergne—occupied each.

From here follow the directions to the Knights' Refectory. This cryptlike hall with its three massive pillars supporting the vaulted ceiling is one of the finest examples of thirteenth-century Crusader architecture. The ground has been excavated around the base of the third pillar to reveal a secret tunnel, which the Crusaders discovered during their building work. Archaeologists now believe it was originally a sewer dating back to well before the birth of Christ. The knights further developed it for use as a communicating passage, and it is thought that other sections, yet to be excavated, may reach as far as the sea.

Walk through the one-hundred-yard-long tunnel, which is narrow, and in places the roof is rather low, but lighting has been installed. The tunnel eventually leads out into further sections of the Crusader headquarters, where there are more vaulted ceilings. The area immediately ahead was probably used as their hospital. On the way out into the daylight notice on either side of the passageway inscribed stones, which have been removed from Crusader tombs.

Mount the wooden stairway, completing the tour of the Underground City, turn right at the top, then shortly right again into a long covered passageway where there are a few craft shops. Follow the passageway toward the daylight, and when outside, turn left.

ROUTE TO THE KHAN EL-UMDAN AND THE HARBOR

Seventy yards away is a large open space. Cross this, keeping to the left, and in the far left-hand corner turn to the left. Within ten yards turn right, descend the steps, then turn right again into a covered street with shops on either side. Walk along this street for a hundred yards, and at the end turn left. Continue ahead for forty yards, then turn right to reach another open area. Proceed toward the harbor, but divert to the right to walk under a five-storied tower, which leads into the Khan el-Umdan (Inn of Pillars), commonly known as the Camel Market, although camels are no longer traded here. On all four sides are granite columns that Ahmed el-Jazzar removed from Caesarea when in 1785 he rebuilt this merchants' inn. The khan originally belonged to the city-state of Genoa. Notice the large octagonal trough in the center of the courtyard. Return to the entrance and turn immediately right to walk to the picturesque fishing harbor, where there is much to see.

If time is not at a premium, it is well worth walking along the south walls beyond the harbor. For the more adventurous there are also two other *khans* and several churches to explore, but a map is essential.

Opening Times:

Mosque of Ahmed el-Jazzar: no admission during Muslim times of prayer

Crusader Headquarters (Underground City): June 16–September 14—8:30–6:30; Fridays closes 2:30. September 15–June 15—8:30–5:00; Fridays closes 2:00

Khan el-Umdan: always open

Souvenir Shop: none

Toilets: almost opposite the Knights' Halls

Custodian: The Old Acre Development Company

Telephone: Crusader Headquarters (04) 9911764

MEGIDDO

Megiddo is an archaeological site of extreme antiquity, which occupied a strategic position on the southwest edge of the Plain of Jezreel commanding the trade routes between Egypt in the south, Asia Minor in the north, and

Megiddo is an ancient archaeological site. The Canaanites built this large circular altar of unhewn stones nearly five thousand years ago. *(Allan Weinert)*

Babylon in the east. Within the impressive mound (*tel*), twenty stratas of human habitation have been revealed. The site fell into disuse four hundred years before the birth of Christ.

Through the centuries so many bloody battles had been fought on the plain that the name Armageddon (a corruption of the Hebrew for Hills of Megiddo) came to symbolize the battle to end all battles— the final conflict between good and evil, as foretold in the Revelation of St. John the Divine 16:16.

Access

Megiddo lies twenty-one miles southeast of Haifa, just north of the intersection of Routes 65 and 66; twenty-one miles from Caesarea; and thirty-one miles from Tiberias.

You can complete a tour of the *tel* itself as suggested below, including the detour, in about an hour, but allow a little extra time to visit the museum room.

History

Megiddo dates from about 4000 B.C. during the Neolithic Period (late Stone Age), when its earliest inhabitants lived in caves hewn out of the bedrock. A thousand years later the first of a series of Canaanite cities was built on the site. Among the discoveries from this period is a large circular pagan altar dating from 2800 B.C. and part of a defensive wall ten feet wide and thirteen feet high.

205

In 1468 B.C. Pharaoh Thutmosis III, after a great battle with the Canaanite kings, overran the city. It remained under Egyptian control for the next three centuries, and significant finds from this period include hoards of beautifully carved ivory, gold, and jewelry.

One of its most prosperous eras was during the reign of King Solomon (965–928 B.C.). Megiddo is often referred to as Solomon's Chariot City, although archaeologists now attribute this particular development to King Ahab (c. 875–854 B.C.) who constructed stables to accommodate more than 450 horses. It was Ahab who introduced into Israel the worship of the Phoenician god Baal, thus provoking the hostility of Elijah and the prophets. The impressive tunnel at the west side of the mound, through which water was brought from a spring outside the walls, was also cut during this period. It was the city's lifeline in times of siege.

The battles on the Plain of Jezreel (Esdraelon) are far too numerous to list here, but some are described in the Old Testament. During its turbulent history conquerors destroyed and rebuilt the city many times. Foreign invading armies that passed its walls included Canaanites, Egyptians, Israelites, Philistines, Assyrians, Greeks, Romans, Persians, Turks, and finally the British in 1917 during the First World War. Field Marshal Allenby set up his headquarters at Megiddo to defeat the Turks and thus secured for himself the title of Viscount Allenby of Megiddo and Felixstowe!

Under the auspices of the University of Chicago, a major archaeological excavation took place between 1925 and 1939, when a deep trench was cut into the east face of the *tel,* exposing over twenty layers of civilization, including the five-thousand-year-old Canaanite altar. The late Israeli Professor Yigael Yadin carried out a further series of short investigations between 1960 and 1972.

TOUR

Before commencing the tour, a few minutes spent in the small museum to the right of the entrance with its excellent displays explaining the history of Megiddo is well worthwhile. In a room beyond is a working model of the *tel* at the time of Solomon.

From the gift shop and cafeteria, take the path toward the *tel* and follow the direction signs to the right at its foot. Notice on the left a flight of perfectly preserved steps nearly three thousand years old, which led up to the city gate. Continue ascending the path, and pass through the remains of an even older Canaanite triple gateway. Ascend the wooden stairway and notice on the right the remains of a quadruple gateway dating from the time of King Solomon.

Throughout the *tel* the various features are well marked and do not, there-fore, require a detailed explanation here. Continue the tour by following the arrows until reaching the sign to the north observation platform.

Proceed to the platform, which has two separate viewing positions. The first looks out over the Plain of Jezreel, and against the railings is an orienta-tion plan identifying the main panoramic features. The second overlooks the deep channel cut through the *tel* during the 1925–1939 excavations. The main feature here is the large circular Canaanite altar built of unhewn stones nearly five thousand years ago, with seven steps leading up to it. The archae-ologists uncovered evidence of four temples in this vicinity; one was several centuries earlier than the altar itself. It is thought that by 1800 B.C. the temples no longer existed.

Retrace your steps to the main path, and turn left to reach the grain silo. It is over twenty-three feet deep and is thought to date from the time of King Jeroboam II (793–753 B.C.). Around the inside are two stairways, which al-lowed the grain to be collected at separate points. In King Solomon's time there was a palace beyond the silo. The path to the left leads to the far end of the *tel*, from which there is a different view of the Canaanite altar and sacred area from the opposite side of the archaeological cut. Close by you can also see the ruins of the residence of King Ahab's chariot commander. If taking this detour, return to the silo to resume the tour.

Continue along the main path, bearing around to the left, and make a short detour to view the remains of the stables built by King Ahab for his 450 chariot horses (still often incorrectly attributed to King Solomon). In this area you can see a number of feeding troughs, a few still with their tether-ing posts. Some scholars are of the opinion that the stables were in fact storehouses (as at Masada), and that the troughs were for feeding smaller beasts of burden that brought in supplies. Professor Yadin was, however, con-vinced that they were designed for chariot horses.

Return to the path and continue toward the underground water system. Originally, the inhabitants on the mound depended for their water supply upon an ancient spring that welled up within a cavern at the foot of the *tel*. This rendered them vulnerable in times of siege. To overcome the hazard, an ambitious tunneling project was devised to enable water to be brought safely into the city by an underground route. The work was probably started dur-ing Solomon's reign but was certainly completed by Ahab.

It is interesting to note that the Megiddo undertaking was carried out 150 years before Hezekiah quarried his water tunnel in Jerusalem, and the sev-enty-yard-long tunnel here is very much wider in comparison. The descent to it is now via 183 steep steps. Considering its antiquity, it is an incredible feat of engineering. After a shaft a hundred feet deep was sunk, the task of cutting horizontally through the bedrock was begun from either end, and the two gangs of laborers had only to make a small correction to meet in the middle. At the far end of the ten-foot-high tunnel is the original spring, but now in summer the cavern is often quite dry. From here another eighty steps lead up to a position outside the walls. This opening was sealed upon completion of the tunnel so that invaders could not use it to enter the city.

Unless arrangements have been made to be picked up in the parking lot near this exit, return through the tunnel and across the *tel* to the main entrance.

Opening Times: April to September 8:00–5:00; October to March 8:00–4:00; closes one hour earlier on eve of Shabbat and holidays; closed on Yom Kippur; the tourist "green card" is accepted

Souvenir Shop: behind the reception area and museum; help-yourself snacks and meals available

Toilets: beside the refreshment area

Custodian: The National Parks Authority

Telephone: (06) 6526815

CAESAREA

Roman Aqueduct
Roman Theater
Byzantine Street

The extensive ruins of this once substantial Mediterranean seaport provide some idea of its size and importance in our Lord's time. Caesarea was the provincial headquarters of the Roman administration, and it was here that the procurator, Pontius Pilate, had his residence. For the Christian, it is of great significance because in this city St. Peter baptized the first gentile convert, Cornelius, a centurion in the Roman army. Here, at the home of Philip the Evangelist, Agabus foretold the treatment St. Paul would receive in Jerusalem. Before his trial in Rome, Paul himself was imprisoned in Caesarea for two years.

The main sites are a Roman theater restored to seat a twentieth-century audience of four thousand, a Crusader walled town with its harbor and modern bathing beach, and the Roman aqueduct.

ACCESS

Caesarea is thirty miles north of Tel Aviv and twenty-one miles south of Haifa. It is not prominently marked on some maps because much of the site consists of historical ruins.

FROM TEL AVIV

Take the coastal expressway (Route 2) running north, and in about twenty-seven miles opposite the huge power station on the left look for a sign to Afula and Caesarea. Turn off here, then proceed left under the expressway. At the first junction turn right, and upon reaching the first traffic circle, go straight ahead. At the second traffic circle, exit left, following the signs to the "Old City" and "Theater" until arriving at the parking lot in front of the ruins of the Roman theater(details on page 214).

To visit the Crusader Walled City, continue along the road running parallel to the sea for about a half mile (passing the parking lot and the defensive walls on the left) until arriving at another parking lot straight ahead. (Tour details are on page 212.)

To reach the Roman Aqueduct, drive inland; then in a half mile take the first road off to the left. In two hundred yards turn left again and follow the "Cluster 2" signs to the aqueduct. (Details are on page 213.)

FROM HAIFA

Drive down Route 2 for about seventeen miles until reaching the Zikhron Ya'aqov interchange. Turn off here to drive inland for two miles and join the smaller coastal road (Route 4) running south and marked Zikhron Ya'aqov.

Continue toward Tel Aviv and after six miles keep a sharp look out on the right for a turn off to Caesarea. Drive on this road for one mile, going straight ahead at a traffic circle and then passing under the expressway. Shortly afterward turn off to the right by a modern sculpture. After another two hundred yards turn left at the "Cluster 2" signs to reach the aqueduct. (Details are on page 213.)

To reach the Crusader Walled City it will be necessary to return via the same route as far as the modern sculpture and then turn right. The parking lot close to the defensive walls is about a half mile ahead. (Details for the town are on page 212.)

After exploring the main ruins of Caesarea, continue south along the road running parallel to the sea for about a half mile until reaching the Roman Theater. (Details are on page 211.)

HISTORY

In the fourth century B.C. there was an anchorage here known as "Strato's Tower," named after the principal landmark. A fortified town subsequently developed, and it was conquered a number of times before Roman Emperor Caesar Augustus gave it to Herod the Great in 30 B.C. Herod then undertook a most ambitious development, which he named Caesarea Maritima in honor of the emperor. An impressive artificial harbor was constructed; it was capable of providing anchorage for over a hundred ships and was surrounded by many colonnades and statues. The public buildings included a large theater, hippodrome, amphitheater, and a temple to Augustus. It also had a main thoroughfare nearly eighteen feet wide under which was an advanced sewage system flushed daily by sea water. Herod's town was over three times the size of the area now contained within the walls.

During the Roman occupation tensions ran high between Jews and Gentiles. The historian Josephus records that in A.D. 66, following the desecration of the synagogue, twenty thousand Jews were slain; this massacre was the main cause of the Jewish revolt against Rome. It was from Caesarea that Roman Emperor Titus set out with his army to sack Jerusalem in A.D. 70.

In the third century the writer Origen, who lived in the town for twenty

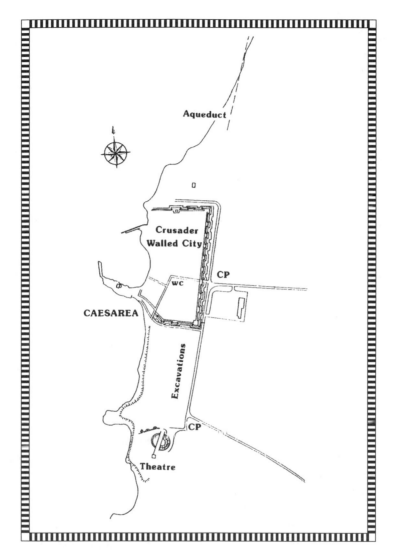

years, founded a Christian library and center of learning here. One of his pupils was Eusebius, who became bishop of Caesarea in A.D. 314. He was the first church historian, and it is due to his records that the position of many biblical sites has been established. At the height of the Byzantine Period the town was over eight times the size of the present area, rivaling Jerusalem itself.

After falling into Muslim hands in A.D. 640, Caesarea declined in importance until the Crusaders captured it in May of 1101 and began some redevelopment. However, following their defeat by Saladin in 1187 at the Horns of Hattin, the town again changed hands on a number of occasions, and it was not until 1251 that some reconstruction, albeit on a much smaller scale, was carried out at the instigation of Louis IX of France. The remains of the large Roman theater, amphitheater, and hippodrome were not included within the bounds of the town, but his impressive walls and defense ditch, reminiscent of many fortresses in France, are still to be seen.

The Marmeluke Sultan, Baybars, finally defeated the French Crusaders only thirteen years after the defensive walls were completed. He destroyed the town, which remained unoccupied until 1878, when the Turks allowed a number of refugees from Bosnia to inhabit the site. Their mosque, a feature of the present tourist area, was in use until this small community abandoned the place in 1948 following the division of the country by the United Nations. It is only in recent years that Caesarea has been excavated and developed as an attraction for visitors.

TOUR

The bridge over the defensive ditch, on the east side of the old town, leads into a covered gateway, which is one of the most complete Crusader structures in Israel and is reminiscent of many castle entrances in Europe. Pass through the covered gateway, then shortly afterward turn left to walk through the foundations of various buildings. Notice, in particular, lying on the ground immediately to the left of the path, a fine marble Roman column, which at some time had a small Christian cross set into it. Ahead are some picturesque arches open to the skies; they formed part of a street. It is not difficult to imagine shops on either side similar to the covered Crusader streets in the Old City of Jerusalem. Soon after walking through the arches, climb the mound of ruins on the right to reach a plateau, where there are further excavations. Continue toward the sea and notice at the highest point the remains of the Crusader cathedral, which was erected on this high ground. The three apses at the east end of the building are clearly recognizable. In fact, the cathedral was never completed because the vaults below, from an earlier period, were unable to withstand the weight.

Other features in the attractive area around the harbor are clearly marked, not least the ruins of the temple that Herod the Great built in honor of Caesar Augustus. Continue along the breakwater to the left and notice how many Roman columns the Crusaders used to reinforce the sea wall. Ahead is a modern restaurant standing upon the remains of a substantial building that was once the Crusader citadel. Some scholars suggest that this might also have been the site of the Roman prison; if this is correct, then it is likely that here St. Paul was detained.

At the time of writing there are extensive archaeological excavations taking place between the Crusader Walled City and the Roman Theater; you can visit these if time permits. Some of the main features are now clearly marked.

AUTHORS' COMMENTS

In addition to a wealth of historical interest there are a number of quality shops, restaurants, and also a bathing beach. Caesarea is a relaxing place by the Mediterranean, in contrast to the more intense pilgrimage centers of Jerusalem, Nazareth, and Galilee.

Opening Times: April to September 8:00–5:00; October to March 9:00–4:00; closes one hour earlier on the eve of Shabbat and holidays; closed on Yom Kippur; retain the entrance ticket for admission to the remains of the Roman Theater; the tourist "green card" is accepted

Souvenir Shop: many shops within the walls

Toilets: at the far east end of the block of shops to the north of the tourist area

Custodian: The National Parks Authority

Telephone: (06) 6361358 or (06) 6361060

Roman Aqueduct

ACCESS

See the instructions on pages 209 and 210. The aqueduct was built to bring a constant supply of fresh water from the foothills of Mount Carmel into the town. The structure beside the seashore has withstood the onslaught of wind and sand for two thousand years and still stands as a testimony to the skill of the Roman engineers. There are, in fact, two aqueducts, each with its own water channel and separate foundations. Herod the Great had the one nearest to the road constructed just before the birth of Jesus, while Hadrian had the other nearer the sea built at the beginning of the second

The aqueduct was constructed to supply fresh water from the foothills of Mount Carmel to Caesarea. *(Allan Weinert)*

century. The total length of the aqueduct was over twelve miles, and for half its distance the water channels were supported on these continuous arches.

There is no admission charge to the area, nor any public facilities. Bathing is prohibited because of the dangerous currents.

Roman Theater

ACCESS

See the instructions on pages 209 and 210. This impressive structure lies about a half mile to the south of the walled Crusader town. From the ticket office, walk diagonally across the sand to the ruins, then pass through one of the archways leading into the tiered auditorium. If there is no wind, you will be able to appreciate the acoustic properties; invariably, there is someone standing on stage to prove the point. The theater has a seating capacity of about four thousand, and the rows have been numbered because concerts are occasionally held during the summer months.

Walk down one of the gangways onto the stage, and behind it and on either side you will see the remains of dressing rooms, rehearsal rooms, and other facilities connected with any theater. Before leaving the site be sure to look at the carvings and statue-remains displayed near the ticket office. Not least among them is an enormous foot, but more important for the Christian is a replica of part of a carved stone bearing a Latin inscription to the effect that "Pontius Pilate, Prefect of Judea, made and dedicated the Tiberieum to the Divine Augustus." This is positive archaeological evidence to confirm the existence of the Roman procurator as recorded in the gospels.

Opening Times: April to September 8:00–5:00; October to March 9:00–4:00; closes one hour earlier on the eve of Shabbat and holidays; closed on

Yom Kippur; retain the entrance ticket for admission to the remains of the Walled City; the tourist "green card" is accepted

Souvenir Shop: small booth by the ticket office

Toilets: close to the north boundary fence between the ticket office and the sea

Custodian: The National Parks Authority

Telephone: (06) 6361358

This Roman Theater has been restored and can now seat four thousand spectators. *(Allan Weinert)*

Byzantine Street

If time permits, it is worth visiting another site outside the Walled City. To the east of the defensive walls, but south of the road running away from the gateway, is part of a Byzantine street in which there are two enormous statues dating from the second to third centuries. The identification of the one in white marble has not been established, but the other in dark granite is thought to depict Roman Emperor Hadrian (A.D. 76–138) and may have been carved in Egypt.

BIBLICAL REFERENCES

Acts 8:40: Philip the Apostle reaches Caesarea
Acts 10: Peter comes up from Joppa to baptize Cornelius
Acts 21:8ff: At the home of Philip the Evangelist, Agabus foretells
St. Paul's treatment in Jerusalem
Acts 23–26: Paul's imprisonment and defense before King Agrippa
and Festus

Part 3

Appendices

GOSPEL REFERENCES

THE UNIDENTIFIED verses refer to the place name only.

ASCENSION, PLACE OF
Luke 24:50–53	The Ascension
(Acts 1:4–12)	The Ascension

BEATITUDES, MOUNT OF
Matthew 5:1–7:27	Sermon on the Mount
Luke 6:17–49	Sermon on the Mount

BETHANY
Matthew 21:17	
Matthew 26:6–13	Jesus is anointed at Simon the Leper's house
Mark 14:3–9	Jesus is anointed at Simon the Leper's house
Mark 11:1, 11–12	
Luke 10:38–42	Martha and Mary
Luke 19:29	
Luke 24:50	
John 11:1–44	Raising of Lazarus
John 12:1–9	Anointing of Jesus by Mary

BETHESDA, POOL OF
John 5:2–15	Healing of the paralytic

BETHLEHEM
Matthew 2:1-12	Visitation of the Magi
Matthew 2:13–15	Joseph's dream and the flight into Egypt
Matthew 2:16–18	Massacre of the Holy Innocents
Luke 2:1–20	The Nativity and the story of the shepherds
John 7:42	

BETHPHAGE
Matthew 21:1–11	Triumphal entry into Jerusalem
Mark 11:1–11	Triumphal entry into Jerusalem
Luke 19:28–40	Triumphal entry into Jerusalem
John 12:12–15	Triumphal entry into Jerusalem

CAESAREA PHILIPPI

Matthew 16:13–20	Peter's commissioning
Mark 8:27–30	Peter's confession of faith

CANA

John 2:1–11	Miracle at the Wedding Feast
John 4:46–53	A healing
John 21:2	

CAPERNAUM

Matthew 4:18–22	Calling of Peter, Andrew, James, and John
Mark 1:16–20	Calling of Peter, Andrew, James, and John
Luke 5:1–11	Calling of Peter, James, and John
Matthew 8:5–13	Healing of the centurion's servant
Luke 7:1–10	Healing of the centurion's servant
Matthew 8:14–15	Healing of Peter's mother-in-law
Mark 1:29–34	Healing of Peter's mother-in-law
Matthew 8:16–17	Healing of many
Matthew 9:1–7	Healing of the paralytic
Mark 2:1–12	Healing of the paralytic
Matthew 9:9	Calling of Matthew
Mark 2:13–14	Calling of Matthew
Luke 5:27–28	Calling of Matthew
Matthew 9:11–13	Eating with tax-gatherers and sinners
Mark 2:15–17	Eating with publicans and sinners
Matthew 9:18–19 & 23–26	Raising of Jairus's daughter
Mark 5:21–24 & 35–43	Raising of Jairus's daughter
Luke 8:40–42 & 49–56	Raising of Jairus's daughter
Matthew 9:20–22	Healing of the woman with hemorrhages
Mark 5:25–34	Healing of the woman with hemorrhages
Luke 8:43–48	Healing of the woman with hemorrhages
Matthew 11:23–24	The impenitent town
Matthew 17:24–27	Payment of taxes—"Peter Fish"
Mark 1:21–28	Healing of the demoniac
Mark 9:33–50	The meaning of discipleship
Luke 4:23	
Luke 10:15	
John 2:12	
John 4:46	
John 6:16–71	Teaching

DOMINUS FLEVIT, CHURCH OF
Luke 19:41–44   Jesus weeps over Jerusalem

EIN KEREM
Luke 1:23–25   John the Baptist is conceived
Luke 1:39–56   Visitation of Mary to Elizabeth
Luke 1:57–80   Birth and naming of John the Baptist

EMMAUS
Mark 16:12–13   Resurrection appearance on the road to
                                   Emmaus
Luke 24:13–35   Resurrection appearance on the road to
                                   Emmaus

GALILEE, SEA OF
Matthew 8:23–27   Stilling the storm
Mark 4:35–41   Stilling the storm
Luke 8:22–25   Stilling the storm
Matthew 14:22–32   Walking on the water
Mark 6:47–51   Walking on the water
John 6:16–21   Walking on the water
Luke 5:1–11   Catch of fish

GALLICANTU, CHURCH OF ST. PETER IN
Matthew 26:57–75   Trial before Caiaphas and Peter's denial
Mark 14:53–72   Trial before the High Priest and Peter's
                                   denial
Luke 22:54–71   Peter's denial and trial before the Council
John 18:13–27   Trial before Annas and Peter's denial

GETHSEMANE
Matthew 26:36–56   Agony, betrayal, and arrest of Jesus
Mark 14:32–50   Agony, betrayal, and arrest of Jesus
Luke 22:39–54   Agony, betrayal, and arrest of Jesus
John 18:1–12   Betrayal and arrest of Jesus

HOLY SEPULCHRE, CHURCH OF THE
Matthew 27:33–28:10   The Crucifixion and Resurrection
Mark 15:22–16:8   The Crucifixion and Resurrection
Luke 23:32–24:12   The Crucifixion and Resurrection
John 19:16–20:18   The Crucifixion and Resurrection

JACOB'S WELL

John 4:4–30	Meeting with the Samaritan woman

JERICHO

Matthew 20:29–34	Healing of the two blind beggars
Mark 10:46–52	Healing of blind Bartimaeus
Luke 10:25–37	Parable of the Good Samaritan
Luke 18:35–43	Healing of the blind beggar
Luke 19:1–10	Story of Zaccheus

JORDAN, RIVER

Matthew 3:1–12	Baptisms by John
Mark 1:2–8	Baptisms by John
Luke 3:2–17	Baptisms by John
Matthew 3:13–17	Baptism of Jesus
Mark 1:9–11	Baptism of Jesus
Luke 3:21–22	Baptism of Jesus

NAZARETH (IN CHRONOLOGICAL ORDER)

Luke 1:26–38	The Annunciation
Luke 2:39–40 & 51–52	Childhood of Jesus
Matthew 13:53–58	Teaching in the Synagogue
Mark 6:1–6	Teaching in the Synagogue
Luke 4:16–21	Teaching in the Synagogue
Luke 4:23–30	Jesus is rejected and expelled
Matthew 2:23	
Mark 14:67	
John 1:45–46	

PATER NOSTER, CHURCH OF

Matthew 6:5–15	The Lord's Prayer
Luke 11:1–4	The Lord's Prayer
Matthew 24 to 25	Jesus foretells the destruction of Jerusalem and his return in judgment

SILOAM, POOL OF

John 9:1–12	Jesus gives sight to a man born blind

SOWER'S BAY

Matthew 13:1–9	Parable of the Sower
Mark 4:1–9	Parable of the Sower
Luke 8:4–8	Parable of the Sower
Matthew 13:18–23	Parable explained
Mark 4:13–20	Parable explained
Luke 8:11–15	Parable explained
Matthew 13:24–30	Parable of the Wheat and the Weed
Mark 4:26–29	Parable of the Wheat and the Weed
Matthew 13:31–32	Parable of the Mustard Seed
Mark 4:30–32	Parable of the Mustard Seed
Matthew 13:33	Parable of the Leaven

TABGHA

Matthew 14:13–21	Feeding of the five thousand
Mark 6:30–44	Feeding of the five thousand
Luke 9:10–17	Feeding of the five thousand
John 6:1–13	Feeding of the five thousand
Matthew 15:32–39	Feeding of the four thousand
Mark 8:1–10	Feeding of the four thousand
John 21:1–24	Resurrection appearance including the commissioning of Peter

TABOR, MOUNT

Matthew 17:1–8	The Transfiguration
Mark 9:2–8	The Transfiguration
Luke 9:28–36	The Transfiguration

TEMPLE AREA (IN CHRONOLOGICAL ORDER)

Luke 1:5–25	The Angel Gabriel appears to Zechariah
Luke 2:22–39	Presentation of Jesus in the Temple
Luke 2:41–52	Jesus with the teachers in the Temple
Matthew 4:5–7	Temptation—the Pinnacle of the Temple
Luke 4:9–12	Temptation—the Pinnacle of the Temple
Luke 18:10–14	Parable of the Pharisee and the Tax Collector
Matthew 21:12–13	Jesus drives the traders out of the Temple
Mark 11:15–17	Jesus drives the traders out of the Temple
Luke 19:45–48	Jesus drives the traders out of the Temple
John 2:13–17	Jesus drives the traders out of the Temple
Luke 20:1–8	The authority of Jesus
John 2:18–21	The authority of Jesus

John 7:14–52	Teaching
Luke 20:9–16	Parable of the Tenants in the Vineyard
Matthew 21:14–17	Blind and crippled healed in the Temple
Matthew 23:38 to 24:2	Destruction of the Temple foretold
Luke 21:5–7	Destruction of the Temple foretold
Matthew 27:3–10	Judas's remorse
Matthew 27:51	The veil of the Temple torn in two
Mark 15:38	The veil of the Temple torn in two
Luke 23:45	The veil of the Temple torn in two
Luke 23:52–53	The Disciples in the Temple after the Ascension

UPPER ROOM

Matthew 26:17–30	The Last Supper
Mark 14:12–26	The Last Supper
Luke 22:7–38	The Last Supper
John 13 to 17	The Last Supper

VIA DOLOROSA

Matthew 27:1–32	Jesus before Pilate; the Way of the Cross
Mark 15:1–21	Jesus before Pilate; the Way of the Cross
Luke 23:1–31	Jesus before Pilate; the Way of the Cross
John 18:28–19:16	Jesus before Pilate; the Way of the Cross

ZION, MOUNT (TRADITIONALLY SOMEWHERE ON THE MOUNT)

Luke 24:36–49	Resurrection appearances to the Disciples
John 20:19–29	Resurrection appearances— "Doubting Thomas"
(Acts 2:1–47)	Pentecost

BIBLIOGRAPHY

Brownrigg, Ronald. *Come, see the Place.* London: Hodder and Stoughton, 1985.

Corbo, Virgilio. *The House of St. Peter.* Jerusalem: Franciscan Printing Press, 1972.

Duncan, Alistair. *The Noble Heritage.* London: Longman Group, 1974.

Freeman-Grenville, G.S.P. *The Beauty of Jerusalem.* London: East-West Publications, 1983.

Hoade, Eugene. *Guide to the Holy Land.* Jerusalem: Franciscan Printing Press, 1984.

Kenyon, Kathleen. *Digging up Jerusalem.* London: Benn, 1974.

King, Laurence. *Church of the Holy Sepulchre.* 1944.

Kollek, Teddy and Moshe Pearlman. *Pilgrims to the Holy Land.* London: Weidenfeld and Nicholson, 1970.

Ludwig, Gumbert. *The Basilica in Nazareth.* Commissariat of the Holy Land: 1986.

Martin, James. *A Plain Man in the Holy Land.* Edinburgh: St. Andrew Press, 1978.

Murphy-O'Connor, Jerome. *The Holy Land Archaeological Guide, The.* Oxford University Press, 1986.

Prag, Kay. *The Blue Guide to Jerusalem.* London: A & C Black, 1989.

Richards, H. J. *Pilgrim to the Holy Land.* Great Wakering: Mayhew McCrimmon, 1982.

Wilkinson, John. *Jerusalem As Jesus knew it.* London: Thames and Hudson, 1978.

Yadin, Yigael. *Masada—Herod's Fortress and the Zealot's Last Stand.* London: Weidenfeld and Nicholson, 1966.

Copyright Acknowledgments

We are grateful to the following for permission to quote lines from the undermentioned hymns as "prayerful thoughts" at the end of each reading:

Josef Weinberger Limited © 1960 "Lord Jesus Christ" Patrick Appleford (from *Hymns for Today,* No. 58).

Mowbray, a division of Cassell plc: "O dearest Lord, thy sacred head" H. E. Hardy (from *Hymns Ancient & Modern New Standard,* No. 391).

Stainer & Bell Ltd: "When I needed a neighbour" Sydney Carter (from *Hymns for Today,* No. 100), and "When Jesus came to Jordan" F. Pratt Green (from *Hymns for Today,* No. 193).

Oxford University Press: "Forgive our sins, as we forgive" Rosamond Herklots (1905–87) (from *Hymns for Today,* No. 29), and "Rise and hear! the Lord is speaking" H. C. A. Gaunt (1902–83) (from *Hymns for Today,* No. 176).

The Revd. Basil E. Bridge: "Jesus, Lord, we pray" (from *Hymns for Today,* No. 142).

Also to the National Parks Authority, Tel Aviv, Israel, for permission to use their plans of Masada and Caesarea.

We have endeavored to establish and make contact with all copyright owners. However, we apologize to anyone who has been overlooked and will make every effort to rectify omissions in future editions.

FIRST LINES OF HYMNS
USED AS PRAYERFUL THOUGHTS

INDEX

About the Authors

NORMAN WAREHAM AND JILL GILL worked together for a children's charity for more than thirteen years. During his vacations Norman led a number of Christian groups to the Holy Land, and he became increasingly aware of the need for a really practical guidebook. On retirement, he and Jill began working on their first book, *A Pilgrim Guide to the Holy Land Gospel Sites*, which concentrated exclusively on the places mentioned in the four gospels. When the time came to reprint, they decided to add a number of non-Christian sites to encompass most of the places included in a typical pilgrimage itinerary, and the title was changed to *Every Pilgrim's Guide to the Holy Land*.

Norman has served Canterbury Cathedral in a lay capacity for the past seventeen years and continues to lead Holy Land pilgrimages. Jill has served her parish church on the outskirts of London for more than twenty years and has visited the Holy Land both as a pilgrim and in researching this guide.